CONTEMPORARY BLACK THOUGHT

CONTEMPORARY BLACK THOUGHT

THE BEST FROM
The Black Scholar

EDITED BY

ROBERT CHRISMAN

&

NATHAN HARE

The Bobbs-Merrill Company, Inc.

INDIANAPOLIS / NEW YORK

The Bobbs-Merrill Co., Inc.
INDIANAPOLIS / NEW YORK
Copyright 1973 by Black World Foundation
All rights reserved
ISBN 0-672-51821-X cloth
0-672-51822-8 paper
Library of Congress catalogue card number 72-89702
DESIGNED BY VINCENT TORRE
Manufactured in the United States of America

Contents

Introduction

I

CULTURE

II

FAMILY

III

POLITICS

IV
ECONOMICS

Introduction

Politics and culture have reciprocal functions, the achievement of one enhancing the reality of the other. What man would do he must first think, and the thoughts of man in turn are influenced by what exists and what has been done. While the direct relationship of politics to culture tends to be obscured in most contemporary American thought, it is constantly probed, analyzed and discussed by the intellectuals, practitioners and theoreticians of the black liberation movement. This is a natural consequence of the realization that, to be effective, oppression must subdue political and cultural identity.

The need for an independent journal of black studies and research was quite clear: one that not only would enhance black culture but would serve as an independent instrument for the expression of contemporary black thought. *The Black Scholar* was formed in response to that need.

Endorsed by a wide range of black intellectuals and activists, *The Black Scholar* emerged at a time when there were serious schisms in the black movement over the questions of revolutionary nationalism versus cultural nationalism, race consciousness versus class consciousness, and integration versus separation. Crystallizing the concepts involved and drawing parameters for future discussion therefore became a primary goal for *The Black Scholar,* and it is to these ends that the journal has addressed itself. Further, it is the intention of *The Black Scholar* not only to provide a forum for these discussions but also to be an independent instrument for the expression and enhancement of black culture. We feel that the essays selected here are representative of the major trends in black political and cultural thought.

It is appropriate here to define the term "culture" and its precepts as we understand them. In "A Dialectical Approach to Culture," Sékou Touré states:

> By culture, we mean all the material and immaterial works of art and science, plus knowledge, manners, education, a mode of thought, behavior and attitudes accumulated by the people both through and by virtue of their struggle for freedom from the hold and dominion of nature. . . . Thus culture stands revealed as both an exclusive creation of the people and a source of creation, as an instrument of socio-economic liberation and as one of domination.

Culture is a vehicle for developing, shaping and organizing a people and their consciousness, representing their collective values, esthetics, ethics and laws as well as their spiritual directions. It has a special role in the national futures of colonized and enslaved peoples. Typically, colonization destroys the balanced relationship between a people's culture and their political economy. The victimized people must submit to an antagonistic political and economic pattern established for their exploitation. We are familiar with these patterns—slavery in the United States, the Caribbean and South America; apartheid in South Africa; the indentured labor system and oppression of caste and class in Asia.

But beyond the immediate economic and political colonization lies culture colonization. In terms of consciousness, identity, religion, esthetics and other modes, the victim is forced to identify with the culture of his oppressor, or with a surrogate culture tailored for his oppressed condition. The survival of his intrinsic culture is suppressed, and the creative and positive possibilities of a new culture resulting from the fresh contact of two good-willed peoples is stifled.

Thus for enslaved and colonized peoples the question of culture takes on tremendous importance. Even after total or partial freedom and liberation, the cultural values imposed by oppression can still exist and subvert the economic and political victories achieved through struggle. It is not surprising that African and Asian theoreticians such as Mao Tse-tung and Sékou Touré emphasize the development of revolutionary and cultural values and the decolonization of the mind.

Regardless of the people affected, the task remains the same—the creation of a new culture in consonance with the political and economic changes which have occurred. Once interrupted or greatly diminished by oppression, the native culture cannot return to its former self. It has changed. Nor, if there is a true struggle for liberation, can it conform to that of the oppressor, for neither pure condition exists any longer or is viable. As the Irish poet William Butler Yeats said after the Irish Uprising of 1916, "All changed, changed utterly/A terrible beauty has been born."

It is precisely this intersection of the old with the new, of the liberated with the restrictive, that permeates the essays published here. In all the major categories—culture, family, politics and economics—we find that this dialectic occurs, as the warp and woof upon which contemporary black thought is woven.

Many of the typical assumptions and values of European and American culture are challenged outright and discarded afterward. Very often, Euro-American values and methods are viewed from a radically different perspective and employed in new directions in order to be relevant to the black experience.

With respect to the challenge and dismissal of Euro-American

values, we find that "A Black Value System" by Imamu Amiri
Baraka (LeRoi Jones) emphasizes the resurrection and internalization of traditional African values, African values which existed before colonization and, for Baraka, have helped to sustain Africa during its oppression. In his subsequent thought and political action
Baraka has given root to such values in the contemporary political
and economic fabric of the United States. A foremost exponent of
cultural revolution, Baraka stresses the transformation of consciousness, the development of new language, new names, new rituals,
new behaviors—all of them rooted in African tradition.

Similarly, Ralph Metcalfe, Jr. recovers African origins in "The
West African Roots of Afro-American Music" to create new cultural
perspectives for the Afro-American. Music has been perhaps the
most enduring and indestructible medium for the development of
African and Afro-American cultures and the linkages between them.
For music was and is integral to the core experiences of African tradition and retains its importance in Afro-American culture, with
many of the same forms, functions and styles.

The essay by Eugene B. Redmond, "The Black American Epic: Its
Roots, Its Writers," traces the continuing tradition of Afro-American
literature, a tradition that Redmond maintains is epic, the blues and
their composers being likened to chapters and verses in a continuing
saga. For the black authors of the last hundred years have consciously honored the epic tradition, preserving and expanding upon
its forms. Redmond further stresses the importance of culture for
maintaining the fiber of a given people in this passage:

> Black presence means maintaining an equilibrium: a coolness undis-
> turbed by tokenism or lofty statements; a stoic endurance unobservable
> of those unwritten "stay in your place" signs along the way. For like the
> theme of "The Signifying Monkey," that great black American oral epic,
> black presence is a survival of the soul, a patience paced by discipline.
> "Any black man in the least perceptive must be constantly on the verge
> of insanity," James Baldwin has said. Yet in stoic defiance of inherent
> psychological death, like Ahab stalking the deck of the *Pequod*, the black
> presence, almost invincibly, not only "survives" but is a predominant in-
> fluence on many physical and psychological American actions and atti-
> tudes.

While Redmond acknowledges the importance of the oral tradition in shaping Afro-American culture, William H. Wiggins, Jr. himself a folklorist, traces the development of Afro-American folklore
with reference to the great boxer Jack Johnson in his essay, "Jack
Johnson as Bad Nigger: The Folklore of His Life." A man of epic
proportions himself, Jack Johnson follows in the bad-nigger tradition: a man who is the apotheosis of brute force, intelligence, cun-

ning and rebellious anger, pitched into direct conflict with his oppressor and his values. The wit, the style, the incisive ironic insights into the nature of black-white relations in this country, all are evoked in Wiggins' narration and the folk stories he employs, the folk stories themselves being an aspect of black culture of far greater significance than most Euro-Americans have ever realized.

Equally stimulating are essays in which the standard instruments of Euro-American culture are employed in fresh new directions. In the essays by Nathan Hare, Harry Edwards, Robert Staples and Jacquelyne Jackson we find brilliant and militant sociologists utilizing the instruments of social analysis in new areas for the development of new insights into the black social condition, free from white social mythology and futile exercises in comparative oppressor-oppressed analysis. The mythology itself is explored in studies on super-physicality, impotence and promiscuity among blacks.

Angela Davis, Kenneth Divans and Larry West write of the black woman's role in building black family life during slavery and compare the present prison system with the slavery system. We find these essays particularly ironic and apt because the three essayists were writing from behind prison walls.

This is a collection that yields special satisfaction in the reading. For, overwhelmingly, the works are distinguished by style. There is wit, humor and irony. There is scope and range in concepts, accuracy and precision of thought. These are essays by black writers who are cognizant of the cultural traditions of the Afro-American and who are themselves vigorous participants in the social and cultural renaissance of black America today.

Robert Chrisman
February 1973

I

CULTURE

A Dialectical Approach
to Culture

SÉKOU TOURÉ

The path of tribulations undergone by the concept of culture is, to-day, long indeed! The opinions of "committees of intellectuals" cancel each other out in a sterile dialectic; various "symposia" bring incomprehension and a hollow humanism into a timid encounter with historical truth and the progressive determination of man up against the greatest calamity known to history: imperialism.

In countries where a capitalist regime isolates the general populace from scientific and technical attainments, the intellectual fights to retain his false "freedom" and questions himself in vain about the future of a decadent economic and social structure. He is helpless. He somehow constructs a cultural policy in an attempt to strengthen a society whose upheavals are the undeniable symptoms of degeneration, and instead of using the faded light of his poor autocratic reason to seek a new cultural conscience, he sinks into skepticism or, rather, into the terror of a future overshadowed by capitalism.

European trends have dominated the study of cultural problems in Africa. For a long time latter-day Anglo-Saxon anthropology, concerned with justifying the reactionary ideas of colonialism, cited Africa as the home of backward peoples who should be forced to accept colonialist humanitarian civilization.

History has shown that revolutionary maturity cannot be the object of an edict which imperialism would, in any case, never sign! The Anglo-Saxon school of thought allowed for a pseudo-realism worthy of Hume's successors—a pseudo-realism the reactionary ideological content of which was soon to be exposed. Vierkandt's disciples, "culturalists" such as Grabner and Ankermann, and functional-

SÉKOU TOURÉ is the President of the Republic of Guinea and one of Africa's most eminent revolutionary thinkers. When Kwame Nkrumah was deposed in Ghana, Touré gave him political asylum.

ists like Malinowski, believed they had discovered the basis of our culture. Their empiricism and its hatred of historical materialism produced a flood of disjointed monographs in which the class war and the imperialist's exploitation of our peoples were denied and reduced to an anti-scientific cultural pluralism.

Archaeologists' pickaxes had evidently not reached the African culture, which lay too deeply buried under the irremovable heap of dirt left behind by the colonialists, which our peoples have now succeeded in uncovering. The anxiety to extricate an authenticity which is for obvious reasons indiscoverable gave rise to a fairly accurate representation of the prelogism of Levy-Bruhl, who was already blind! In any case there is no difference of concept between the black man unaware of the logical categories of the classical world on the one hand, and the idea of the essentially sensitive black man as a sort of passive, wax creature, only fit to remain at a primary intuitive level in his perception of the outside world, on the other.

Thus it is no accident that African states still have to dedicate a symposium to a topic such as that which unites us today: "African culture and its realities." We recall that twenty years ago many pages were devoted to another topic which at that time seemed provocative, and that was, "A black man is a human being." It has become today our historical duty to re-establish ourselves in a field such as culture, because we are emerging from a long period of eclipse during which the most elementary attributes of man, notably that of his creativity, were contested and denied to us.

According to a well-nurtured prejudice, Africans took no part in the general task of shaping civilization. Africa is accused of being without history and without culture because it was necessary that this be so. Europeans slaughtered American Indians while at the same time admiring their temples and palaces. They admitted that they massacred the men to take over their land. With their conquests and domination, Europeans destroyed millennial civilizations in Asia, but they never denied the existence of these civilizations as such and never contested the quality of their craftsmanship and their human attributes.

Concerning Africa, Europe's first notion was not to exterminate the men with the sole idea of seizing their treasures, but to treat them as beasts to be sold into slavery and, as they pleased sold on the spot or exported to America, or even killed when their capabilities and selling price no longer assured an adequate profit.

To guarantee the success of such a venture a preliminary step was necessary—that of easing one's conscience and reassuring oneself by thinking that it was a question of dealing with beasts and not human beings. Hence the alleged barbarity of Africans and the denial of their culture and civilization gave birth to their estrangement from the human race.

But time did not stop, and progress continued to strengthen in the face of opposition and exploitation. More attention was paid to the legends, the epic poems and the tales passed by word of mouth from generation to generation of the Griots. Archaeology finally penetrated the various continents, thrusting deep into the depths of history and the soil so as to revive and bring to the surface the remains of entombed cultures.

In fact even without archaeological research and the tales of the Griots, ordinary common sense was adequate to realize the absurdity or rather the class-consciousness of those who managed to imagine a cultureless people.

By culture, we mean all the material and immaterial works of art and science, plus knowledge, manners, education, a mode of thought, behavior and attitudes accumulated by the people both through and by virtue of their struggle for freedom from the hold and dominion of nature; we also include the result of their efforts to destroy the deviationist politics—social systems of domination and exploitation through the productive process of social life.

Thus culture stands revealed as both an exclusive creation of the people and a source of creation, as an instrument of socio-economic liberation and as one of domination.

Culture implies our struggle—it is our struggle.

Culture—as both the expression and the result of the relationships between man and society, and between man and society on the one hand and nature on the other—is found among all peoples and is inherent in the very process of life. A culture is to be found wherever conscious life exists.

Culture is the sum total of the material and spiritual values created by humanity throughout its history. This creation is both continuous and necessary. It is the corollary, the yardstick and the result of man's action to adapt to his environment so that he can both survive and flourish. It is inspired by the instinct for survival at the first stage and by an awareness of the laws of existence at a higher stage. Therefore it first obeys a simple biological law regulating the survival of the individual and the species before obeying a more complex psychological and socio-economic law. Now the instinct for self-preservation and the need for self-fulfillment are common to all societies and peoples. Every people must struggle to exist by creating the material means of its existence.

African peoples, like all peoples, have come along the long road of history through recurrent conflicts whose overall result has been increasing success. The creation of material values, the creation of spiritual values, the creation and development of this global culture progresses continuously in spite of momentary slowing down, stagnation and setbacks. Material cultural production and spiritual cultural production are dialectically linked and exercise a reciprocal influence on each other. But the absolute priority must rest with material production, which itself participates directly in man's concrete action.

For human history has more than once recorded a slackening of spiritual tension, a stagnation of intellectual and political life or even a total annihilation of all intellectual and political activity, but it has never recorded a long-term total interruption of the development of material civilization. This evolution can, of course, slow down but it can never stop, as its stopping would signify the end of man's creative activity, the disappearance of his powers of adaptation, and mean his extinction.

This material production is a matter of vital necessity—a condition and sign of life. Man's material action is the "prime mover," the source of all else. It aims at the satisfaction of needs, first vital, physical needs and then less immediate ones relating to the assertion and enrichment of the personality, the intellectual and moral needs. This action of both men and society is directed against the environment, against man himself and against nature. It is designed to meet the needs of all, and this raises the problem of its efficiency and profitability. To meet the needs of all, material action must have a tactics, a strategy, an intellectual effort to action, a certain degree of planning, both criticism and self-criticism in the light of the results, and a methodology bringing into play a whole series of intellectual operations. Culture is a material and spiritual acquisition, both the product and the price of action.

Creative action springing from a universal imperative and culture, which is its reflection, subject and effect, both constitute universal realities. Wherever there is the necessity of creation, we find culture. As the expression of the relationships between man and society, between man, society and nature, culture poses in the most pressing terms the problem of the dialectic of the general and the particular. Culture is an expression, in particular, specific forms, of a general problem—that of the relationships linking man to his environment.

But these relations in turn take on a specific character determined by geographical conditions, the level of development of productive forces and the nature of the means of production as determined by the historical and social context. The cultural level of a people (including the peoples of Africa), its means of conquering knowledge, its manner of explaining phenomena, will depend on the power that it has gained over natural forces and the degree of objectivity and abstraction attained in the heat of action to gain mastery over ever more perfected techniques.

The specific, particular nature of a culture is a reality; it is one of the attributes of national reality in general and of class reality in particular. It expresses conditions of life shared in common, a similarity of attitudes and of reactions to natural and social phenomena. But there is a general aspect even to this specific particularity. Even if these attitudes and reactions are marked by the irrational at certain stages of historical development, even if they derive from simple emotion at certain points in the action or even if they occur at the level of reflexes, they are fundamentally set in motion and guided by reason with a view to reaching well-defined objectives and finding solutions to well-defined problems. Specific particularity is not specific to African culture, but to every culture.

This specificity is a general reality. But, apart from this general aspect of specificity, culture, by virtue of its content—the expression of man's eternal aspiration to happiness and to the final unfolding of his nature, with ever-increasing power over the environment—culture is in perpetual movement towards the universal. The speed at which culture tends towards the universal is a function of the dialectic of cultural forms and content at a given stage of history.

The universalization of the content of culture in interpreting the aspiration of all peoples will go hand in hand with a greater perfection of its forms of expression, due to the general development of forms and the revolutionization of industrial relations. African culture, like any culture, originated with the African himself and embodies his first preoccupations, his first struggles, his first successes and setbacks.

The course of history and the succession of African culture's development have closely reflected the course of the development of productive forces. Its initial simplicity, low intellectual level and slow rate of progression all reflected the weakness of man's position and the precariousness of his existence. Then over the centuries and down the ages, following the development of productive techniques, culture developed, became diversified, took on shades of meaning and incorporated science, technology, literature, music, dancing and sculpture.

This whole evolution, this progressive qualification is subordinated to reason, to the law of gnoseology, to the transition from ignorance to an increasingly deeper and more exact degree of knowledge. Any anthology of African culture tending to situate it outside the realm of reason, of rational thought, of the law and of gnoseology tends to downgrade it and deviate it from its true end, which is to qualify mankind, and sacrifices it to the myth of singularity and specificity.

African culture neither has nor needs any foundation other than the concrete life of the African. With its roots deep in the innermost life of the people, it expresses the life, work, ideals and aspirations of the African people. It has contributed along with other peoples to the development of science and technology. Prior to the contact with other continents, Africa had begun to smelt metal and to forge tools and weapons. She had learned to weave fabrics. The notion of chemistry had developed through various recipes needed to make soap, indigo, ink; to tan hides, etc.

But, to a far greater extent than science, which was handicapped by the persistence throughout the ages of a low level of technology, African art, African literature, African sculpture, music and dancing will occupy or already occupy an important place in humanity's cultural heritage. The reality of African culture needs no further demonstration, but its infinite realities are still to be discovered, recorded and described.

On the other hand, in Africa as elsewhere, culture reacts upon those producing it (man and society) at the same time as it is produced and developed.

Culture is an accumulated experience which modifies man in a linear, progressive and quantitative manner but with additional qualitative phases of mutation. The result is a new man, a new society, more skillful and more apt, integrating to an ever-increasing extent the means and the end of action, and perfecting to an ever greater extent technology and means of action.

Experience, acquired by and for action, becomes an inexhaustible source of energy; both the instrument and the guide of present and future action. Culture appears then, at one and the same time, as a creation and a means of creation of man and society, as an expression of the dialectical relationships between the creator and his creation. It is clearly apparent in its real light, that of a factor determining and conditioning all else. The conquest of culture has obliged man to mobilize all his physical and intellectual resources. Once it was conquered, culture became a flame animating and intoxicating the conqueror, man. So it is scarcely an exaggeration to say that man equals the culture that formed him and which inspires his behavior and action.

The fact of a culture conditions both the existence of the people and their exercise of sovereignty and power. For us, to speak of culture is to fight, and, although history has very edifying examples to offer, such as those which dominate the formation of feudalism, we have chosen to carry the data of this combat forward into the present era.

Everyone knows what a foul use was made of culture by the predatory powers in the course of modern history, in their appropriation, among other things, of the African peoples.

After having laid their hands on the essential elements of the culture of their own people, the upper classes of the colonialist powers used this weapon in their endeavor to dominate and exploit our continent.

It was first of all necessary to legitimize the various kinds of pillage and colonial domination in the eyes of established morality. To this end the natural difference between our culture and that of the peoples of these powers was used to justify and accredit the ignominious assertion that we did not have any culture and that a culture should be bestowed and imposed upon us.

Here started the crusade for humanization through the culturalization of the "marginal" peoples, of the peoples which have remained at the stage of "raw material-peoples," of peoples waiting to be manufactured in the Big Factory of civilized men. And presently, so as to ensure that colonization was everlasting the colonizers introduced the systematic indoctrination of native workers, which contributed to the smooth functioning of the Big Factory.

The corps of "colonial elites," "men of culture," natives of any level, of any experience and political hue, was created.

On the eve of the disintegration of the colonial empires an "intellectual elite" emerged. It was opposed to the old "colonial elite," but subjectivist in the nature of its opposition.

This new elite tried to make use of all available means. It had suffered from the racist blows that imperialism has dealt to Africa, but it had not understood that although ideology and racist practices may be an effective weapon when wielded by imperialism which is an active racism and a non-culture in history, that racist ideology used by those who are in revolt cannot be but a double-edged weapon which, in the last resort, is profitable only to the imperialist enemy. Therefore, Holy Negritude, be it Arab-Berber or Ethiopian-Bantu, this Negritude is objectively an ideology auxiliary to the general imperialist ideology.

The Master transforms his slave into a Negro whom he defines as a being without reason, subhuman, and the embittered slave then protests: as you are Reason, I am Emotion and I take this upon myself. This is how we loop the loops. The Master assumes his pre-eminence, and the Slave his servitude, but the latter claims his right to weep, a right which the Master grants him.

A reconciliation has come about, and one understands easily why the imperialist propaganda system, press, radio, cinema, etc., goes to such trouble to spread the comforting concept of Negritude. Negritude is actually a good mystifying anaesthetic for Negroes who have been whipped too long and too severely, whipped to a point where they have lost all reason and become purely emotional.

As serious analysis shows, the colonial situation is by no means contested by this elite, and that, objectively speaking, far from mobilizing and arming the subjugated peoples, it gives the colonizers an easy conscience by accrediting the existence of certain liberty of thought and action within the colonial system.

From this point of view, the intellectual elite, while being subjectively in opposition, objectively completes the arsenal of colonial domination. While the latter appropriates popular culture for its own profit, it deprives the colonized people of its best defensive and offensive weapons, an autonomously created culture nurtured by themselves.

The combination of two circumstances: a people deprived of its own culture on the one hand, and the tremendous development of science and technology (elements of culture) by the imperialist, made a certain kind of culture into a deadly weapon in the hands of the neo-colonialist, at the time the former colonies were attaining national independence.

It must be admitted that the frightened attitude of many African governments towards cynical imperialist arrogance, the helplessness of the peoples who were victims of neo-colonialist coup d'etats, were a result of the fact that these peoples had been deprived of their culture. The most powerful weapon for the rape and renewed subjugation of our peoples now available to imperialism and neo-colonialism is a certain kind of culture.

The invincible weapon, defensive against imperialism and colonialism and offensive for the complete emancipation of our peoples, is culture which has once again become the creation of an entire society and the source of all progressive creation.

This analysis leads to the conclusion that culture, a superstructure born from an infrastructure, which it modifies and qualitatively transforms in its turn, is the reality of a class of ideological classes.

One should not mistake this expression for a form of neo-idealism: by ideological classes, we are referring to classes which are by no means born from a simple economic and social stratification; we are faced here with a fundamental choice between two and no more possibilities which are mutually exclusive, viz. between:

1—The ideology of domination, and prostration under domination.

2—The ideology of struggle against any kind of domination and of the complete sovereignty of the people, power being exercised by and for the people.

All the activities of the Guinean Democratic Party are based on this second ideology which is manifest in all the aspects of life without a single exception.

Thus it is understood that culture is a field of action where man, society, nature, and peoples confront one another. In this merciless combat, the reconnoitering and conquering of ground are essential for victory. The superiority of arms is a superiority of culture, at least in its material and technical aspects. And it is this superiority in the production of culture which enables a people to dominate other peoples and impose its spiritual culture on them.

Culture is a more effective weapon than guns for the purpose of domination. For it was scientific, technical and technological culture which produced the guns. The prerequisite for any domination, exploitation and oppression is the denial to the oppressed man or people of his or their human attributes and therefore, in the first instance, cultural activities.

Before conquering, dominating and subjugating a people, the ruler asserts the superiority of his culture and civilization and proclaims its civilizing mission to those he has declared arbitrarily and unilaterally to be barbarian, savage, uncultured, and without civilization. The rulers take it for granted that the understanding of nature with a view to exploiting it in order to promote technical advancement is their exclusive privilege, their property. But opinions more authoritative and more justified than those of imperialism, colonialism and neo-colonialism stated that nature was understandable to any individual and that man, provided he was aware of the historical significance of his existence, was capable of penetrating further every day into the secrets of nature and increasing his power over it in order to increase his control of it.

What is important, at a given historical moment in the process of the knowledge and control of natural forces, is not so much the quality of knowledge and its conformity to the absolute truth as the way men and people are aware of their abilities and possibilities for understanding, and of their unfailing will to progress. In this process, the characteristic factor is an attitude, a turn of mind leading to self-reliance and confidence in the people. Acquired knowledge and the degree of truth which characterized it belong to a quantitive factor linked with facilities used in research, experiment, and application.

This is a historical stage in development which each people will achieve more or less quickly according to their means, the prerequisite being once again the belief that what is unknown can be known. No people are more gifted, more intelligent than others, but there are differences in historical contexts. Imperialists and exploiters blinded by the will to exploit are incapable of understanding this primary truth. Their culture is made up of guns, whips, hard labor and training which deny, humiliate and depersonalize those under the colonial yoke.

For the bourgeoisie and its colonialist allies, masses must be kept in ignorance, for ignorant individuals can distort culture if they attain it. Peasants and workers are incapable of preserving cultural values, let alone creating new ones. This propaganda has been proved to be absurd in those countries where socialism is being introduced. Revolution is the only way to ensure that science and culture will thrive and not decline.

Culture, through art, literature, techniques, etc., is the image of men's activity. Thus, hunt dances imitate the movement and pace of the game hunted. The stylized choreography of the African savannah hunter imitating the lion or the elephant, even so far as to include its appearance, is aesthetically poor only in the minds of the exploiters who hate all that is connected with the people. War is a hunt where man is the game, and culture is an imitation of war episodes. The dances of the Sofas of Samori or the "tudos" of the Damel Tagne lat Dior, the Boko (challenge dances) of a N'Beur-Kat (Senegalese wrestler) like the famous wrestler Modum Khule (who actually existed) are real masterpieces, especially when accompanied by songs and gestures of attack like those of the phalanges mentioned by Stanley. Culture is the image, the record of both experience and the techniques of production.

Sayings, proverbs, tales and folk songs express the wish for a bountiful production and the experience of mastery over nature; hence the naive materialism of peasant cultures co-existing with the idealism arising from their ignorance.

Authors as perspicacious as Frazer, in their rejection of historical materialism, were not able to account scientifically for magic. The experience of the fight against nature enables man to acquire knowledge. But given his limited means and sometimes even the implacable hostility of physico-chemical determinism, the major secrets of nature are all the more difficult to penetrate in that their world is unknown. Magic then becomes a conjuration, and rites reproduce gestures acquired from experience, which are regarded as valuable if occult creatures are favorable. Hence man invokes the experiences aiming at limiting damages, natural disasters, and at killing beasts which destroy the crops, etc.

Should development stop at that stage, it would lead to ignorance. Imperialism soon found out that its power lay in this. It had to transform us into scared, helpless beings facing natural and historical necessities. Kept in such an ignorant state, oppressed peoples are prey to prejudice and terror before invisible powers which are all the more alienating in that they are closely linked with their culture. Misery and physical decline are given an explanation except when this latter unveils the monstrous responsibilities of the imperialist exploiters.

Culture is the synthesis of people's activities. To fight together against diseases and hunger, to control nature and to widen the scope of knowledge are the tasks of the whole of mankind. Scientific and technical culture is the highest manifestation of collective creativeness. It has led to the eradication of several natural scourges.

From the historical point of view, no culture can be free of a class content. Unless it is a fake to camouflage some stupidity of the ideologists of exploiting regimes, every culture follows a well-defined political line. African feudalism for example did not experience private land control while, on the contrary, it was the case in Europe, where the lords came to consider themselves as the owners of the land they were entrusted with simply defending against possible invaders. That is the origin of the collective nature of peasant dances, where the gestures cover the whole range of free agricultural activity.

Culture, like all social phenomena, is characterized by class struggle. Cultural power, the container and contents of economic and political power, is thus a powerful oppressive weapon in the hands of the exploiters. Culture for the people has rightly been considered as the *bête noire* of the ideologists of capitalism.

It is logical for capitalistic exploitation to deny workers access to the culture they have created. Thus it is that sociologists, reactionary historians, with a view to justifying such a monopolization and to praising it, put forward the theory of the development of culture by an elite. The idea is that mankind is indebted to a handful of such brilliant individuals as Darwin, Einstein, Shakespeare and Beethoven for its achievements in art, science, technology and literature. Of course, tribute should be paid to these men. But if it is true that their active existence is a proof that culture is created by an elite, how can one explain that individuals endowed with equal genius did not exist in the days of the Leakey man or Sinanthropus?

Science has never been a one-man concern. It is usually retorted that, in the past, a scholar used to work by himself. In fact a scientist can make discoveries or inventions and enrich the heritage of mankind only in a favorable social and cultural context. Nowadays, the method of scientific research has altered. The scientist forms part of a team. The "demonstration" of this method has not yet led to the realization that collective work was a necessity due to the complexity of problems and the scope of modern science. It is also due to the fact that capitalism aims at monopolizing and exploiting brigades of brains. But as far as we are concerned we are fully aware that this method, of which capitalism considers only the effects, is the very basis of scientific inventiveness. Besides, scientific workers are the perpetuators of the efforts of past generations.

It is here that I and the poet Victor Hugo are in agreement. I wrote: ". . . one discovery may fundamentally or partially question a scientific principle previously considered sacrosanct and which had therefore prevailed till then . . . undoubtedly it is the law of continuous advance which prevails." Hugo wrote: "Science is continuous scratching with fruitful results; science is a ladder. . . ." The foundations of culture have been created and the conditions for its progress are created by the working masses which are the makers of history.

Literature and art have thrived for a long time in the form of folklore: epic poems, legends, tales, proverbs, songs served as a basis for writers. Painters and artists drew inspiration from the applied arts created by the people; popular art is an inexhaustible treasury of patterns and methods, a source of exaltation for writers and artists. It generates and feeds the national form of the art and literature of every country; science stems from the people's genius.

Consequently, culture is not the privilege of those exploiters who, by depriving the masses of the benefits of science and culture and by keeping them in ignorance, have found a justification for their class supremacy. For intelligence and talent are not the privilege of a class; the force of the spirit, talent and will of thousands of workers is reflected in all cultural creations.

Culture, a weapon of domination, will be one of liberation. In this instance, one must fight on ground of the enemy's choosing but one where the issue of the fight will be governed by an adequate weapon: popular culture. The imperialists use cultural, scientific, technical, economic, literary and moral values in order to justify and perpetuate their regime of exploitation and oppression. The oppressed peoples also use cultural values, but of a nature contrary to the former, in order to fight more successfully against imperialism and in order to free themselves from the colonial regime.

Resistance, and then the offensive, will be organized, first of all, in the cultural field. Colonized man must first recollect himself, critically analyze the results of the influences to which he was subjected by the invader, which are reflected in his behavior, way of thinking and acting, his conception of the world and society and in his way of assessing the values created by his own people.

In the first place, he must undertake to reconquer his own personality by denying the cultural values which have depersonalized him, by de-colonizing his own mind, his customs and his attitudes, by dismantling the philosophical systems justifying dominations, particularly Levy-Bruhl's notorious myth of the primitive and pre-logic mind as opposed to the intellectual and moral superiority complex of the colonizer. The colonized man must free himself from his inferiority complexes and embody man in what he represents of absolute values, aspirations to the universal.

This first stage of liberation, of struggle for the liquidation of the various complexes of the colonized man, is not to be dissociated from the following stage—that of the reconquest of lost values, of possessions denied and lost, attributes of a sensible man who thinks and acts in a dignified way and is aware of his potentialities. Nature abhors a vacuum, even on the cultural level. One cannot extirpate from the mind of colonized man the culture which has been imposed upon him and which has poisoned him, except by offering him a substitute culture, namely his own culture, which implies an action to restore to life, re-valorize and popularize that culture.

However, this action is possible only in the larger framework of the struggle for national liberation and social promotion. Culture cannot flower properly without putting an end to the causes which have been stifling it; but conversely the cult of cultural authenticity, the struggle for the reconquest of this authenticity by activating the awareness of popular masses and their mobilization, activates the process of political and social liberation, as well as forging the nation through the creation of a melting pot in which the simple citizen is formed without any consideration of tribe or race.

This free man within a free people who has rediscovered his physical and mental balance can thenceforward assume the entire responsibility for his own destiny. He can and must widen boundlessly the bases of his cultural heritage, diversify them, direct them in order to clarify any action likely to be undertaken with a view to improving the conditions of existence and prosperity. The imperialists have dominated and oppressed peoples because of a technical superiority they had previously acquired. The peoples in turn, animated by the conviction that the faculty of research, discovery and invention is the thing most fairly shared among men, will throw themselves into the battle for sciences and technics. Scientific culture, the ideal means of domination and production of goods, is a factor for progress in the creation of material culture and spiritual culture.

Yes, culture is an instrument of freedom, an anti-imperialist, anti-colonialist, anti-neo-colonialist weapon, a means of dominating nature, always providing it is a progressive, revolutionary culture created and consumed by the people on the basis of popularization. Only such a culture frees man of himself, of his egoistical tendency, of the vanity and pride and the fear which inhibit him—only such a culture frees and promotes a people by reconciling them with their authentic nature and opening for them the way to the future and the universal.

Today, national liberation and the edification of socialism are scheduled in the program of revolutionary Africa. All kinds of imperialists, colonialists, neo-colonialists, armies of ideological puppets, traders of peoples have taken fright when confronted with the determination of our masses, and vilify socialism and present it as an ideology of terror. The only reason for such a display of anti-revolutionary force is our determination to free Africa from the lust of imperialism, our determination to build an Africa having nothing to do with the exploitation of man by man.

However, we would be supporting a determinism similar to a wait-and-see policy and to fatalism, if we limited our victory to the eradication of imperialism and its self-destruction. For, while such a system bears in itself the germs of its own destruction, history teaches us that the duration of the regimes of exploitation of man by man depends on the intensity of intervention and the cultural level of the oppressed peoples. It is therefore important to create revolutionary conditions in order to enable citizens to give the best of themselves. Culture, being a synthesis of people's activities, is a power whose democratic mastery provides the masses with unexpected capacities of ideological and material creation and improvement.

It was through cultural power that the Master managed to justify and maintain his political power and economic domination over the Slave. It is through usurpation of cultural power—in the form of science, technology, methodology, art and a certain conception of the world—that neo-colonialist imperialism is still controlling many governments and exploiting the peoples it is supposed to help.

The other aspect of the elite's monopoly is that it cripples culture; capitalism, which is only concerned with the creation of a wealthy upper class, cannot stimulate culture. There is neither a unilateral economic determinism nor idealism to assert that the weakness or the death of several civilizations is due not to irascibility or to a so-called original moral insufficiency of man, according to ill-omened bourgeois philosophers, but to the fact that culture was the monopoly of a small minority; the scientific and technical power of this minority was the perfect expression of the frailty of such economic and cultural systems. Only a creative people can make culture advance, provided that the social system enables the democratic assimilation of the techniques and that the enrichment of a universal cultural patrimony becomes the people's monopoly. Democratization of science and culture is thus the fertilization of progressive civilizations.

Only the revolutionary movement can restore to culture its humanistic essence.

Culture is then understood in its two basic aspects:

· It means domination of physico-chemical determinism for progressive purposes.
· It means revolutionary orientation of society.

The Cultural Revolution implies the total emancipation of the people; consequently the Cultural Revolution is the radicalized revolution.

One cannot talk of revolutionary socialization of the means of production when the people, who are the rightful owners, are uneducated and incapable of improving upon that of which they have been deprived. The revolutionalization of culture supposes two basic aspects:

· Culture is available to masses and is a democratic process which is the means of qualifying the masses.
· By widening the intellectual qualification, revolution creates new conditions for the fecundation of culture and science. Once the people are aware of what they create, and know they are responsible for the improvement of social relationship, they are ideologically capable of undertaking the construction of a society free of the exploitation of man by man.

Revolution democratizes culture to its very core, making it serve all of society and not just the elite. The democratization of culture enables many people to reveal their talents in all fields of scientific and artistic endeavor, and it creates the conditions that enable these talents to flourish.

Artistic creation cannot remain outside the struggle, aloof from politics, because each writer, each artist, whether he likes it or not, expresses the interests of his class in his work. The socialist revolution throws off the monetary yoke from culture and permits the creation of works for the vast popular masses and not just for the flattering of the personal tastes of a handful of stupid gluttons.

The cultural and technical aspects of a society are a part of the whole of the revolutionary cause. Lenin wrote that they are "a little review and a little screw" in the general mechanism of the revolution. Revolutionary culture is a powerful fighting weapon and a material force for the people. Before the revolution, it constitutes an indispensable part of the battle-front of total revolution. Science and culture fit perfectly into the general mechanism of the struggle, as weapons of unity and education for the destruction of the enemy, with one heart and one will.

"An army without a culture is an ignorant army, and an ignorant army can never defeat its enemy," wrote a contemporary philosopher. Africa must join the Cultural Revolution. But what are the principal tasks of the Cultural Revolution? Cultural Revolution does not mean the denial of all culture of the past; rather it is the continuation of everything that was beautiful because it was of the people in spite of the will of the exploiters. It is therefore a question of:

· Choosing permanent and sound values from the cultural heritage and rejecting everything that is useless and reactionary, the outmoded mores, the bad traditions, the superstitions, and alienating and inhibiting attitudes such as Negritude.
· Transforming culture from the privilege of an elite into a culture that belongs to the people.
· Elevating the cultural and scientific level of the working class to ensure the continued progress of the production forces.
· Re-educating and completing the training of the older intellectuals who can still be salvaged, because once man has freed himself from the narrowness of the petit bourgeois, he can always be perfected.
· Creating a new type of intellectual.
· Committing the whole people irrevocably to the building of socialism.

The revolution restores to the people what they created during the secular class struggle, returns to the masses the scientific and technological acquisitions achieved by their labor, and defines constantly the means of struggle against imperialism, colonialism and neo-colonialism.

Given adequate material and dimensions, our people become invincible, raise higher the flag of freedom and better exercise their historical role of eradicating imperialism permanently.

Here, presented as briefly as possible, is an African sample of Cultural Revolution.

During the 22 years of the heroic struggle of the Democratic Party of Guinea against colonialism, feudalism and imperialism, pride of place is due to the fight for the restoration and assertion of the cultural assets of the works of civilization created by the millenary genius of our peoples, shamelessly scouted by the most criminal aggression of imperialism, cultural aggression.

Indeed, more than the military invasion and armed occupation of the mother country, more than the looting of our riches and the destruction of our country's social institutions, the lowering and denaturing of our civilizations seemed to our people to be the most unbearable expression of the colonialist imperial regime.

During the most intense period of separate citizenship and hard labor, in the prisons and the death camps, the proud people of Guinea, chained and gagged, have been continuously rejecting the cultural assets of the colonizers. In their moral and physical poverty, they remained haughty and aloof to assimilation, proclaiming forcefully with determination the undying authenticity of their culture and rejecting at the same time the caricature of civilization in the name of which the authorities in occupation enjoined them to renounce their personality.

Our people have never accepted the inevitablity of colonization. They were aware of the fact that our continent had been in ignorance of Europe, Asia and America for millions of years and that, during the long centuries of furious struggle against nature, our ancestors, facing the multitudinous difficulties connected with survival and improvement, produced cultures and civilizations which stand today, in many fields, as the finest achievements of human creation.

They were aware that, during these remote ages, our ancestors discovered the secret of the techniques and laws of agriculture and pastoral life; that they discovered and mastered numerous secrets of nature; that they devised methods of education and information in relation with the requirements of their development; that they codified the rules of social organization and ethics; that they organized trade, erected cities, created armies, founded empires and states.

Thus our people know that they were the worthy repositories of human culture, assets in the defense and perpetuity of which so large a number of our ancestors—forever immortal—gave their lives; our people did not kneel to the cultural mystification of the authorities in occupation.

For a people animated by such an awareness of history, there could not be any compromise: it was a question of totally rejecting the colonial system of imperialism and its criminal ideology as well as all the values it defends.

We must, in and by a struggle, re-create a new society based on the values which glorify the memory of its heroes.

We must restore to the concept of culture all its meaning and all the importance that it should have never lost: that of being at the same time the specific creation and collective property of each people concerned, the factor of identification, cohesion and improvement of societies, the means for the mastery of nature, the source and the surest defender of people's power, and the pre-eminent weapon against any foreign intrusion.

This is how, throughout the centuries, were maintained the concept and reality of African Culture, for the perpetuation of which millions of Africans gave their lives, among whom history mentions the prestigious names of Samory, Alpaa Yaya Lat-Dior, Sundiata, Biton Koulibaly, Behanzin Abdelicader.

On August 2nd, 1968, I started, in the name of our people, the socialist Cultural Revolution, an event with far-reaching consequences.

Although, in the course of the construction of an essentially democratic society, the exercise of political power by the people must be accompanied by a mastery of the economic power, this alone is not enough. Experience taught us that when the people do not control what they create, if they are not aware of the finality of their daily activities, the acquisitions of the revolution and all the prospects for the improvement of society are still watched by the internal and external counter-revolution. Science, technology and culture in the widest sense are now the property of the people and enable the masses to assume irreversibility of the permanent and ever-improving revolution.

So it is that some intellectuals without any revolutionary political philosophy and some theorists who are prisoners of a unilateral dogmatic materialism think that the idea of the revolution conscience-in-movement, used by our Secretary-General in his analysis, is a form of neo-Hegelianism, because for Hegel the conscience was just an absolute idea wandering in quest of undiscoverable contents. For us this conscience is not an evanescent form; for our party, idealism is rather in the conception of a socialist society which gave birth mechanically to popular science and culture without which, however, the edification of socialism is a compromise.

We reject this theory for two fundamental reasons. First, at a time when imperialism brandishes science and technology like a scarecrow, at a time when imperialism in Vietnam, in Africa, in the Middle East shamelessly scorns universal reprobation by its aggression and maintenance of neo-colonialism, the people must be more than ever the masters of nature and society. Second, culture and technology, together forming cultural power in the hands of a "comprador bourgeoisie," are the most deadly weapons of the counter-revolution.

Therefore, although adequate political and economic conditions produce the possibilities of changing society, the economic and political power remains fragile as long as the methodical, scientific development of the future by the people has not been achieved. The growth of revolutionary movement depends on the scientific and ideological level of the people.

One might be tempted to put this conception of the cultural

reality prior to the material edification of socialism to the account of objective neo-idealism. This is wrong—we have clearly adopted the analysis of Marx and Engels: the superstructures result from the material basis and influence it dialectically. This analysis, chiefly put forward by Engels, was an immediate answer to the class spies of historical materialism.

It is through a serious study by the light of the new data on the African revolutionary movement that we discovered a characteristic of the superstructures which seemed to have passed unnoticed so far: culture is at a given time a social process, an infrastructure. Therefore it can be easily understood that once cleared out of its idealistic contents and impalpable synthetic data, culture, now including science and technology, is the stake for a ruthless class struggle.

This is why, forged by twenty years of fight, the people of Guinea, as early as the 8th Congress of its national party, the DPG, after several sessions of the National Revolutionary Council, and the decisive one of the Central Committee on August 2nd, 1968, started the socialist revolution with its cultural phase.

Our Cultural Revolution operates in all fields of national activities.

At the level of the masses, all the inhabitants of our country must become literate before October 2nd, 1971, the end of the literary campaign. In a second stage, literate persons will receive supplementary courses of two kinds: the knowledge and the know-how acquired at the end of this vocational and intellectual qualification correspond to the 9th school year in our system (lower certificate in the Colonial system).

At the level of public services, institutes, specially organized schools, and production unit committees are the promoters of the courses; a ministry created for this purpose is entrusted with the standardization and distribution of courses.

Each rural political and economic unit has its own PRL (Pouvoir Revolutionnaire Local—Local Revolutionary Administration).

We have established that state centralization is the worst manifestation of bureaucracy; in the long run it impedes localization of the functions of the state; the revolution becomes a collection of principles in a vacuum. Directives, mobilizations and manifestations are characterized by a discontinuous periodicity in contrast with the need for continuity in the development of the Revolution.

The PRL represents the revolutionary state in the hands of the people who thus have a real control of bodies which are notably concerned with practical achievement. Not only does the state no longer maintain a plethora of civil servants who might well take over the revolution at their level, but the activities of those who are in service necessarily come partly within the sphere of the PRL.

- the economy
- public works
- education and culture
- health
- civil status and justice
- communications
- defense of the revolution

The objectives laid down in each sector are attained by the masses by means of specialized brigades.

We may well expand a little on education and culture. Each political and economic cell, and we have over eight thousand such basic cells, has its various cultural unit; each has an artistic group and sporting groups. Artistic competitions between local committees or between sections of the Party provide opportunities for cultural activities rich in stimuli for mass mobilization and particularly for the rehabilitation of African art. After making a selection at basic committee level, the sections of the Party become shock troops meeting one another in friendly strife each year during the National Artistic fortnight. Prizewinning plays and other forms of artistic creation, after being checked for ideological soundness, become part of the teaching material available for training and education. As far as we are concerned, the play *Et la nuit s'illumine*, the theatrical expression of the recent epic of our people, which is our country's entry at the present competitions in Algiers, together with another tragedy *The Siege of Sikasso*, are quite the equal of *Le Cid, Iphigenia* or *Othello*.

As regards its functioning, the PRL has been adapted to the structure of the Party and the State, as regards both its organization and its various offices.

As we have said, the PRL represents the Revolutionary State in country districts. This has proved beneficial in abolishing urban bureaucracy and planting the roots of the revolution in the countryside.

On the economic front, no hierarchy in government service is exempt from participating in the annual agricultural campaign, the final aim of which is to abolish economic blackmail by turning the slogan, "Produce to be self-sufficient," into a reality. It is also the best method of re-educating the old-style intellectuals towards a real instead of a lip-service identification with the ideals of the Popular Revolution.

As regards education, the schools are closely coordinated in the process of transforming individuals and society and are known as

CER (Centre d'Enseignement Revolutionnaire—Centre for Revolutionary Education), covering all four stages of schooling, from the primary school to university level.

Education, now in revolutionary mould, follows a dialectical line: It starts with social, geographic and political realities; on the basis of these initial data, it draws up plans for transformation; these plans are carried out on the land made available to the CER.

In the Republic of Guinea today each scholastic establishment, right up to university level, is a production unit working one or more forms and at the same time an administrative unit, self-governing through its Council, all the members of which, save one, are pupils. Today we already have a number of self-sufficient units, and State financial support for the others is ever more strictly reduced. Thus the CER is a fertile cell in the forefront of socialism.

It is not a simple school, but a centre of economic and ideological radiation, the crucible in which the New Man is formed. Not only does it represent in the countryside, for example, the most successful creation of the revolution, but every one of the 8,000 Basic Committees of the Party has a CER attached to it, which thus becomes a centre of research and of scientific and technical extension.

Pedagogically speaking, the curricula have been shorn of all that was useless and ideologically false. This makes it possible to devote far more time to productive activities, which in some cases account for 75 percent of the programme.

In each district and in the Federation there exists a Council for Revolutionary Socialist Culture, directly concerned with the close integration of the schools with the life of the people.

As part of the revolutionizing of our educational system, we considered that the moment had come to end our linguistic inferiority complex—a tenacious heritage of colonialism. The re-establishment of our native tongues is held to be a potent factor in shaking off alien influence and in bringing ideological freedom and therewith the self-confidence of which colonialism had robbed us.

Accordingly, from the earliest classes onwards, these national languages are not "lessons" or "subjects" but tools—the vehicles for transmitting scientific and technical knowledge. In the higher classes, including the 4th stage—High Education—the national languages are compulsory subjects not merely for the faculty of Social Sciences, but for the technical faculties also. The national languages are, at this level, provisionally compulsory subjects because they are intended, in our plans for a Cultural Revolution, to be the tools of education in uprooting mental structures foreign to the genius of our people.

All this is not easy; we have our difficulties, but they are far from

insurmountable. The class struggle following the path of anti-im-
perialism cannot be a simple affair. But our difficulties are the less
formidable because in education, as in all other fields, no decision
is taken until it has been discussed in a thoroughly democratic manner in the Party framework. From the first to the fourth scholastic
cycle, the people have a voice in all matters; the people cannot be
wrong and may oppose a perfectly justified decision if they have not
been consulted or if they are not convinced that the decision is right.
This principle is dear to us.

At all levels, the CER is directly administered by the pupils and
students themselves, through a Governing Council which is not only
an administrative body but also a technical component of the Party,
functioning with well-defined attributes. In all cycles of education
the headmaster is not the potentate of yesterday but an adviser, a
member of the Council who takes part, on the same footing as the
pupils, in the collective management of the funds voted by the
State or earned directly by the production of the CER. The Council
maintains discipline and has the whole responsibility for the cor-
rectness of financial dealings. The teacher is no longer a figure de-
claiming dogmatically from behind his desk, but a militant spirit
carrying out his tasks in revolutionary education.

It is no internal contradiction but the logic of our socialist lean-
ings which has prompted us to democratize the administration of
our educational establishments and the relations between masters
and pupils, professors and students. In an hour when youth is causing age-old and "proven" systems to totter, our young people, satisfied and with no further claims, no longer ask the dramatic question, "What shall I be tomorrow?"

Our youth are not merely implicated in the exercise of power,
which is denied, incidentally, to their comrades in bourgeois countries, but they exercise power effectively and exclusively. Today the
struggle—often bloody—of youth in support of its claims, which is,
by the way, a heightened aspect of the class struggle in many economic systems, does not exist in Guinea. Our youth, entirely devoted to the struggle against imperialism and against the clique of
counter-revolutionaries, demands, instead, supremacy over nature.
Armed with the Party ideology, these young people strive rather to
rid historical necessity of its fatal character by becoming the effective masters of the future.

We have been well aware that a revolutionary movement without a coherent and scientific ideology is a dangerous compromise
doomed to fail. Therefore the Party ideology is at the heart of all
our activities, whether productive, scientific, technical, literary or
other. For us ideological training is absolutely imperative. It is

above all for us the essential implement enabling us to create, in Guinea, the African Society, the New African Man, an artisan conscious of possessing a culture, the crucible of United Africa and an original contribution to universal culture.

That, Comrades, is what we are doing in Guinea, in the name of Africa.

Our history and our culture were completely destroyed when we were forcibly brought to America in chains. And now it is important for us to know that our history did not begin with slavery's scars. We come from Africa, a great continent and a proud and varied people, a land which is the new world and was the cradle of civilization. Our culture and our history are as old as man himself and yet we know almost nothing of it. We must recapture our heritage and our identity if we are ever to liberate ourselves from the bonds of white supremacy. We must launch a cultural revolution to unbrainwash an entire people . . .

Armed with the knowledge of the past, we can with confidence chart a course for our future. Culture is an indispensable weapon in the freedom struggle. We must take hold of it and forge the future with the past.

MALCOLM X

2

The West African Roots of Afro-American Music

RALPH H. METCALFE, JR.

Much controversy surrounds the American black man's African heritage. Some scholars assert that little if any concrete proof exists that Afro-American culture is not wholly a product of that people's experiences in the West. We should harbor no false notions of academic objectivity. White scholars develop their theories from an ethnocentric point of view, evaluating alien cultures by white Western standards. Because of the racism that permeates the very fabric of American society, the attempts of Afro-Americans to present their history and culture in an ethnocentric frame of analysis have been suppressed and overlooked in white academic circles.

Just as no man has the right to determine another man's future, no man has the right to interpret another man's past. White anthropologists devote lifetimes to the study of the black man's origins, yet little attention is paid to the tribes of cavemen of the Caucasus mountains. Far from being an exception, the subjects of African music and the roots of Afro-American music contained therein have been grossly misinterpreted by Western scholars. Their tools of analysis are incorrect and insufficient. The tribal tonalities that the Western musicologist interprets within the Western chromatic scale were in existence long before the Western scale was ever written down.

Though progress toward truly objective cultural analysis is being made, it is minimal. The failure of Afro-Americans to develop a cultural viewpoint concerning our own heritage and that of the white man would not only be incorrect, it would be disastrous. We do not question the existence of the musical links between Mother

RALPH H. METCALFE, JR. received the B.A. in economics from Columbia University in June, 1970. Interested in a wide range of black experience, Metcalfe has published previously in *The Black Scholar* (April, 1970, "Chicago Model Cities and Neocolonization").

Africa and her children, held in bondage here in the United States. Our knowledge of this link is not merely a symptom of a newly popular slogan such as "Black is beautiful." Brother John Wesley Work commented on the same concept in 1915:

Thirty centuries ago, amidst the dawning civilization of the Mediterranean shores, science taught that the earth was a circular disc surrounded by the ocean. Contemporaneous legends told of the swarthy Ethiopians living in two divisions; one in the East, the land of the rising sun, and the other in the extreme West, the land of the setting sun. Consequently the Ethiopians dwelt in perpetual light. . . . Ruthless centuries have not overcast that brightness, nor have they destroyed the soul happiness of the Son of Light. His soul is a song. He expresses his every experience, his whole life, in terms of melody, and he passes through the Valley of the Shadow of Death with a song upon his lips.[1]

It is obvious, therefore, that we seek to determine not whether the blues has anything in common with African music, but rather what elements of the music of the Sons of Light survive here among those in this land of darkness.

The history of the Afro-American people begins with the Atlantic slave trade. The census of 1790 showed a slave population of 697,897, with almost all slaves living south of the Mason-Dixon line.[2] Most of the Africans brought to America as slaves came from the Guinea Coast, from an area bounded on the north by the Senegal river, stretching to the eastern border of modern Nigeria. Elements of the Ashanti, Dahomey, Bini, and Yoruba peoples were captured and sold into slavery. These groups, "composites of many small groups, welded through a long process of conquest into more or less homogeneous kingdoms, (they) share many traits in common." [3]

It is true that American slaves were robbed of much of their culture by their masters. During the early period of slavery drums were prohibited, as were religious worship and song. Eventually the slaves were allowed to sing happy songs, but the singing of any tune of sorrow was punishable by the master's whip. Families and tribes were consciously dispersed throughout the South. The knowledge of these various forms of oppression should not prevent us from realizing that there was a set of interrelated West African traditions in the common past of the early slaves.

In studying African music it is important to understand something

1. John Wesley Work, *Folksongs of the American Negro*. Nashville: Fisk University, 1915, p. 7.

2. Daniel P. Mannix and Malcolm Cowley, *Black Cargoes*. New York: Viking, 1952, p. 68.

3. Melville J. Herskovits, *The Myth of the Negro Past*. Boston: Beacon, 1958, p. 61.

of the nature of the society that produced it. Surely the European music of the seventeenth century differs markedly from that of the twentieth century. There are two reasons for believing that music is and was one of the most stable aspects of West African society: the existence of a reasonably cohesive musical system in Africa, and the fact that music is one of the most strongly functioning parts of African society. In 1959, Herskovits and Bascom noted that, "songs referring to battles of the eighteenth century are still current in Nigeria." [4]

It is probable that the West African music that has been studied in the twentieth century is very similar to that which was being played and sung during the time of the slave trade. An even more stable element of African societies than music is language. In the Bantu languages, *Nommo* is the word for the "life force" contained in the spoken word. The belief is that

> The vital force that carries the word issues from the mouth in a water vapour which is both water and word. . . . Yet this *Nommo*, which effects conception and then calls for birth, is not sufficient to produce a complete human being. . . . For the new-born child becomes a *muntu* only when the father or the "sorcerer" gives him a name and pronounces it. Before this the little body is a *kintu,* a thing; if it dies, it is not ever mourned.[5]

Nommo is the power of the spoken word and is not limited in significance to the birth of a child. It is a building block of strategic importance in the foundations of the African ethos:

> Thus all the activities of men, and all the movement in nature rest on the word, on the productive power of the word, which is water and heat and seed and *Nommo,* that is, life force itself.[6]

The lyrics or words of an African song must then be analyzed in a different light than Euro-American verse. "The song is the *Nommo* which does not reflect but creates the mood." [7] The African singer does not describe a mood to his listeners; rather, he creates a mood and puts his audience in that frame of mind. In his book, *Blues People,* LeRoi Jones tells us that in some African languages, the meaning of a word can be changed simply by altering the pitch of the word. Moreover, it is a recognized theory that the natural inflections of speech were the ultimate origin of the concept of scale and melody in music. Without exceptions, the folksongs of the Yoruba people are sung to the tonal inflection of words.

4. William B. Bascom and Melville Herskovits (eds.), *Continuity and Change in African Cultures.* Chicago: University of Chicago, 1959, p. 12.
5. Janheinz Jahn, *Muntu.* New York: Grove, 1961, pp. 124-125.
6. *Ibid.,* p. 126.
7. *Ibid.,* p. 224.

Not only did the African have a different experience than the European, but we have seen that he also had a different method of expressing his experiences than the Western musician. The understanding of this difference is central to the study of any aspect of black music, especially to the study of the blues, which shows greater African influence than either rhythm and blues or so-called "jazz." Different means of expressing an idea can also be observed in the instrumental music of both cultures. The European tradition is one of preciseness, the articulation of exact notes and meters in perfect imitation of those described on the score. Even improvisations are composed of exact steps and measures. The black musician talks through his instruments, producing musical inflections to represent vocal ones. The musician plays from "beneath" a note, through the note, and "above" the note. He passes through the arbitrary point on the Western scale known as a note and instead plays a whole range of sound. The Bantu tradition of sliding from tone to tone survives in the blues to this day.

Each West African tribe would have its own songs and its own way of playing them. Usually a unique set of tones would make up the tribal tonality in which all of their music was performed. These tonalities were passed down to each succeeding generation of musicians from the last, a situation which we shall see paralleled in the southern United States and later in northern urban centers.

The power that the music of Africa held over its people was harnessed in several useful ways. When an African would become sick, the physician would go to him accompanied by a band of musicians who would play all night and as long as necessary to cure the patient or to send him into the next life.

It is not unlikely that in this custom is to be found the origin of the singular custom of "settin' up." . . . This nocturnal song-service . . . is held when a negro is supposed to be dying. The singers, men, women and children of all ages . . . sit about on the floor of the larger room of the hut and stand outside at the doors and windows, while the invalid lies upon the floor in the smaller room. Long into the night they sing their most mournful hymns and anthems, and only in the light of dawn do those who are left as chief mourners silently disperse.[8]

Perhaps the most well-known African idiom is the work song. Years of slavery in this country preserved the work song if nothing else. Africans and Afro-Americans enjoy working rhythmically, in order to make their task easier. In West Africa there are songs of courtship and songs of challenge or scorn between a man and a woman as well as work songs. There are African work songs about

8. Henry E. Krehbiel, *Afro-American Folksongs*. New York: Schirmer, 1914, p. 107.

fishing, hunting, and weaving. "The men sing and their music seems irresistible; for their bodies sway, and their hammers rise and fall to the perfect time of their tune and the work goes on with happiness, interest, and power." [9]

Usually each work gang would have its songs led by a type of foreman or leader who would do no work. Professor Work noted this custom among the Kroo people:

Among the Kroo tribes it is a custom to change farms frequently, because their god forbids their cultivating the same farm during successive years. Consequently, every year new lands must be opened up, necessitating the felling of trees. Three or four surround a tree to cut it down. Gala leads a song but does no cutting. This Gala is the leader of all songs and shouts. In war time he stands in the midst of his warriors, hurls his spear into the air, catches it again and leads a shout, which is a vigorous kind of song, telling of the valor of their ancestors, and describing what they themselves are going to do in war . . . [10]

As of yet, Afro-American culture has not enjoyed achievements of nearly the same magnitude as those of many African societies. The work songs produced in this country, therefore, are less elaborate than their African counterparts. There is no mention of the glorious deeds of ancestors in war, for the Afro-American people have yet to fight their own war. Black Americans working for a railroad, laying track would sing:

> *Leader:* Oh boys, can't you line her?
> *Gang:* shack-a-lack-a
> *Leader:* Oh boys, can't you line her?
> *Gang:* shack-a-lack-a
> *Leader:* Oh boys, can't you line her?
> *Gang:* shack-a-lack-a
> *Leader:* Ev'ry day of the week we go linin' track.

The "shack-a-lack-a" response of the work gang was a phonetic imitation of the sound made by the pieces of track as they were pushed into line with long metal poles. When the leader shouted, the gang would rest; then as they chorused the reply, they would pull back on their iron bars in unison, moving the piece of track an equal distance throughout the length of the gang.

White people in particular and white society in general had been defining black culture long before white scholars began their studies of the black man's heritage. Even before it was generally acknowledged by whites that black people have a culture (if it is generally acknowledged now), slave masters were controlling the social cus-

9. Work, *op. cit.*, p. 8.
10. *Ibid.*

toms of their slaves. The desires of the slaves were accorded secondary importance behind the slave master's drive to maximize profits. Blame must fall squarely upon the shoulders of the capitalist system that black people in this country were allowed to sing work songs, but were not allowed to engage in ceremonial songs such as those used in the practice of "settin' up." The work song made the workers more productive, while "settin' up" merely drained them of energy that could be used to the master's benefit.

Nevertheless, the work song is an integral part of the Afro-American musical tradition. Few work songs are sung today, but there are many blues songs that illustrate the Afro-American's current attitude toward work and working conditions. In 1960, Mississippi-born Jimmy Reed recorded perhaps the best-known of these songs in his "Big Boss Man."

> Big Boss man, can't you hear me when I call?
> Big Boss man, can't you hear me when I call?
> Well you ain't so big, you just tall, that's all.
>
> You got me workin' boss man, workin' around the clock,
> I want a little drink of water, but you won't let Jimmy stop.
>
> Big Boss man, can't you hear me when I call?
> Well now you ain't so big, you just tall, that's all.
>
> Well I'm gonna get me a Boss man, one gonna treat me right,
> Work hard in the daytime, rest easy at night,
> Big Boss man, can't you hear me when I call?
> Well you ain't so big, you just tall, that's all.[11]

Here the degradation of having to ask the white man for permission to take a drink of water is surmounted by the boss' inhuman refusal. The brother is not lazy; all he wants is a fair deal—"Work hard in the daytime, rest easy at night." Respect is a two-way street, and by failing to respect his employee or slave, the boss loses the respect of the worker. Jimmy Reed realized the reality of the situation in the line "Well you ain't so big, you just tall, that's all." The boss is not big in the sense of being big-hearted. He is tall because he is over the worker; he has greater power behind him. This line is almost religious in significance in that it tacitly acknowledges the strength of good and the weakness of evil. He is not big enough to resist the power of right; he is vulnerable in his thin, unprotected tallness. "Big Boss Man" documents the recent realization of black people that the "Boss Man" can be had.

By the time that Afro-Americans had arrived at this level of consciousness, the system which oppresses them had become more so-

11. Bluesway Records.

phisticated. Black people have been hit harder by the economic
fluctuations of this system than any other ethnic group in America.
The continual shortage of jobs becomes more acute in times of
recession or depression, as chronicled by Chicagoan J. B. Hutto in
his blues, "Things Are So Slow."

> I went to work this morning, was all set to start.
> My boss looked up and said to me, "son it weighs my heart."
> *Chorus:*
> Things are so slow don't think we need you no more.
> He told me things are so slow,
> I don't think we need you anymore.
> I had to tell my wife, she didn't fuss.
> Finance took the car, we'll have to ride the bus.
> I had a dream last night, I was standing in a great big line.
> A line like they had, folks, in 1929.[12]

Not only is the brother denied an opportunity to work, but he
must go home and explain to his wife why he can't fulfill his function as a provider. It is in this form that the African work song
survives today. The prevalent social conditions of the day do not
produce glorious deeds of ancestors to be honored by later generations; rather, unemployment and degradation of the head of the
black family are discussed.

One of music's most fundamental functions in African society was
that of social control. In the kingdom of Dahomey, musicians enjoyed less royal sanction than in other African societies. They would
therefore resort to "songs of allusion," topical songs about current
events which were used to spread news and sometimes for extortion.
Songs were used in the court, however, as a means of preserving
history.

"Songs were and are the prime carriers of history among this non-
literate folk. In recounting the ritual associated with the giving of offer-
ings to the souls of those who were transported into slavery, this function
of song came out with great clarity. The informant at one point could not
recall the sequence of important names in the series he was giving. Under
his breath, to the accompaniment of clicking fingernails, he began to
sing, continuing his song for some moments. When he stopped he had the
names clearly in mind once more, and in explanation of his song stated
that this was the Dahomian method of remembering historic facts. The
role of the singer as the "keeper of records" has been remarked by those
who visited the kingdom in the days of its autonomy.[13]

12. Chance 1165, Blues Classics BC-8.
13. Alan P. Merriam, "African Music," in Bascom and Herskovits, *op. cit.*,
p. 321.

The Afro-American people have no palaces, no royal courts. There are certain blues songs that tell of great disasters, and list the people who were involved. The incomparable Howlin' Wolf (Chester Burnett), now living in Chicago, recounts a famous fire that took place in Mississippi in his "The Natchez Burning."

Chorus:
Did you ever hear about the burning that happened way down in Natchez, Mississippi-town?
Did you ever hear about the burning that happened way down in Natchez, Mississippi-town?
The old building got to burning, there was my baby laying on the ground.
Sally Jones was there, Louiza was there, Rosa Mae was there, Louise was there.
Did you ever hear about the burning, that happened way down in Natchez, Mississippi-town?
I looked up and it was burnin', there was my baby layin' on the ground.[14]

The African forerunner of the Afro-American bluesman was the *griot.* These *griots* or *guéhués* as they were sometimes called were a large caste of Saharan-Sudanic musicians, similar to the European traveling minstrels. They would travel from village to village, singing and playing a lute (a stick over a gourd covered with skin with a string strung over the stick), an ancestor of the guitar, telling of the current events in the area. Though they were generally liked, these musicians were sometimes looked down upon by the African social system of which they were a part. In February of 1884, Henry Krehbiel received a letter from Lafcadio Hearn, then in West Africa, telling him of "the strange history of the *griots,* who furnished so singular an example of musical prostitution, and who, though honored and petted in one way, are otherwise despised by their own people and refused rites of burial." [15]

Here perhaps is at least part of the reason why the urban bluesmen of today are viewed with such contempt by certain segments of the black community. Of course, the blues are thought of as the music of slavery, the unpleasant memories of which all black people would certainly like to forget. Yet the urban blues singer does not want to return to slavery. He wishes to escape the past also, but he is faced with the harsh reality that slavery is not over. Many Afro-Americans find this reality hard to face, and they therefore develop a dislike for anyone who reminds them of it. Attitudes such as these prompted Junior Wells to remark, "As soon as people find out that you're a musician, they automatically think you a sissy, drink wine, or eat pussy."

14. Chess 1744.
15. Krehbiel, *op. cit.,* p. 38.

We can see marked similarities between the African *griot* and Afro-American bluesman traditions. It would be naive to assume that bluesmen consciously set out to become *griot* or *griot*-like figures. In 1936, Maud Cuney-Hare gave us a most concrete link between the two traditions in her study, *Negro Musicians and Their Music:*

A peculiar class of professional musicians which may be found nearly everywhere in Africa make their appearance decked out in the most startling apparel—feathers, roots, and bits of wood, with other emblems of magical art. Whenever a listener is discovered he begins at once to recite details of his travels and experiences, in a chanting recitative. The Arabs have bestowed upon them the name of hashash (buffoons). . . . In the Senegal, minstrels who frequent market-towns have what is called a song net made of a fishing net. On this all manner of things are tied— tobacco pipes, bits of china, birds' heads, feathers, reptiles, skulls and bones, and every object bespeaks a tale. The passerby selects an object and asks the price for the song. Bargaining ensues: finally a price is agreed upon and the purchaser listens to the song. The saying is that when these singers die, they are put into trees. The fantastic "song net" reminds one of a home owned by a very aged colored couple in a Tennessee city of the United States. . . . The trees in front of the house are literally covered with bits of brightly colored glass, glazed crockery, parts of broken earthen-ware and scraps of gaily flowered china—broken pieces of every known article of a crockery store—and these fastened in the trees! Was it possible that this aged man and woman were the progeny of Senegal minstrels? No one could give me an answer to the riddle.[16]

The position of the *griot* on the social ladder ranged from high to rock bottom in various parts of West Africa. Certainly, at his lowest social ebb, the *griot* could not have occupied as low a position in his society as the black man does here in America. Black people have been deprived of the opportunity to participate in the social, political, and economic functioning of the society of the United States. Education has been denied to this whole ethnic group. For these reasons, blues singers in the past have not been conscious of these forces, and their music has not dealt with them. Because they did not exist politically, black people produced no political songs. Prevented from participating in political relationships, all that was left to the Afro-American community were personal relationships. The blues is thus a personal music; when it deals with politics it does so on a personal level. The resultant form of politico-personal blues is exemplified in "Korea Blues" by J. B. Lenoir:

Love you baby, yes I always will,
Love you baby, yes I always will,

16. Maud Cuney-Hare, *Negro Musicians and Their Music.* Washington, D.C.: Associated Publishers, 1936, p. 18.

Took you downtown, baby, bought you some shoes,
Love you baby, know what to do.

Went to the army, I stayed two long years,
Fought twelve months in hot Korea,
Sent my money to my wife and child,
She didn't even write me or send a line,
Got back home on the fourth of July,
Knocked on her door and she made me cry.

Hey hey hey, hey hey hey,
Woa yeah, woa yeah, woa yeah yeah, woa yeah,
Ooooh wee, did me wrong,
Woa yeah, woa yeah, woa yeah yeah,
You gonna get it, you gonna get it.[17]

J. B.'s negative reaction to his experience with the Korean War is anything but ideological. He has no complaint about his experiences in Korea; he tells us of the pain that having to go to Korea produced when he got back. He does not consider the international implications of the war, but rather its inter-personal ramification. His audience is told about the Korean War in a way that is relevant to their lives. The bluesman does not deal with social, political, or economic theory. He deals with the personal realities of the situation. J. B. Lenoir offers no social theory to explain his wife's infidelity. The facts are simple and clear: his wife needed a man and he had to leave her for two years. He ends by saying, "you gonna get it," giving us a graphic example of how external oppression breeds violence against one's own people; indeed, against one's own wife.

The African *griot* was not always despised. "In some Western Sudanic states the king's authority was diminished by the influence of a caste-like group of minstrels, 'griots,' who had acquired a monopoly of state traditions." [18] More often, he spent little time if any in large towns, traveling more in a circuit of nearby villages. As recently as 1969, in the area of the ancient kingdom of Mali, Frederic de Saint Michel observed that among the Mande peoples, comprised of the Bambora, Malinke, and Khasonke tribes,

. . . you can find, with only a few variants, the same instruments and the same musical genres. Sometimes, in the evening, friends and neighbors gather round the head of a family and listen to the *strict* recounting his genealogy to the accompaniment of his *cora* or *dan*, telling of the bravery of ancestors and the deeds of the great chiefs who founded the society. . . . The *cora* is a harp-lute with 21 strings, stretched in two

17. Parrot 802.
18. J. Lombard, "The Kingdom of Dahomey," in Daryll Forde and P. M. Kaberry, *West African Kingdoms in the Nineteenth Century*. London: International African Institute, 1967, p. 80.

rows along a long shaft. The sounding box is a half gourd covered with
skin.[19]

An examination of African musical instruments and the most popular blues instruments reveals another dimension in the link between
Africa and the blues. The *griots* all played stringed instruments; the
lute, the *cora*, or the *dan*. The guitar is without question the main
instrument of the blues. It, along with the harmonica, lends itself
particularly well to the "ranges of sound" that take the place of notes
in the blues. The strings of the guitar and the reeds of the harmonica
can be "bent" to produce a wide range of sound around the Western
note which they were designed to produce. The destruction of the
Afro-American family unit and the original African tribal structure
by the slavemaster made it impossible for the slave's musical culture
to remain intact. Just as the steel drums of the Caribbean originated
from a lack of the original drums, so the use of the harmonica and
especially the guitar came to be popular among Afro-Americans.
The amount of significance attached to the guitar itself as a blues
instrument is subject to much debate. Some Euro-American students of the blues believe the European guitar to have been a
major influence in the original African music.[20]

There was also in Africa a strong tradition of guitar-like instruments,
and most of the early accompaniment styles in the blues seem to have
grown from the rhythmic finger picking styles that had been developed
in West Africa. The instrument was introduced into Africa by the Portuguese in the fifteenth or sixteenth century in its earliest European form
as the small "machet" or rabequina. Using this as a model the African
musicians built crude guitars that were called rabekin, ramakienjo,
raamakie, rampi, rabeuquin, or ranke.[21]

Excavations found exclusively in a small central section of Africa
have turned up relics from the neolithic period, among them the
ground harp, the earliest known stringed instrument. The ground
harp is composed of a pit in the earth, covered with bark. Beside the
pit:

... a tall flexible rod is stuck in the earth and pulled way over by a
string fastened from its end to the back lid of the pit. The instrument is
either struck or plucked, sometimes by several persons simultaneously.

A similar instrument of comparable age is the ground-zither. It is
comprised of:

19. Frederic de Saint Michel, "West African Cultural Traditions Still Strong
in Music of the Mande Peoples," *Muhammad Speaks*, June 27, 1969.
20. Samuel Charters, *The Bluesmen*. New York: Oak, 1967, p. 19.
21. Curt Sachs, *History of Musical Instruments*. New York: W. W. Norton,
1940, pp. 54-55.

A pit dug in the ground and covered with a piece of bark as a sound-board. A string is stretched horizontally between two posts; another string tied to the middle of the first and acting as a bridge runs vertically to the bark lid, serving the string into two acoustical sections.[22]

It therefore seems ludicrous to assume that the introduction of a Portuguese proto-guitar into Africa in the fifteenth or sixteenth century would have a very profound effect. No doubt some African musicians did build models of the rabequina, out of musical curiosity if nothing else. It is an insult to all peoples of African descent to assume that the Portuguese instrument had far-reaching effects on the music of a people who had been playing ground harps since neolithic times, and among whom the lute had been flourishing for centuries. Finally, let us not forget that the North African Moors controlled the southwestern tip of Europe for 400 years during the first millennium A.D., before Portugal was Portugal.

We have touched upon a few of the many social traditions of West African music that find parallels in Afro-American blues. Evidence of this link exists not only in the social functions of the two different styles of music and in the instruments that are most commonly used in both, but also in several "musicological" characteristics of West African music and Afro-American blues. Similarities in the approach to playing the "notes" or tones have already been observed. A direct and irrefutable connection also exists between the verse form in both idioms. Most blues verses fit the rhyme scheme a-a-b. Usually the first line is repeated, adding emphasis to the statement and deepening the mood. The third line is the punch line, explaining the significance of the first two lines and completing the thought of the verse. This form seems to be a direct descendant of the most common type of West African song which Western musicologists call "antiphonal." As in the work song, there is a leader and a chorus. The leader will sing a line, sometimes two, and will then be answered by the chorus with a second or third line or with a refrain that remains constant throughout the song. This call and response song form has carried over into the relationship between the voice and the instrument of a single unaccompanied musician. In the blues the voice often accompanies the instrument, the same relationship that has been widely observed in West Africa. Here originates the twelve bar format of most blues songs. There has been a degree of departure from the twelve bar blues in some of the more recent urban blues. A guitar player from Chicago, Magic Sam (Samuel Maghett), has been playing a lot of sixteen bar blues. Of course the dividing lines between blues, rhythm and blues, and so-

22. *Ibid.*

called "jazz" are not arbitrarily concrete, and the recent beginnings of cross-fertilization in these three different areas account for some of this departure from the twelve bar form. The vast majority of blues, however, both past and present, still exhibit this African characteristic.

The technique of falsetto singing in the blues and in black music in general is often misunderstood by the unfamiliar listener. Charles Keil, the sociologist-musicologist author of *Urban Blues*, explains,

Falsetto singing comes directly from Africa, where it is considered to be the very essence of masculine expression. The smallest and highest pitch drum in a West African percussion ensemble or "family" is designated the male drum because its tone is piercing and the role it plays is colorful, dynamic, and dominant. The falsetto techniques of a West African cabaret singer are sometimes undistinguishable from those employed so effectively by Ray Charles, B. B. King, or the lead voice in a gospel quartet. . . . I should like to stress again, however, that an Africanism argument may be both relevant and interesting, but it is not necessary to establish this point. Negro women jump and shout when B. B. King cuts loose with a high falsetto, that is really all we need to know.[23]

There are at least two particularly interesting references in the lyrics of certain blues tunes.[24] B. B. King sings, in a tune entitled, "You Put It On Me,"

They say there ain't no woman that a man can trust,
That they all use juju and gooby dust.
But I'm glad, glad, glad, I'm so glad, you put it on me.

The reference to "gooby dust" comes from the African word *gooba*, which is a kind of African nut. Jones explains,

In Africa the ground-up *gooba* was used to conjure with, and it was thought to give one person power over another if the ground *gooba* (goober dust) was spread around the victim's hut. In the South, peanut shells spread in front of someone's door supposedly caused something terrible to happen to him.[25]

It seems reasonable that folk superstitions would be one of the most resistant elements of African culture to the oppression of slavery. If the master heard one of his slaves using the word *gooba* or "gooby," he would probably categorize it as either a mispronunciation or as the ignorant mumblings of a savage.

The "original" Sonny Boy Williamson, Willie "Rice" Miller, recorded a blues in Chicago in 1955 called "Fattenin' Frogs for Snakes," which would hardly have been acceptable during the era

23. Charles Keil, *Urban Blues*. Chicago: University of Chicago, 1966, p. 27.
24. Quincy Jones and M. Angelou, Bluesway BLS-6022.
25. LeRoi Jones, *Blues People*. New York: Morrow, 1963, p. 35.

of official slavery. Sonny Boy uses the symbols of the frog and the snake to evoke a feeling for an exploitative relationship in which he finds himself on the losing end.

It took me a long time to find out my mistakes,
It took me a long time, long time to find out my mistakes,
   spoken: It sure did man,
But I bet you my bottom dollar, I'm not fattenin' no more frogs for snakes.

I found out my downfall back in nineteen hundred and thirty,
   spoken: I started checkin'.
I found out my downfall back in nineteen hundred and thirty;
I'm tellin' all my friends now I'm not fattenin' no more frogs for snakes.
Here it is nineteen an' fifty seven, I've got to correct all my mistakes.
   spoken: Oh, man.
Here it is nineteen and fifty seven, I've got to correct all my mistakes;
I'm telling my friends including my wife and everybody else I'm not fattenin' no more frogs for snakes.[26]

The meaning of the song is clear. It is a masterpiece in the simplistic straightforward style of the poet-laureate of the blues, chronicling his arrival at a new level of consciousness after thinking about a problem for twenty-seven years. For our purposes here, however, the significance lies in Sonny Boy's use of the frog and the snake. These two creatures are represented widely in Ashanti art. Their meaning is two-fold. The Ashanti used the frog and the snake to symbolize the pitfalls of evil, the frog having to be careful not to be eaten by the snake. Of particular significance, however, is that the Ashanti also interpreted the two symbols as a warning to the king not to harbor too much disdain for the people or to tread upon them as upon a serpent, lest the king receive a fatal wound. Sonny Boy had been naive, his efforts toward accomplishing his goal in life had been thwarted at every turn. His positive gestures turned out to have no more significance than that of a frog being fattened for a snake, to be eaten eventually when the frog had gotten big enough. Even though there is a reversal of roles here—as Sonny Boy identified with the frog and the Ashanti identified with the snake—the similarities of the two anecdotes, one from West Africa and the other from Mississippi, are striking.

Unlike Euro-American music, the music of West Africa is a powerful social force. There is music for weddings, music for funerals, music for work, music for courtship, and the historical music of the *griot* caste, each serving a specific social function.

There is then in Ghana a clear awareness of the emotional value of music which is utilized in a practical way to meet the requirements of social life. There is evidence from anthropological monographs that this is

26. Checker 864, LP 1437.

so in other African societies. Considerations of enjoyment are always at
the forefront, for music and dancing constitute a dominant avenue of
dramatic expression. The music of workshop is not cultivated merely out
of a dread of the gods but because it is emotionally satisfying. Aesthetic
pleasure is looked for even in the dirge.[27]

It has been necessary for our purposes here to skim over some
of the basic characteristics of the relationship between West African
music and the blues which is a subject for many volumes and a
fundamental step in understanding the nature of the urban blues.

27. J. Nketia, *African Music in Ghana.* Evanston: Northwestern University,
1963, p. 9.

3

The Black American Epic:
Its Roots, Its Writers

EUGENE B. REDMOND

> Before he deserted the streets of Har-
> lem and the fuel in his furnace died at
> curfew, my Afroirishjewish Grandpa
> said: "Between the dead sea Hitherto
> and the promised land Hence looms the
> wilderness Now: although his confi-
> dence is often a boar bailed up on
> ridge, somehow, the Attic salt in man
> survives the blow of Attila, Croesus,
> Iscariot and the Witches Sabbath in the
> Catacombs of Bosio."
> —MELVIN TOLSON, from GAMMA
> in Harlem Gallery
> "Art is the signature of man."
> ROMENETHA WASHINGTON

For the moment it is enough, perhaps, to lament the lack of information detailing those aspects of African culture that stayed, in one
form or another, with the African made slave in America. There has,
however, always been more than conjecture to go on (though today
too many unread youth feel free to guess at relationships between
the then and now or, as the poet might put it, the "now and now"),
for many scholars have observed, studied and placed their findings

EUGENE B. REDMOND is a professor of Black Studies at Sacramento State College, Calif. Widely known as a poet and editor, Redmond has taught at Oberlin
College and Southern Illinois (East St. Louis). His poems have appeared in
Tambourine, New Black Poetry, Negro Voices: An Anthology of Negro Poetry,
and other anthologies. He is editor of two collections of the late Henry Dumas'
works, Poems for My People and Ark of Bones and Other Stories. Redmond's
most recent volume (1970) of poetry is Sentry of Four Golden Pillars, House
of Truth, East St. Louis.

at the disposal of the general public. Personal background, then, combined with studies, allows us to state that folklore (especially animal stories and fables), song styles, tonal utterances and many general practices and customs tie the black American to his African starting point.

A prerequisite to embarking on a discussion of the origin, growth and development of an indigenous Black American Epic is an understanding of the ingredients characterizing epics in all times: elevated communal folk expression; general, and on occasion specific, detailing of a people's lifestyle carved by the pen of one viewing his subject through the collective eye and mind; a heroic best-foot-forward picture of a race, personified and embodied in the protagonist, e.g., John Henry!

Tracing the genealogical table of the Black American Epic sends us back. Margaret Walker, in "Sorrow Home," finds the other end of the natal cord:

> My roots are deep in southern life;
> deeper than John Brown or Nat
> Turner or Robert Lee. I was sired
> and weaned in a tropic world. The
> palm tree and banana leaf, mango
> and cocoanut, breadfruit and
> rubber trees know me.

A fusion of physical Africa and the southern United States, held together by black spirituality, sets an epic mood as does Countee Cullen's poem "Heritage":

> What is Africa to me:
> Copper sun or scarlet sea,
> Jungle star or jungle track,
> Strong bronzed men, or regal black
> Women from whose loins I sprang
> When the birds of Eden sang?

Back. We go back to capture the spirit and letter of winds that put the music to the black epic, style that instills rhythm, color and sights that make it picturesque, faith, discipline, tolerance and strength that make it *endure*. "Heritage" is a revelation: a way of becoming for Cullen who recalls African past/present and masterfully juxtaposes Western ideology (his training) with "popular" myths about Africa. Epic in stature, the poem is carefully formed, colorful and lyrical, with personified Africa given heroic proportions and the noblest virtues. A search, then, for the epic carries one, as we shall see, psychologically inward. Cullen, overcome by the fire and force of his imagination, of poetic truth, has his "body" cry out:

"Strip! . . . Come and dance the Lover's Dance!" Exquisite paradox
also comes through as this poet reflects on "heathen" African gods,
notes his "Conversion" to Christianity, and longs for home—confess-
ing that ". . . although I speak/With my mouth thus in my heart/
Do I play a double part. . . ."

For My People, Miss Walker's winner of the Yale Series Young
Poets award in 1942, gives due—and, really, unavoidable—tribute to
the great protagonists that "people" the black experience from the
spirituals right up to Filthy McNasty and Killer Joe, contemporary
folk heroes associated with, and popularized by, jazz music. That
African-classic, cool, stoic self is the mainstuff of Miss Walker's
volume. Divided into three sections, the first portion of the book includes such poems as "Dark Blood," "We Have Been Believers,"
"Lineage," and "Today." Viewed as multi-voice folk expression, For
My People becomes a powerful literary folk fabric with the several
characters merging to one "people." This magnificent volume ends
on a note of optimism. There is no total blues here. The foundation
for going on has been built by ancestors ". . . full of sturdiness and
singing. . . ." In the third section, "The Struggle Staggers Us," but:

> Out of this blackness we must struggle forth;
> from want of bread, of pride, of dignity.
> Struggle between the morning and the night.
> This marks our years; this settles, too, our plight.

Uprightness is the picture; uprightness that fuels endurance, that
approaches stoicism in its seeming indifference to stillborn democracy
and death. Is it a curious uprightness? Where does it come from? In
his The Negro Spiritual Speaks of Life and Death, theologian
Howard Thurman pulls at the roots of what this writer has called
"black stoic presence." We recall these lines from a slavery time
spiritual:

> Oh Freedom! Oh Freedom!
> Oh Freedom, I love thee!
> And before I'll be a slave,
> I'll be buried in my grave,
> And go home to my Lord and be free.

And Dr. Thurman supplies an explication:

Obvious indeed is it here that death is not regarded as life's worst
offering. There are some things in life that are worse than death. A man
is not compelled to accept life without reference to the conditions upon
which the offering is made. Here is something more than a mere counsel
of suicide. It is primary disclosure of an elemental affirmation having to
do directly, not only with the ultimate dignity of the human spirit, but

also with the ultimate basis of self-respect. . . . Here is a recognition of death as the one fixed option which can never be taken from man by any power, however great, or by any circumstance, however fateful. . . .

For the slave, from whose mouth and mind the first epic unfolded, death was a stopping off point—a rest, if you will—from his brutal and harsh reality, from what Langston Hughes was to call, in 1926, *The Weary Blues.* Yet, as "The Struggle Staggers Us" makes clear, any rest, actual or symbolic, was carefully paced. There was room to "stagger" but none to halt!

We have mentioned the first ard third sections of *For My People* without taking note of the sandwiched second which deals with a particular kind of secular religion found in the Black Epic. Traditional epics, from *Chaka* (uniter of the Zulus) to *The Song of Roland* to *Beowulf,* have central characters of "heroic stature." The hero may be an accumulation (mentally and physically) of the most desirable traits of the race, but he emerges as a single man: a sort of classic tragedy figure. The above pattern holds, also, for the Black Epic.

However, in the latter, the hero often embodies traits deemed "criminal" by the larger society. Outsiders view him as a subcultural character within a "subculture." Actually, however, he is quite revolutionary (the nature of this man is *revolution*)—understanding well, and at once, that survival depends on wits. (One book popping up with increasing frequency during discussions on this subject nowadays is Iceberg Slim's *Pimp,* a rather "icy" saga of a black man educated in the school of hard knocks and advocating a hard line on women in the "fold.") And while not every one of these often too loosely called "revolutionaries" is what blacks consider an ideal epic character, the vivacity of black oral literature has kept many of them before the eye-screens of generations. Miss Walker's renderings, then, give us no new characters. Her work is exceptional in that she has the poet's power to color and shape many of these cultural folk images. The indigenous, enduring black folk rap, then, is populated with witches, tyrants, befrienders of young children, the strong, the stoic, the quick-witted, the mysteriously wealthy, the very religious folk: a moving mosaic on the historical, psychological, religious, political black experience.

Poems in the second section of *For My People* include "Molly Means," "Bad-Man Stagolee," "Pappa Chicken," "Kissie Lee," "Yalluh Hammuh," "Two-Gun Buster and Trigger Slim," "Teachers," "Gus, The Lineman," "Long John Nelson and Sweetie Pie," and "Big John Henry." All are characters in the moving folk portrait—collectively and individually forming the epic: African graphic and oral carryovers brought into relief against the Western tradition.

Here, new language emerges from an ear (sounded for tone) forced to utter foreign non-musical phrases ("Joshua Fit de Battle of Jericho," "I'm jes as misabul as I can be," "One mo' ribber to cross"). Here, also, is the cool gait, stoic indifference, symbolized and typified in modern times by, among others, Trumpeter Miles Davis ("The birth of the cool"). Mosaic. Complete with everything except recognition!

The Tradition and Its Impact

The 500–600 spirituals existing today in written form, and the numberless others living on the tongues of the old folk, constitute the first Black American Epic. These songs were blacks' first literary-artistic contribution to America. And together they from a grueling, smelted praises-and-happy song of the Ulyssean mentality—and of wanderings, in fact, like those of *Invisible Man* or Rufus Thomas, driven, riveted in class, in *Another Country*. Consider, even, the titles of Langston Hughes' autobiographies: *The Big Sea* and *I Wonder As I Wander*. The spirituals are personal, individual statements set to the needs of an enslaved people. James Weldon Johnson (preface to *The Book of American Negro Spirituals*) said the individual developers of these early songs (poems) were spiritually and rhythmically influenced by the group. A hierarchy of bards, Johnson points out, included the song maker (writer) and song leader. Much less available than the leader, the maker had to pick graphic phrases, pitch tunes true, remember lines and maintain a strong voice. The "new" tradition of Richard Wright, James Baldwin, Ralph Elison and Henry Dumas is not too far removed from the voices or the defiant mood of the song makers and singers of yesteryear. Nor is it, when examined closely, lacking in African influences. In "Dark Blood" Miss Walker clears the rubbish from the view back:

> There were bizarre beginnings in old
> lands for the makings of me. There
> were sugar sands and islands of fern
> and pearl, palm jungles and
> stretches of a never-ending sea.

> There were the wooing night of tropical
> lands and the cool discretion of
> flowering of plains between two
> stalwart hills. They nurtured my
> coming with wanderlust. I sucked

fevers of adventure through my
veins with mother's milk.

Someday I shall go to the tropical
lands of my birth, to the coasts of
continents and the tiny wharves of
island shores. I shall roam the
Balkans and the hot lands of Africa
and Asia. I shall stand on mountain
tops and gaze on fertile homes
below. . . .

Imagination and genealogy colored with anticipation! The epic
poet's truth coming through, tuned and timed on tradition and
knowledge of it! Baldwin, on his way back home (literally speaking), pays tribute of blood and sweat and song to the tradition—to
his ancestors. His works, from end to end, reflect his debt to the
makers of the old slave songs, the creators of that vast body of folklore including animal stories, work songs, joy songs, blues, fables,
anecdotes and dances. A "called" preacher himself, Baldwin had to
Go Tell It on the Mountain. But his message, like Malcolm's, was
more than "Jesus Saves" or "You May Have All Dis World, But
Give Me Jesus." He stood on the high peak viewing the behind and
before. And in *Tell Me How Long the Train's Been Gone* he has
the hero reflect on African ancestor worship.

The saga cycles and epic literature also received germination in
the old-time preacher who assumed a more revolutionary role as
the people's struggle widened and became more complex. Dr.
Martin Luther King, Jr. was a digestion of the old and the new.
Academy-trained, steeped in the old Southern Baptist tradition,
thrust into leadership in the civil rights era, he returned—without
a doubt—to storytelling, that rich folk warehouse of black literature.
He hurled the most graphic phrases from pulpits, Chicago streets
and southern jails; wrote with the poetic eloquence of James Weldon Johnson; led songs like the old preachers used to do. And
rightly so. Noted Johnson (preface to *God's Trombones*):

The old-time Negro preacher has not been given the niche in which
he properly belongs. He has been portrayed only as a semi-comic
figure. . . . It was through him that the people of diverse languages and
customs who were brought here from diverse parts of Africa and thrown
into slavery were given their first sense of unity and solidarity. He was
the first shepherd of this bewildered flock. His power for good or evil
was very great. It was the old time preacher who was the mainspring
of hope and inspiration for the Negro in America.

The epic, as Johnson says in so many words, owes much of its
philosophy, its style, its development—in fact its coming into being—

to the old-time preachers and, by inference, the spirituals. Carter G. Woodson, in *History of the Negro Church*, describes the popularity and crowd-attracting power of black preachers who ebulliently sermonized from pulpits as far back as 1773. Looked up to and highly respected, these preachers resembled, in voice and action, African tribal chiefs, medicine men and wise elders. One cannot fail to see the picturesque relationship between, say, Dr. King, the poetic sermons in Johnson's *God's Trombones*, and the refined, delicious imagery in *For My People* where in "Dark Blood" we find "Sugar Sands," "fern and pearl," "wooing nights," "flowering plains," and "fertile homes." Johnson's "Negro Sermons in Verse" *(God's Trombones)* is a veritable painting of sights and sounds: "pine tree pointed his finger to the sky," "split the air with their wings," "darkness rolled up on one side," "I will be thy mouth and I will be thy tongue." And when Dr. King sees freedom in terms of "mighty" waters "rushing" and mountainous roars, we cannot help but get the graphic quake. Can we?

Great folk epics rise from life just as great folk heroes are born out of urgency, chaos, leadership need, challenge and human fastidiousness. The roots of stoic black presence combined, grew, knitted to produce the vast material and the many themes for the indigenous epic. And the more aware blacks become of the roots, of these historical threads in the quilt, the better will be the modern sagas. In 1922 Johnson's preface to the first twentieth century anthology of black poetry *(The Book of American Negro Poetry)* explained and defended the artistic existence of black people. Correctly, he started at the beginning: with rhythms, the spirituals, folklore. He was later to note (preface to *Trombones*) that black oral sermons were a "fusion of Negro idioms with Bible English; and in this there may have been, after all, some kinship with the innate grandiloquence of their old African tongues." The basis of the black preacher's fondness for big words, Johnson explains, was love for the "sonorous, mouth-filling, ear-filling phrase because it gratified a highly developed sense of sound and rhythm in himself and his hearers." That peculiar connection, then, between the written and the spoken word is sometimes elusive to those who do not understand and have not taken the time, in the words of poet Henry Dumas, to "Listen!"

The anthology preface displays Johnson's own concern for, and knowledge of, the tradition to which he must adhere if he is to have a valid voice. This pioneer pointed out "creations" of the "American Negro . . . summed up under four heads": (1) the Uncle Remus stories, collected by Joel Chandler Harris; (2) "spirituals" or slave songs "to which the Fisk Jubilee Singers made the public and the musicians of both the United States and Europe listen"; (3) the cakewalk, and (4) the ragtime—dances. Paris called the cakewalk the "poetry of motion," and Johnson said its influence was evident on "any American stage where there is dancing." Things have not changed that much since the Twenties! Johnson's comment holds for American dance stages today. In fact the same can be noted for much of the so-called "popular" American culture. For decades, America has found its rhythmic lifestyle in the "action" of the blacks. Each new temporary subculture takes its music, language, pattern of dress—in general, its lifestyle—from black Americans. In one of my poems, "The Barbarians," I have labeled the above practice "Imitating the naked pain of black captives."

James A. Emanuel (*Negro Digest*, August, 1969) reports that during the Harlem Renaissance of the Twenties, many whites went to that mecca to "forget the war and to engage their new Freudian awareness by escaping into exotic black cabaret life." The psychological interaction of blacks and whites deserves much treatment by "native sons." And some have already made inroads into this many-sided, complex thing. At his best, it has been said, the writer *is* a psychologist. *Perhaps.* Listen to Conrad Kent Rivers' "Watts" in *The Still Voice of Harlem:*

> *must I shoot the*
> *white man dead*
> *to free the nigger*
> *in his head*

Psychologically, the hugeness of black artistic output—and its rather embarrassing effects—has moved from the dance stages of American cabarets and ballrooms to the stages of the American mind. Yet the epic hero in black America remains the ogre, as we observed earlier, the nightmare in the "other" America. United States recognition of black epics, and the culture that produced them, has been through— for all it is worth—the back door, after a sorting out of "undesirables" has taken place. The folk tradition which is strengthened daily, and which is the wellspring of the black epic, was forged early. It had to be and Johnson's rangy prefatory comments in the anthology shows the elements that went into that forging.

From the powerful preachers and songmakers to W. C. Handy, the Memphis genius who wrote "The St. Louis Blues," the voice of black poetry was receiving life and purification. "A black poet is a preacher!" the Henry Dumas joyously announced in 1968. And in his exceptional eulogy to Dr. King ("Our King Is Dead"), Dumas leaped full-blown from tradition when he said: "To be a Black King in America means you must know how to die!" Presence. Uprightness. If no bridge exists for a crossing, Dumas said in a letter to a friend, then you "build one." (Do the undo-able!) Indeed the black American expressed the desire and determination to live in spite of death. A way of saying "I'm one with the past and the future." In its most contemporary posture, the epic is still transfused from the roots of that early fart in death's face. When, on a ghetto corner, a young black spokesman raps: "Man, wut'n no way in hell we was 'spose to make it," his strut and his indifference to the avid-eyed cop reaffirm what he knows—he did make it, America not-withstanding.

The Voice

Because he dealt almost exclusively in folk material, Langston Hughes is perhaps the greatest of the modern epic "writers." We do not discount W. E. B. DuBois' *Souls of Black Folk*, Ellison's *Invisible Man*, Baldwin's *Notes of a Native Son*, Wright's *Black Boy* or Melvin Tolson's overpowering *Harlem Gallery*. But Hughes' mammoth output, his work with the language, his range, his power and his endurance mark him as a seer deeply rooted in his tradition, a true folk poet. The creation of Jesse B. Semple, the Harlem folk philosopher, was, alone, a germinal force in much writing that followed it. Like Johnson, Hughes knew his place. As originator of the practice of reading poetry to jazz, he not only stitched backwards and forward in his lineage and idiom, but wrought a new force in the now obscenely exaggerated concept of multi-media. When Dr. King announced "I have a dream," had he not heard "Montage of a Dream Deferred" or "Let America Be America Again"?

> *Let America be America again.*
> *Let it be the dream it used to be.*
> *Let it be the pioneer on the plain*
> *Seeking a home where he himself is free.*
> *(America never was America to me.)*
>
> ❋ ❋ ❋
>
> *Yet, I'm the one who dreamt our basic dream . . .*
> *O' I'm the man who sailed those early seas*
> *In search of what I meant to be my home—*
> *For I'm the one who left dark Ireland's shore*
> *And Poland's plain, and England's grassy lea,*
> *And torn from Black Africa's strand I came*
> *To build a homeland of the free.*

At age 19, Hughes spiritually united the black world in his poem "The Negro Speaks of Rivers." He grew strong in the WORD as he traveled, studied, wrote and got firmer footing in the roots. In the words of Johnson (preface), Hughes "dug down into the genuine folk stuff" and used it as a source for cultural motifs and inspiration. He works especially well with blues and worksongs. But typical of the real giant, Hughes is at home in the most intellectual of company. He is cynic ("ain't no back/To a merry-go-round!"); full of race consciousness ("They'll see how beautiful I am/And be ashamed—," "Night coming tenderly/Black like me"); reminiscent ("My soul has grown deep like the rivers"); cognizant of miscegenation and the plight of the mulatto ("I wonder where I'm gonna die/Being neither white nor black"); colorfully descriptive ("Flavor of Harlem mine!/Walnut or cocoa,/Let me repeat: Caramel, brown sugar,/a chocolate treat") and folkly realistic ("And life for me ain't been no crystal stair").

The widest read, most often quoted, most imitated all-around writer in the black community, Hughes was the first of our race to live solely on his literary talent and is regarded internationally as the "Poet Laureate" of black people. "There comes this song/I do not understand," was Hughes' reference to Africa in the Thirties. But by the Sixties, he not only was praising and siring the concept and distribution of Negritude but was editing anthologies of African prose and poetry.

It was clear that the young Langston who did not "understand" became "aware"—indeed he had to, once he reached the end of the teleological line of black lineage in America.

We have called the epic a mural, a mosaic. True! With all the beauty, nostalgia and power normally associated therewith. No technical rules have been given for the pairing of oral and written black literature. But there is an explanation. Responding to an interview published in a pamphlet by Illinois Bell Telephone, poet Gwendolyn Brooks said the theme of race in her poetry "is organic, not imposed. It is my privilege to present Negroes not as curios but as people." Miss Brooks, then, supplies the answer to the thorny question of why juxtapose the oral and the written. They are organically linked, a body of work. The indigenous Black American Epic is either a stitch or an entire fabric, depending on when, how and where you view it. Here, we are talking about a self-portrait—dressed up in Sunday-go-to-meeting clothes; about the sum total of trials, loves, religions, politics, heroic feats, and battles. We mean the songs of Countee Cullen and of Smokey Bill Robinson, who sings "Way Over There," "I'll Try Something New," "The Love I Saw in You Was a Mirage," and "The Tracks of My Tears." We are talking about how Sterling Brown continued a tradition by seeking out folk epics and ballads as sources for poetry: "Stagolee," "John Henry," "Casey

Jones," and "Long Gone John." Robert DeCoy's *Nigger Bible* explores the genealogy of Jody Grind, and Lou Rawls in "South Side Blues" gives a more modern characterization of the Jody Grind-John Henry syndrome. In a poem "Invasion of the Nose," I tried to strike a contemporary resemblance to that celebrated folk hero, simultaneously admired, envied and criticized:

> *His nose was his radar,*
> *His eyes icy darts that moved faster than speed-of-sound jets.*
> *He could rap like a pneumatic drill*
> *Or croon like Smokey Bill when the occasion arose.*

Today perhaps he wears iridescent, pastel clothes and, maybe, silk and colored underwear, but black youngsters would rather dress like him than Brooks Brothers. He is a throw-back to John Henry and to "Pappa Chicken" of whom Miss Walker sings:

> *Pappa was a sugah daddy*
> *Pimping in his prime;*
> *All the gals for miles around*
> *Walked to Pappa's time.*
>
> * * *
>
> *Pappa's face was long and black;*
> *Pappa's grin was broad.*
> *When Pappa Chicken walked the streets*
> *The gals cried Lawdy! Lawd!*
>
> * * *
>
> *Pappa smoked his long cigars—*
> *Special Pappa brands—*
> *Rocks all glis'ning in his tie;*
> *On his long black hands. . . .*

Regardless of the intellectualness of epic writers, epics—in order to be such—must continue to spring from the roots, must stretch on the canvas of life, must be mosaics and murals, mirrors of the mass and public life of the people, admitting individual sketches—a Malcolm here, Jody Grind there, Nat Turner called to his tasks, DuBois gathering and digesting modern technology for the people along with his memorable *Souls of Black Folk*, Hughes painting pictures of black beauty and reminding America of her madness, Tolson mastering the language to an incredible degree and subtly signifying at America's psychological paralysis. Black presence means maintaining an equilibrium: a coolness undisturbed by tokenism or lofty statements; a stoic endurance unobservable of those unwritten "stay in your place" signs along the way. For like the theme of "The Signifying Monkey," that great black American oral epic, black

52 I/CULTURE

presence is a survival of the soul, a patience paced by discipline. "Any black man in the least perceptive must be constantly on the verge of insanity," James Baldwin has said. Yet in stoic defiance of inherent psychological death, like Ahab stalking the deck of the *Pequod*, the black presence, almost invincibly, not only "survives" but is a predominant influence on many physical and psychological American actions and attitudes. And so, just as in the African experience of the past and the present, the Black American Epic illuminates and defies the ancestral spirits, capturing—as it were—the spirituality of the quintessential black life force.

After Shakespeare, Pope and Arnold in the academies, black writers and students of literature find they have to begin a laborious —but rewarding—job of tracing their own roots (a chore not considered respectable in most American public school systems and institutions of higher learning). These searchers of the "self" carry on a new love affair with their past. Often, some are so "staggered" on the hearing of "their" ancestors' achievements that Western training clutters should-be respect with doubts and cynicism. This is especially true of some of the sons and daughters of Negro middle class attending expensive liberal arts schools; it is also true of many young black writers today, screaming and distorting black reality and performing such sacrilegious abortions as purposely corrupting word spelling under the guise of doing something "new." Some of these writers also find it fashionable and quite profitable to market flamboyant and grossly inaccurate "black" language. The worst of these offenders (may school help their soul!) implicitly say black people are monosyllabic, rap-sick fools. And we have yet to see today anything near the poetic footage of the Harlem Renaissance. But to return, the epic is a form of ancestor worship in that it enshrines the best characteristics of a people and passes them on in legend and myth. In a strongly oral language—such as Black American—this legending and myth-making is especially true, although the practice, generally, occurs in all cultures, among all people. The Black Epic need not include names, dates or actual places. As Cannonball Adderley has said, "Hipness is not a state of mind. It is a fact of life." So is black experience: yesterday, today and tomorrow. And it is from lineal personification of the black experience that the Black American Epic derived, grew and will continue to grow.

4

Jack Johnson as Bad Nigger: The Folklore of His Life

WILLIAM H. WIGGINS, JR.

Jack Johnson was a man.

This flamboyant black champion who has been called many things, e.g. show off, fool, speed demon, hero, race man, and many variants of nigger, such as smart, black or uppity, by both his detractors and defenders; but both of these hostile camps agree—the former reluctantly and the latter enthusiastically—that he was a man. For example, though the great majority of white Americans, and many respectable Negroes as well, cringed at the thought of his chaotically colorful, amoral life style outside the ring, the majority of them had to grudgingly admit that his actions within the ring reflected traits of manhood, e.g. physical courage and the inner spiritual ability to endure great hardships to achieve a goal. On the other hand, the controversial life of fast cars, white women and good times that Jack lived outside the ring personified those traits which combine to make a man for many blacks. But, perhaps, most important of all is the fact that Jack Johnson was very serious about establishing and maintaining his crown of manhood. For once in a moment of rare poignancy, he said to his biographer, John Lardner, "When you write about me remember that I was a man, and a good one." [1]

This paper will make a folkloristic investigation of Jack Johnson and his life style. The writer will attempt to substantiate two hypotheses in this article. First, he will defend the claim that an

WILLIAM H. WIGGINS, JR., a teaching associate and a folklore doctoral candidate at Indiana University, is currently conducting research into black oral history and folklore throughout the South, on a grant from the Rockefeller Foundation.

1. Finis Farr, "Black Hamlet of the Heavyweights." *Sports Illustrated*, June 15, 1959, p. 76.

oral tradition did spring up around Jack Johnson; and second, he will show how many of the folklore themes which circulate in the black community reflect many facets of Jack Johnson's life style.

Jack Johnson was his own man; he refused to allow anyone, white or black, to determine his place in society or the manner in which he should live. His most recent biographer, Finis Farr, wrote this description of his personality: "With Johnson, one never could be sure what he would say or do; and this from a Negro made white people nervous when it did not anger them." [2] This definition sounds very much like Samuel M. Strong's definition of a "bad nigger." He wrote, "The 'bad nigger' refuses to accept the place given to Negroes." [3] And, in another real sense, Johnson's personality sounds very much like Roger D. Abrahams' definition of the "hard-hero" as being that hero in the black community who "is openly rebelling as a man against the emasculating factors in his life." [4] Abrahams cites Railroad Bill, Stackolee, John Henry, and the Bully of the Town as examples of this "hard-hero." This does not fit Jack Johnson as well as Strong's "bad nigger" because Abrahams contends that the "hard-hero" is frustrated in his attempts to strike back at white society and, as a result, turns his anger inward on himself and other black men.[5] This is not always the case with Jack Johnson and the "bad nigger." They welcomed and often instigated direct confrontations with the white society's stereotype of the Negro's role and place in American life. Jack did it by aspiring for and winning a title which had been reserved for white men only, and the "bad nigger" does it by living a fast and violent life which is in many ways the antithesis of the slow and fearful white stereotype. In the next section we will look at some of the junctions at which the life style of Jack Johnson and the "bad nigger" meet.

There are at least four ways in which the life style of Jack Johnson and the "bad nigger" agree: (1) an utter disregard of death and danger; (2) a great concentration on sexual virility; (3) a great extravagance in buying cars, clothing, etc.; and (4) an insatiable love of having a good time. Let us look at these four traits in greater detail.

Both Jack Johnson and the "bad nigger" were fearless men; they did not fear dying. This idea is present in many ways in the life of Jack Johnson. For example, one early indication of his fearless na-

2. Finis Farr, *Black Champion: The Life and Times of Jack Johnson.* New York, 1964, p. 42.

3. Samuel M. Strong, "Negro-White Relationships as Reflected in Social Types." *American Journal of Sociology,* LXII, 1946, p. 24.

4. Roger D. Abrahams, "Some Varieties of Heroes in America." *Journal of the Folklore Institute,* III, 1966, p. 35.

5. *Ibid.,* p. 346.

ture was his admiration of Steve Brodie, the man who jumped off the Brooklyn Bridge and lived to tell about it. In fact, Jack Johnson so admired Brodie that he traveled by freight car from Galveston, Texas to New York City just to meet him.[6] His early years as a hobo also demanded this type of attitude from him. But, perhaps, the greatest example of fearlessness in Jack Johnson's life was the reckless abandon that he used in driving his expensive cars. He appeared in court on traffic charges at least twenty times and was in more than six serious accidents prior to the crash that killed him in 1946. Here is a typical incident recorded in the *Chicago Defender* under the headline: "Jack Johnson: Ex-Champion Pugilist Is a Real Fiend for Speed." A portion of the story, which was told by R. E. Wortham, the director of Jack Johnson's first film, "For His Mother's Sake," is reported in this manner:

As soon as they were seated, Jack, in the face of a blinding sleet storm, opened up and according to Wortham, that machine must have gone at an 80-mile clip. "I just held my breath, . . . and it was hard enough doing that, for Johnson forgot all about traffic regulations and the driving sleet. That machine must have had invisible wings, for it practically flew under Johnson's steering. My hair stood on end all through the trip, and I for one want it emphatically understood that while I like Jack Johnson, he will never again entice me to take an auto ride with him." [7]

There are parallel accounts in Negro folklore where this note of disregard for death is struck. During slavery, death was often pictured as not something to fear, but in some instances as the only honorable way out of the hell of slavery. J. Mason Brewer has collected the proverb: "De quickah death, de quickah heaben." And when he asked the informant what it meant, she smiled and sang these lines from a spiritual:

> Oh Freedom, Oh Freedom,
> Befoh' Ah'd be uh slave
> Ah'd be burned en mah grave
> An' go home tuh mah Jesus an' be saved.[8]

Another example of fearless defiance is contained in this anecdote called "Leonard Allen," included in B. A. Botkin's collection of folk history, *Lay My Burden Down*. Leonard is described in this manner:

I was scared of Marse Jordan, and all of the grown niggers was too, 'cept Leonard and Burrus Allen. Them niggers wasn't scared of nothing.

6. *Ibid.*, p. 10.
7. Anonymous, "Jack Johnson: Ex-Champion Pugilist Is a Real Find for Speed." *Chicago Defender*, March 11, 1922, p. 7.
8. J. Mason Brewer, "Old-Time Negro Proverbs." *Publication of the Texas Folklore Society*, XI, 1933, p. 102.

If the devil hisself had come and shook a stick at them, they'd hit him back. Leonard was a big black buck nigger; he was the biggest nigger I ever seed. And Burrus was near 'bout as big. And they 'spised Marse Jordan worse 'n pizen.

As the story progresses, Marse Jordan is home from the Civil War and is angered by Leonard's remark: "Look at that goddam soldier. He fighting to keep us niggers from being free." The informant re-tells Leonard's death this way:

Old Marse flung her off and took the gun from Pappy. He leveled it on Leonard and told him to pull his shirt open. Leonard opened his shirt and stood there big as a black giant, sneering at Old Marse. . . . He . . . shot a hole in Leonard's chest big as your fist. Then he took up Miss Sally and toted her in the house. But I was so scared that I run and hid in the stable loft, and even with my eyes shut I could see Leonard laying on the ground with that bloody hole in his chest and that sneer on his black mouth.[9]

I also remember two somewhat similar anecdotes that my father's father told me. Both took place in Georgia during the early 1900's. The first one evolved around a black carpenter. While he was busy completing one job, this carpenter was rudely approached by a prominent white citizen in the town who demanded that the car-penter stop what he was doing and begin work on his job. The Negro politely refused and said he would get to the job next. This did not satisfy the white man, because he continued to argue that the Negro should begin work on his job now. Finally, in anger the black carpenter told him to take his business elsewhere. This reply so angered the white man that it caused him to kick the black man in the seat of his pants. The black man stopped working, picked up his tools and went home without saying a word. He got his gun, re-turned to the store and killed the white man. He and his family hid out until night and made their escape to Chicago.

The second story is centered around the notion that all blacks look alike and/or have no individual dignity or worth. This low estima-tion of the Negro's worth is clearly reflected in this couplet which was popular during the 1870's when the Chesapeake and Ohio Rail-road was being built:

> Kill a mule, bury another,
> Kill a nigger, hire another.[10]

The hero of this story was James E. Jones. The sheriff came into the black community with a warrant for the arrest of James A.

9. B. A. Botkin, *Lay My Burden Down: A Folk History of Slavery*. Chicago: the University of Chicago Press, 1945, pp. 194-195.
10. Louis W. Chappell, *John Henry: A Folk-Lore Study*. Jena: 1933, p. 34.

Jones. He stopped in front of James E. Jones' house and yelled for him to come out, because he was under arrest. James E. Jones came to the front door of his house carrying his baby in his left arm and said he was not coming because he was not James A. Jones. The sheriff got angry and said, "Nigger, you better come on out here before I blow your brains out! James A. or James E. is all the same to me." Again James E. Jones refused. This so angered the sheriff that he jumped out of his car and headed for James E.'s gate. As the sheriff approached the gate, the Negro told him not to trespass on his property because if he did, he would shoot him. By this time, the sheriff was in such a rage that he whipped out his pistol and began to shoot at the two figures framed in the doorway. As his shots were whizzing around James E. Jones, James E. calmly reached above the frame of the door, pulled down his rifle, and killed the sheriff. The next day he escaped with the help of the black undertaker who got him past the road block by hiding him in a casket and driving him out of town. These are just a few examples from the black oral tradition which talks of a black who fears neither death nor the white man.

A second major characteristic shared by Jack Johnson and the "bad nigger" is the equating of manhood with sexual virility. Jack Johnson was married four times and had many mistresses. He always seemed to be in trouble either because of or over some woman. Early in his life he was tricked out of all his belongings by one. He was shot in the foot by one jealous woman. He fought numerous brawls over the honor of his wife, Etta Terry Duryea, as they toured Europe in 1911. And, finally, his downfall and conviction under the Mann Act was the result of sensational testimony given by one of his former lovers, Belle Schreiber.

Jack Johnson's flaunting of his white mistresses in the face of white society was bitterly denounced by whites and respectable Negroes, such as Booker T. Washington. The latter denounced Johnson publicly, but the former created and enacted national and state laws dealing with sexual morals and mixed marriages. George Schuyler eulogized Jack Johnson in this manner: "To stop him [Johnson] from making money, federal laws were passed preventing interstate traffic in prize-fight films and the transportation of women over state lines for allegedly immoral purposes.[11] Roi Ottley contends that, in addition to the Mann Act, many states passed laws forbidding mixed marriages between Negroes and whites, and other federal bills were introduced which failed to pass. He wrote:

11. George Schuyler, "Views and Reviews." *The Pittsburgh Courier*, June 22, 1946, feature page.

His [Johnson's] marriage to a white woman—one of three—caused bills against interracial marriages to be introduced in Wisconsin, Iowa, Kansas, Colorado, Minnesota, New Jersey, New York and Michigan. Bills were brought before Congress with penalties ranging from imprisonment to castration.[12]

Very few Americans had the liberal outlook of this unknown fan who wrote this letter to the editor of the *Chicago Defender:* "Jack Johnson has paid his debt to the government and should be let alone. If he married a white woman, she was willing and that was their business." [13]

This theme of the tabooed white woman appears in many genres of black folklore. There are two instances in which the white woman appears in the John cycle of tales. The first one, "The Fight," was collected by Richard Dorson. In this folktale John beats Jim by slapping the master's wife in front of the large crowd gathered for the fight. Jim is so frightened by this unorthodox behavior that he runs off. When the angry master asks him why he slapped his wife, John replies, "Well, Jim knowed if I slapped a white woman I'd *a killed* him, so he run." [14]

This second folktale, "Putting Hand Under Old Mistress' Dress," is more sexual in nature:

I tell you 'nother funny joke 'bout Henry Johnson. He had to clean up most of the time. So. Mrs. Newton's dress was hanging in the room up on the wall, and when he come out he said to old Uncle Jerry, he said: "Jerry, guess what I done," and Jerry said: "What?" And Uncle Henry said: "I put my hand under Old Mistress' dress." Uncle Jerry said: "What did she say?" Uncle Henry say: "She didn't say nothing." So Uncle Jerry 'cided he'd try it. So he went dragging on into the house. Set down on the floor by Old Mistress. After while he run his hand under her dress, and Old Master jumped up and jumped on Jerry and like to beat him to death. Jerry went out crying and got out and called Henry. He said: "Henry, I thought you said you put your hand under Old Mistress' dress and she didn't say nothing." Uncle Henry said: "I did and she didn't say nothing." Jerry said: "I put my hand under her dress, and Old Master like to beat me to death." Uncle Henry said: "You crazy thing, her dress was hanging up on the wall when I put my hand up under it." [15]

This theme of the tabooed white woman is evident in these two recent illustrations of black folklore. The first one, "Discretion," is

12. Roi Ottley, *Black Odyssey.* New York, 1948, p. 207.
13. Anonymous, "Letter to the Editor." *The Chicago Defender,* July 8, 1922, p. 10.
14. Richard M. Dorson, *Negro Folktales in Michigan.* Cambridge, 1956, pp. 55-56.
15. Botkin, *op. cit.,* p. 9.

set in Atlanta and concerns a distressed black man who has jumped off one of Atlanta's skyscrapers to commit suicide. On the way down he saw he would hit a white woman, "so he curved and went right back up." [16]

The second one recalls the danger of lynching which looms over a mixed love relationship in many southern parts of America:

A Negro was a helper in a construction gang. A white lady passed. The Negro said, "Lawd, will I ever?"
He was overheard by a white man who said, "No, nigger, never."
The Negro said, "Long as there's life there's hope."
The white man said, "Yes, long as there's a nigger there's a rope, too." [17]

This seems to be a widespread piece of folklore. In my native Kentucky this story ends with the line, "Yes, and long as there's a tree there's a rope." But the message of the white woman being off limits to black men is not changed.

Finally, this legal and social sexual isolation from the white woman has helped produce a black sexual myth. In this trend of thought the black male is desired by the white woman because of his superior sexual drive. Paulette Cross has recorded this interesting response from one of her informants concerning the black sexual myth and the concept of manhood.

Cross: Oh yes, I remember, not too long ago, that I had gone to hear the lecture on the "supposed myth of black sexual superiority" and you told me at that time I should have stood up during the lecture and told everyone that black men are sexually superior. Don't you remember telling me that?
Informant: Oh, yeah, you started expounding about the sexual myth, and I said you should have just told the lecturer that all of it's true, you know. Because it is true despite how it became true, you know, uh—no matter what you say about well uh—a person's body is a person's body. But if it's wrapped up in somebody's mind that this particular body is superior uh—more superior than this particular body and everybody thinks that, then the body is superior. It's like God you know, everybody thinks there's a God. [18]

This idea of the white woman desiring the black man's body because she believes he is a superior sexual lover is widespread in

16. Langston Hughes and Arna Bontemps, *The Book of Negro Folklore.* New York, 1958, pp. 504-505.
17. Arthur J. Prange, Jr. and M. M. Vitols, "Jokes Among Southern Negroes: The Revelation of Conflict." *Journal of Nervous and Mental Diseases,* 136, 1963, p. 164.
18. Paulette Cross, "A Collection of Jokes Told by Black Americans about White Americans and Interviews with Kenneth Newsome and Rockie Taylor." Classroom presentation, Folklore 201, Indiana University, December 15, 1969, p. 4.

popular belief and Afro-American folklore. A white coed at Boston
University affirmed her belief in "the ancient legend of black supersexuality" with this statement: "A lot of girls feel that black guys
really have it [supersexuality]. You see this all around the colleges.
It's a very sexual thing." [19] A black male classmate of this girl mused
over the white coeds' belief in the black sexual myth, too. He said,
"What is it that white girls want from me? Do they think we're that
different, that we're some kind of animal? Why do so many of them
chase us?" [20]

In black folklore there is the story of John the Numbskull, who
could not take advantage of a "good thing." It goes like this:

The boss' white wife was hot to trot for John. She tried every way possible to get him alone so that she could give him a piece. Well, one day
she saw her chance. She got on her horse and rode into the forest with
John trailing behind. When they got waaaaay back in the woods, she got
off her horse and told John: "Do everything that I do." John said: "O.K."
Well, she took off all her clothes and John took off all his clothes, too.
Then she lay back on the ground and said: "Allright, big boy, get in the
saddle and go to town!" John got on the horse and rode into town buck
naked.

However, there are folktales and jokes in Negro folklore in which
the black man does "take care of business" in a most virile manner.
The connection of this virility with the blacks' concept of manhood
is reflected in this segment of Paulette Cross' informant's response:

And uh—it's just that black people have been conditioned to, you know,
responding physically and white people have been conditioned to intellectualize across the experience and over the experience, you know, and
try to pretend that a man is defined by his ability to use fourteen syllable
words, instead of his ability to beat somebody's ass, you know. And if
you're superior in this aspect of the body, the strength of the body, then
I suppose quite naturally you'll be superior sexually, you know. And even
if this weren't true, it's so hung up in everybody's mind, black and white
in America, that for all practical purposes all the mythology is true.[21]

A folkloristic expression of the black male's supersexuality is this
joke collected by Paulette Cross:

There was this honky family and this man had a daughter who had
just turned sixteen. And her father had always promised her that when
she turned sixteen that he was going to have her satisfied. So his daughter
said, daddy, daddy, you know what you told me, that when I turned sixteen you were going to have me satisfied. So her father said all right. So

19. Anonymous, "Boy, Girl, Black, White." *Time,* April 6, 1970, p. 74.
20. *Ibid.,* p. 74.
21. Cross, *op. cit.,* p. 4.

her father went down to the corner to look for a suitable man. First, he sent a honky man to his daughter but she say, daddy, he too little. Next, he sent a Jew man to his daughter but she say, daddy, he too fat. Finally, he sent a black man to his daughter and she said that he was just right. So the girl's father waited on the corner. He was waiting for them to get through. So after a while it was about twelve o'clock midnight. And finally his little son came runnin' down to the corner and said, daddy, daddy, you know that black man you sent home, well, he done satisfied sister, sister Sue, Mary Lou, he done packed me and he waitin' on you, so get you ass on down there.[22]

This final joke marks the ultimate progression of the white woman —black man theme in black folklore. They have moved from the strained taboo relationship of the John cycle to this most intimate contemporary relationship. And, in so doing, this theme has caught up with the love life of Jack Johnson—truly a man ahead of his time in this regard. It is very clear that his sexual life style was the forerunner of today's "bad nigger."

A third trait which is present in both the life of Jack Johnson and in the "bad nigger" is that of extravagance. Both of them spend money as if it were "going out of style." Jack Johnson made big money and he freely spent it on big cars, expensive clothes and other expensive items. In addition to the huge purse he made in the Jim Jeffries fight, Jack Johnson commanded, and quickly spent, large entertainment fees. For example, he was booked into the Howard Theatre in Washington, D.C. for $5,000 per week.[23] In addition to these large fees, Jack Johnson demanded and got large advances. For example, he demanded a $1,500 advance from the Howard Theatre,[24] and $4,500 from another promoter.[25] This latter sum was quickly spent on an expensive car and five $100 suits. Finis Farr aptly summarized Jack Johnson's extravagant living in this statement: "Outside the ring Johnson continued to cut a fashionable figure with his dozens of well-tailored suits, his handmade shoes, and his racing cars." [26] Many of these material items appear in black folklore.

Perhaps the most obvious subject is the expensive car and the troubles it often causes its black owner. The author recalls two anecdotes which were often told by his mother and younger brother. The former taught at Prairie View College in Texas during the late 1930's. She recalls that parking lots in nearby Houston would not

22. Cross, *ibid.*, p. 13.
23. Perry Bradford, *Born with the Blues.* New York, 1965, p. 159.
24. *Ibid.*, p. 159.
25. Anonymous, *The Chicago Defender*, May 6, 1922, p. 1.
26. Farr, *op. cit.*, p. 72.

park an expensive car if it was driven by a black man. This is how she recalls one of her colleagues getting around this prejudice:

> Whenever Phil went into Houston, he would carry a chauffeur's cap on the front seat of his Roadmaster Buick. And just before he turned into a downtown parking lot he would quickly put on this hat. As he got out of the car, he would say, "Park this car for Mr. Jones" (his name was Jones) and leave to do his shopping. It worked every time.

What was told as a local anecdote really has national significance for the black community in America. An example of this was the nationally televised retirement ceremony given by the Boston Celtics for K. C. Jones. Among the many gifts that he received was a new Cadillac car. And one of the most poignant and at the same time ludicrous moments was when Jones' long-time friend and team mate, Bill Russell, gave him a black chauffeur hat. Jones put it on and everybody laughed. But the writer and his wife, plus Bill Russell and many other blacks who witnessed that moment, were "laughing to keep from crying." For in this event the spirit of Jack Johnson and the "bad nigger" had been resurrected again. Once again a black man had refused to stay in "his place." That chauffeur's cap was a reminder of how things used to be for black men who dared to own expensive cars in America.

But things have not completely changed. My brother told me this joke about a black man who was driving "down home" to Mississippi for an annual reunion.

> This Negro was going back to Mississippi in style, Jim! He bought him a "Hog" with all the accessories on it. Man, this Cadillac had air horns, white-walls, power windows, power brakes, power steering, power's mamma!
>
> He loaded up the trunk with all his fine clothes and lit out for the "sip." As he drove through Kentucky with his shades on, everything was cool. But when he got on the other side of Nashville going into Memphis, he started thinking about Mississippi. And the closer he got to Memphis, the scareder he got. So when he got to Memphis, he parked his Cadillac and caught a bus into Mississippi.

A well dressed black man is another sight that many whites do not want to see "down there" in the South. Hylan Lewis makes this incisive observation concerning a southern white community's concept of black man's "place" regarding dress and attitude. It says:

> There are certain pressures that operate from the white community with respect to dress and manner. The Negro is aware of these pressures even if he doesn't always bow to them. The Negro male who dresses well consistently (i.e., without overalls or work clothes on week days), or who in his bearing or manner does not suggest a certain deference or humility,

or the Negro who wears glasses, is in danger of being labeled a "smart nigger." The least he can expect, no matter what his occupation or interest, is to be called (with some degree of patronage) "preacher" or "teacher." As one young Negro put it, "They don't like nobody who don't wear overalls and don't work like digging ditches. If a man dress decent, he's a smart nigger." [27]

The importance of the well-dressed black man is seen in many of the toasts and caps collected by Roger Abrahams in *Deep Down in the Jungle* and Lou Rawls' monologue spieled prior to his singing the street hustler's song, "World of Trouble." In his rapping introduction Rawls describes the well-dressed hustler's suit. In Abrahams' book even many of the animals, especially the signifying monkey, are clearly described from their Stacey Adams shoes to their "stringy brim" hat. The author also remembers how angry one of his friends, Jeff Downey, became when one of his white co-workers asked him where he was going to preach. When Jeff asked him what he meant, he laughed and said, "My daddy told me the only colored men who wear ties in the middle of the week are colored preachers." Jeff works as a clerk in a Louisville, Kentucky bank—a position which requires that he wear a tie! My father also recalled a similar experience. He rode a cab home from work. During the drive he had a pleasant conversation with the white cab driver. As he was paying the driver his fare, the driver asked, "You're a preacher, aren't you?" My father said, "No," and asked why he believed him to be a minister. The driver replied, "Well, during the ride you never cussed; you're carrying a briefcase, and, besides, the only colored men who wear ties on week days are preachers."

This notion of the black man's inferior place in life is evident in these lines from the song, "I Went to Atlanta":

> *I went to Atlanta, Never been dere afo'*
> *White folks eta de apple, Nigger wait fo' co'.*
> *I went to Charleston, Never been dere afo'.*
> *White folks sleep on feather bed, Nigger on de flo'.*
> *I went to Raleigh, Never been dere afo'.*
> *White folks wear de fancy suit, Nigger over-o'.*[28]

Against the background of such social repression, it is easy to understand how a dashing historical figure like Jack Johnson and a cool folklore character like the "bad nigger" would be heroes to millions of black Americans because their exploits and manner of

27. Hylan Lewis, *Blackways of Kent*. Chapel: 1955, p. 54.
28. J. Mason Brewer, *American Negro Folklore*. Chicago: Quadrangle, 1968, p. 189.

living afforded them the vicarious experience of leaving their inferior "place."

The fourth, and final, characteristic that the life styles of Jack
Johnson and the "bad nigger" have in common is the love of a good
time. They are both hedonists "to the bone." Jack Johnson's life
seems to have been one big party. Usually he traveled with an en-
tourage of well-wishers and those just along for the ride. He truly
loved to drink. In fact, his trademark was the sipping of champagne
or some other expensive intoxicant through a straw.[29] Jack Johnson
was a black man who loved "to let the good times roll."

There is a constant thread of this theme woven into the fabric of
Afro-American folklore. For example, in the John cycle there is the
often collected story of John and his friends having a party in the
Big House while ol' marster is away on a trip. However, the party
ends in confusion when John's wife recognizes ol' marster masquer-
ading as one of the slaves. And when John gives the word, everybody finds the nearest escape route. A variant of a recent folktale
which also extols the virtues of a good time is this one entitled
"Saturday Night."

A Yankee once bought a plantation in Mississippi and there were many
things he could not understand about the Negro plantation hands. Among
these things was the importance of Saturday to them, the importance of
drawing money on that day, of having the day off and night free to go
in town. So finally the Northerner asked one of the very old men who
worked for him about it and the answer he got was, "Lord, sir, all I can
tell you is that if you was ever a Negro one Saturday night, you'd never
want to be a white man in this world agin." [30]

The thought of this punch line is found in many other folktales.
Richard Dorson recorded the one about a lumberyard worker who
was asked to work overtime. The worker refused the boss' urging
despite his raising the pay. Finally, when the boss asked why they
could not work on Saturday night, he replied in a manner similar
to the above. The writer also heard this variant from his mother:

This old Negro got drunk every Saturday night and every Monday
morning he was standing before the judge. One Monday the judge got
tired of seeing this man before him, so he asked him, "Why is it that
eeeeeevry Saturday night you get drunk and thrown in jail?" The Negro
smiled and said, "Your honor, if you was a nigger just *one* Saturday night,
you'd never want to be white again!"

The catharsis of Saturday night's fun is a part of Negro folklore
and is reflected in the lives of Jack Johnson and the "bad nigger."

29. Farris, *op. cit.*, p. 25.
30. Hughes and Bontemps, *op. cit.*, p. 509.

For they give bone and marrow to this line from "Stormy Monday Blues:"

> The Eagle flies on Friday,
> and Saturday I go out to play.

Jack Johnson is worthy of folklore studies, not only because his life style is that of the "bad nigger," but also because there are some items of folklore which have sprung up about him. There is very little in the way of oral sources, but many of the written accounts of his life contain what seem to be literary fragments of folklore. As one might expect, the majority of these items dealt with his life as a boxer. First, there is a constant reference to his boasting and talking, while fighting, to his opponent and those at the ringside. For example, before fighting Kid Cutler in Philadelphia he warned the crowd to get there early, because he would end it soon. In many ways, this type of boasting recalls the words of Cassius Clay before the Archie Moore fight:

> Don't block the aisles, don't block the door,
> Because Archie will fall in four.

And in the historic Jeffries fight Johnson is reputed to have let Jim hit him as hard as he could in the stomach and then whipped him unmercifully for the remaining rounds. In the Burns title fight he answered the shout that Burns would win with the boast, "A hundred to one he don't black my eye." [31]

His style made others boast about him, too. George Schuyler remembers him this way: "A master of balance, he [Johnson] could whip a man by merely looking at his feet, and often delighted T. A. Dorgan (Tad), the sport cartoonist, by completely turning his back on an opponent when the latter was off balance, and kidding with reporters in the press rows." [32] Many old timers boast about Jack's quickness of hands. One said Jack could catch his opponent's blows in his hands like a baseball player.[33] Another friend claimed, "Jack was so fast he could block a punch and hit you with the same hand." [34] And, finally, still another friend recalled, "He could predict every blow. He'd tell you he was going to hit you in the eye, and he would. He'd say he was going to hit you in the mouth, and he would. He was the most scientific fighter the world ever produced." [35]

Jack was always looking for a way to outsmart his opponent. Dur-

31. Farris, op. cit., p. 60.
32. Schuyler, op. cit.
33. Farris, op. cit., p. 67.
34. Ibid., p. 6.
35. Ibid., p. 8.

ing my college career I heard this Jack Johnson story told by my classmate Cullen Maiden, who was a former Golden Gloves fighter from Cleveland, Ohio:

Man, Jack was too smart for them white fighters. He'd get them in a corner and pin their arms at the elbow joint between his thumb and index finger. Then he would smile sweetly and kiss them on the cheek. Man, this would make these fighters so mad they would forget about boxing and come out swinging wild. And that was all old Jack wanted. He'd step inside their leads and counter punch them to death!

Story fragments centering on his great strength were also numerous. In two fights he knocked out his opponent despite the fact that on one occasion he had been drunk for several days before the fight,[36] and in the other he had subsisted on a weakening diet of crackers and tea for several days prior to the match.[37] His vicious knockout of Stanley Ketchel has given birth to many versions as to what really went on. In one account Johnson "struck Ketchel so savage a blow that it tore off his front teeth at the gums and stretched him senseless." [38] A second account describes the savageness of Johnson's blow this way: "The punch landed square on Ketchel's mouth. It dropped him as if he'd been hit by a falling steel girder. He was out for a whole hour. When he recovered he found that all of his front teeth were missing." [39] A third account is equally graphic. "The punch dropped Stanley as if he'd been maced. It landed on his mouth, broke off all his front teeth at the gums and stretched him senseless. Later, while musing over the attempted doublecross in his dressing room, Jack picked two of Ketchel's teeth out of his right glove." [40] There are also many stories surrounding the Jeffries fight. Two of them are that he broke three ropes during one training session [41] and that Johnson hit Jeffries so hard he knocked out Jeffries' eye.[42]

In addition to these extraordinary boxing skills, the investigator collected stories about Jack's super deeds outside the ring. One example is his jumping backwards ten feet from a standing start and this soon after recovering from a broken leg.[43] A second example are these two accounts of his tremendous appetite. On one occasion he is reputed to have eaten "a sizeable steak, a bushel of German-

36. *Ibid.*, p. 55.
37. *Ibid.*, pp. 24-25.
38. *Ibid.*, p. 65.
39. John Durant, *The Heavyweight Champions.* New York, 1967, pp. 58-59.
40. Anonymous, "Ketchel's Dream of Glory." *Sports Illustrated,* October 18, 1954, pp. 80-81.
41. Anonymous, *The New York Times,* July 1, 1910, p. 3.
42. Brandford, *op. cit.,* p. 159.
43. Farris, *op. cit.,* p. 11.

fried potatoes, and a stein of rye." [44] And at another time he had a dinner which consisted of "a dozen hot biscuits drenched in butter; then came five glasses of milk, a steak, and for dessert a platter of lamb chops." [45] And this third example has definite overtones of folklore. This is his physical asset of speed afoot. Johnson is reputed to have "engaged in a foot race with a kangaroo and ran the animal to death. He also chased and caught a rabbit, and captured a greased pig." [46] Johnson's behavior sounds much like that of the black who ran so fast he heard the bullet twice, once when it was fired and once when he passed it; [47] or the Negro who was running from the Klan and outran a bus, train, and finally a deer, which he asked if the Klan was after him, too.

There are some collected oral narratives which deal with Jack Johnson. J. Mason Brewer published this song, "Jack Johnson and Jim Jeffries," in *Worser Days and Better Times*:

> *Amaze an' Grace, how sweet it sounds,*
> *Jack Johnson knocked Jim Jeffries down.*
> *Jim Jeffries jumped up an' hit Jack on the chin,*
> *An' then Jack knocked him down agin.*
> *The Yankees hold the play,*
> *The white man pull the trigger;*
> *But it make no difference what the white man say,*
> *The world champion's still a nigger.*[48]

This fight was the greatest event that had happened to the black race since the Emancipation Proclamation. No other day since the "Day of Jubilee" had had such a positive effect upon the black American's self image and his ability to compete on an equal basis with the white man. When Jack Johnson met Jim Jeffries they were representing more than their own personal interests; they were representing the hopes and fears of their respective races. This racial dimension is evident in a front page cartoon carried by the then five-year-old *Chicago Defender*. It showed Johnson in the ring facing the black race's real opponent of racial prejudice. This notion of Johnson being a race champion is also reflected in the fact that black churches across the country opened their doors for special prayer services on the night of the fight.

The same was true of Jim Jeffries. He was looked upon by his white followers as the champion who would restore "the natural order of things" by soundly whipping this "bad nigger" Johnson.

44. *Ibid.*, p. 25.
45. *Ibid.*, p. 18.
46. *Ibid.*, p. 57.
47. Hughes and Bontemps, *op. cit.*, p. 135.
48. J. Mason Brewer, *Worser Days and Better Times*. Chicago, 1965, p. 178.

The day before the fight *The New York Times* carried a very revealing cartoon. In the ring the artist has sketched the two fighters in contrasting stereotypes. Jim Jeffries is positively portrayed as the strong white champion, complete with a bowed belt tied around his trim waist. He is disdainfully glaring at what the artist conceived Jack Johnson to be. Russom's sketch of Johnson is the negative stereotype of the ape-like Negro man. Johnson's figure has a small, ape-like head, resting on large shoulders, from which extend massive ape-like arms which touch the floor. The third person in the ring is a fat, fashionably dressed promoter who has extended his right hand, holding a silk hat, toward the audience. In the faces of this crowd we see the open hostility that many whites had for Johnson. In the foreground there are two white men with clenched fists raised in anger. But perhaps the most revealing character is a white woman who is standing and shouting insults at Johnson, while in her left hand and stuck in her hat are American flags.[49] The meaning is clear: Jim Jeffries, for many whites, represented all that was good and American. Roi Ottley was correct when he wrote: "When Johnson met Jeffries at Reno, Nevada, July 4, 1910, he was in fact fighting the white community; the ex-champion had been hailed as the 'White Hope.' "[50]

This concept of a "white hope" was first conceived in Australia after Johnson defeated Burns in 1908 to become the first black man to wear the world's heavyweight crown. Jack London, reporter for *The New York Herald,* wrote these scathing words after describing how uneven the Burns fight was—he depicted Jack Johnson as "a grown man cuffing a naughty child." This is how his column ended: "But one thing now remains. Jim Jeffries must emerge from his alfalfa farm and remove the golden smile from Jack Johnson's face. Jeff, it's up to you!"[51] But there were "white hopes" before Jim Jeffries, some of whom were Al Kaufman, Victor McLagen, who later became a movie star, Tony Ross, Billy Delaney, Philadelphia Jack O'Brien, and the already discussed Stanley Ketchel.[52] All of these men suffered the same fate; they were not only defeated by Johnson; they were physically abused and their fans were made to eat "humble pie" vicariously by the smiling Johnson who took these fighters' best efforts and then taunted them publicly in the ring, while inflicting much pain before the inevitable knockout.

Like the outcome of his fights with these "white hopes," there is no doubt that Jack Johnson was the reason for the development of

49. Anonymous, *The New York Times,* July 3, 1910, p. 14.
50. Ottley, *op. cit.,* p. 206.
51. Farr, *Black Champion,* pp. 61-62.
52. Farr, *American Heritage,* p. 65.

the notion of a "white hope." Edwin B. Henderson defines "white hope" in this fashion: " 'the great white hope' . . . generally means some hero who is called upon to gain victory for his admirers against great odds, when all else seems lost. Something like a St. George called upon to slay the dragon." Next he gives Jack Johnson full credit for establishing this concept: "The man who inspired that expression ['the great white hope'] was a black man—Jack Johnson, who was the first Negro heavyweight champion of the world." [53]

It is difficult to imagine the amount of racial hatred that was directed toward Jack Johnson prior to the Jeffries fight. Because of the racial overtones of the fight, Johnson had to train under the watchful eye of a guard who ṣat at the foot of the stairs leading to Jack's apartment, armed with a cartridge belt and a big .44 pistol in full view. At the gate, just before the fight, several large piles of pistols were confiscated from angry white fans as they entered the arena. And, *The New York Times* reported: "A lot of talk is going around that hot-headed individuals might draw and create a disturbance if Johnson happened to knock out Jeffries." [54] The most amazing thing about this historical drama is that this real threat of danger and death did not affect Jack Johnson at all. Like the "bad nigger," Johnson looked death in the eye and laughed as he continued to openly do all of those things which many white Americans hated. For example, he kept his white women in his guarded upstairs apartment, and in the ring he showed contempt for the hostile crowd and Jeffries by dividing his time between taunting them and savagely whipping Jeffries for fifteen rounds. After the fight, Johnson left for Chicago in his private railroad car, accompanied by friends, the white woman who would become his second wife, and the largest amount of money ever earned by a black man. Johnson, the "bad nigger," had not only met great odds and won, he had done it "his way." He had smashed the myth of white supremacy and given black men all over America a new vision of themselves. Little wonder that items of folklore began to appear in the black community concerning Jack Johnson.

I was told this Jack Johnson folktale by my father:

It was on a hot day in Georgia when Jack Johnson drove into town. He was really flying: Zoooom! Behind his fine car was a cloud of red Georgia dust as far as the eye could see. The sheriff flagged him down and said, "Where do you think you're going, boy, speeding like that? That'll cost you $50.00!" Jack Johnson never looked up; he just reached in his pocket and handed the sheriff a $100.00 bill and started to gun

53. Edwin B. Henderson, *International Library of Negro Life and History—The Black Athlete: Emergence and Arrival.* New York, 1968, p. 17.
54. Anonymous, *The New York Times*, July 1, 1910, p. 3.

the motor: ruuummm, ruuummm. Just before Jack pulled off, the sheriff shouted, "Don't you want your change?" And Jack replied, "Keep it, 'cause I'm coming back the same way I'm going!" Zoooooom.

This was Jack Johnson, always his own man. In conclusion, one can call him a hero. For as Abrahams defines the term: "A hero is a man whose deeds epitomize the masculine attributes most highly valued within such a society." [55] And certainly during his lifetime, as well as now, one of the major characteristics of manhood within the black community was the courage to stand up to the white man in words and actions. His life-long, valiant struggle against those governments, customs, and individuals who sought to force him into an inferior "place" caused the Irishman R. J. Coad, founder of the Washington Square Art Gallery and editor of the scholarly journal, *The Soil*, to say of Johnson, "After Joe, Whitman and Emerson he is the most glorious American." [56] But perhaps the greatest tribute he received was to affectionately be called a "bad nigger" by millions of black Americans. For in their jokes and songs about Jack Johnson they are really saying that in the first half of this century the word of their folklore became flesh and dwelt among them. His name, like the simple inscription on his tombstone, was: Johnson.

55. Abrahams, *op. cit.*, p. 34.
56. Farr, *Sports Illustrated*, pp. 76-77.

5

A Black Value System

IMAMU AMIRI BARAKA (*LeRoi Jones*)

· *Umoja* (Unity)—To strive for and maintain unity in the family, community, nation and race.
· *Kujichagulia* (Self-Determination)—To define ourselves, name ourselves, and speak for ourselves, instead of being defined and spoken for by others.
· *Ujima* (Collective Work and Responsibility)—To build and maintain our community together and to make our brothers' and sisters' problems our problems and to solve them together.
· *Ujamaa* (Cooperative Economics)—To build and maintain our own stores, shops and other businesses and to profit together from them.
· *Nia* (Purpose)—To make as our collective vocation the building and developing of our community in order to restore our people to their traditional greatness.
· *Kuumba* (Creativity)—To do always as much as we can, in the way we can in order to leave our community more beautiful and beneficial than when we inherited it.
· *Imani* (Faith)—To believe with all our heart in our parents, our teachers, our leaders, our people and the righteousness and victory of our struggle.

The 7 principles are 7 because the number is a meaning-symbol for this world. As a throw of dice it speaks of spiritual concepts and scientific principles. It is because of this that the seventh day was the culmination, as a period of devotion and meditation, for the 6

LeRoi Jones (Imamu Amiri Baraka), poet, playwright and jazz critic, is author of *Blues People, Black Music* and *Home*. His plays include *The Dutchman, The Toilet* and *The Slave*. His poetry has appeared in many leading magazines, among them *Harper's, Negro Digest* and *Liberator*. Baraka co-edited with Larry Neal the anthology *Black Fire*. Active in Newark politics from the Newark rebellions of 1967 to the election of its first black mayor, Kenneth Gibson, in 1970, Baraka has been a powerful force in organizing the black community of that embattled city. Since that time, Baraka has been instrumental in building the Congress of African Peoples and establishing Pan-African unity. He was elected its Chairman at the 2nd International Congress of African People, which was held in San Diego, California, in September, 1972.

days of divine work. Sun-Day. So Maulana speaks of spiritual concepts and scientific principles embodied as a morality system—complete in itself, as a contemporary black philosophy old as the sun.

The 7 principles are the spine and total philosophy of the US
organization. They are simple in what they say, but total in that they
evoke all the levels of meaning associated with philosophical systems.

The 7 principles are "10 commandments" yet more profound to
us—US because they are pre and post 10 commandments at the same
time. If there is *Umoja*, for instance, thou cannot kill, steal, bear
false witness, commit adultery, or any of the things the Western
world thrives on. The commandments are fulfilled by the initial need
of blackness for unity—oneness.

But unity is political too. The meaning vibrates as a totality.
Spiritual unity is the needed completion of physical and mental
unity. (The doctrine is made up of the 3 sides of the ancient pyra-
mid—physical, mental and spiritual—in each of its statements. The
three pyramids of the US symbol meaning "our traditional greatness," and by this, our traditional understanding.) The 7 principles
are solutions to the political dilemma of black people. I would say
solutions to the political dilemma of all men, but I recognize we are
different by virtue of our concerns and the context of our lives.

We, the different peoples, are as different rays of light, each bent
to particular articulation of the initial life force, and at different
stages of evolution (self-consciousness). All men would benefit by
the 7 principles. But the black man has created them out of his
specific need. The balancer of East and West, completer of this
cycle.

Umoja (definition: To strive for and maintain unity in the family,
community, nation and race). We are a *body* of people, the large
Being of Blackness. The many of us are parts of the body. The whole
cannot function *as it will* (Kujichagulia—Self-Determination) if it
is scattered, the head one place, the heart another. Physical unity.
Mental unity. We must think one way of total movement to liberate
ourselves. Each has a function but as complementary parts of a
whole. All organizations, *organs* really, they must function as of the
whole body.

Ujima—Collective Work and Responsibility. All of the organs
must function by the same will. We must have a head with control
over all the organs. The I's must be our many eyes and be a basis
for seeing in all the places.

One being in harmony with itself, this is the first need to be
satisfied before we can deal with an outside world. But it is internal
unity that makes a single will, which is self determination. What we

will be, what we will do, are questions only we ourselves have the proper answers to.

The concept of *oneness* is old and black and spiritual. The One God. And the 7 principles are a religious creed, in its most practical application, a code of common morality.

We need a value system to be predictable in our behavior, Maulana has said. Predictable, meaning stable, pointed toward a single goal. The liberation of our soul, mind and body. A value system is the spine of all cultures. What is good or bad aside from specific interpretation in specific context? Through unity, we arrive at self-determination and can then proceed to collective work and responsibility (in the organs, or as each one teach one, or painting a wall), *Ujima*. The value system selects the goal, we apply ourselves to it, live by it, the rest follows. Why, Moses gave the commandments for the same result, as a best way to live. And they will *raise* us.

So that Maulana Karenga's doctrine is first a value system. It sets forth a value system, to be followed, called Kawaida, literally ("that which is customary, or traditionally adhered to, by black people"). A nation is only as great as that set of values it *actually* practices . . . no matter what it says, e.g., witness America (white and Negro). The value system is how you live, to what end. And Kawaida is, as the doctrine teaches, "a weapon, a shield, and a pillow of peace."

One cannot have a slave's mentality and hope to be free, or one *can hope*, but that will not make anything really happen. The freeing of the mind, before anything else can happen. The people *must actually want* to be free. Want it bad enough to *be* it.

A value system that is itself the way of life of a free man of high morality is what the Kawaida teaches. A morality (more) is *the meaning* of what people do. Culture is how they live, morality is what it means. What it means as cause and effect, past what you or anyone else might *think*. What happens as a result of . . . is what morality directs. And there is a finality to this path-making that is part of the heaviest truth. To live better, you must live better. It is simple and complex.

Kawaida, or the doctrine of Maulana Karenga, is the measure of that "better" life. It is African, because we are African, no matter that we have been trapped in the West these few hundred years. But by the quality of what our lives *meant* we have transformed the West, even transformed the white man. The value system, especially as the Nguzo Saba begins to focus it, can give us the identity, purpose and direction to move to that better life. At each level it is a contrast to Euro-American *morality*, because first it is based on teachings that are superior to the practiced morality of Euro-Ameri-

can civilization. It is also a value system beneficial to black people.
And there is no reason for the practiced value system of Euro-
America to be beneficial to black people; quite the contrary, it has
always been absolutely detrimental to black people. For instance,
the fourth principle of the Nguzo Saba is Ujamaa, collective or
cooperative economics.

But Ujamaa is not, as it has been called, "African Socialism," it is
Ujamaa. If anything, you could say European Ujamaa, but never the
reverse. The reason? Ujamaa is the traditional way of distributing
wealth for the black man. It is an economic attitude older than
Europe and certainly older than the term socialism. Which finally
is another thing, coming from the European definition, since the
European definition is a state that will exist "after the decay of
capitalism." Ujamaa has always been the African *attitude* towards
the distribution of wealth (until the decay that made our kingdoms fall). It has never been a European attitude, but rather a
theory. Can you dig it? (See Julius Nyerere's paper *Ujamaa* in
Uhuru na Umoja.)

The "decay of capitalism" theory is also another aspect of the
European attitude of "world revolution," and do not mistake my
meaning, I am talking about the life style of violence. Vita (violence
or war) in Swah'li equals *life* in Latin. When we say "revolution"
we mean the restoration of our national sovereignty as a people, a
people, at this point, equipped to set new paths for the development
of man. We mean the freeing of ourselves from the bondage of another, alien, people. We are not warring upon our own society
among ourselves. These pigs are no kin to us. We are trying to
destroy a *foreign oppressor*. It is not "revolution" but *National Liberation*.

When you speak of capitalism you speak of the European mind.
We do not want to be Europeans. No, not of any persuasion. Just as
the, as he calls them, "economic radicals" of the twenties tried to
stop J. A. Rogers, whom they called "a black capitalist," from doing
his research and rewriting our destroyed archives, saying Rogers was
"chauvinistic" and suffered an "inferiority complex"; they said he
should be studying people like "Marx, Engels and Lafargue and be
preparing for the worker's utopia which was just around the
corner. . . ." (See Introduction to Rogers' "World's Great Men of
Color, Vol. 1.") *But are not Marx, Engels and Larfargue just another list of "great" men . . . but great white men,* or at least white
men thought great by one particular group of white men? Another
group of white men might give you another list . . . like say Washington, Jefferson, Lincoln, Kennedy, etc. But it is, either way, still a
commitment to Euro-American values, to whiteness.

In order to free ourselves, and this may come as a shock to many "hip Negroes," we are going to have to do it ourselves! For ourselves. Yes, the world will benefit, but they are not going to do it, any more than you helped free the Chinese! If you cannot have faith in blackness, in the black mind and the black man to find a way out of this slavery, you are full of despair, or else emotionally committed to white people. Which is the terrible truth for many of us, even our so-called "revolutionaries." They are so committed to whiteness that they must find a way to make white relevant some way. The Right will not save us so the Left will. This group of white people will not do it, but this other group of white people will. (Do not misunderstand, we will take aid from a scorpion, but we must not confuse our identity. Or try to crawl under rocks with scorpions.)

Another fallacy of many "revolutionaries" is the "right-around-the-cornerism" that Rogers cites and Maulana Karenga always emphasizes as dangerous. There is no such thing. The work of National Liberation is hard and its resolution is to be sought but not fantasized as the result of unprepared spontaneous outbursts of emotionalism. It is work. It will only be achieved by disciplined, dedicated people, with a value system that allows them to persevere and remain healthy and rational and committed for as long as it takes, no matter what happens to anybody or everybody else.

Too often so-called revolutionaries without a black value system like Kawaida do exactly the same things as the oppressor-people, and as I said, they are always emotionally committed to the oppressor people. They speak the same language, think the same things valuable, have the same "taste." In fact they are so much the same they can make alliances that are unnatural as far as the natural life styles of the new peoples are concerned. The bush-smoking, wine-drinking, homo-superhetero-sexual bellbottomed life of the hippy (a truly interracial though white committed phenomenon) is just a phase of death rattle for a culture and a people. The magnetism of the final death will compel to death all those with the jingling matching magnets around their brains.

An epoch passes because it is played out. To imitate the played out is to simulate, and then not to be able to stop, death.

So Nia, purpose. What is your purpose, for anything? For being alive? If you are black your purpose should be the building of Black. The Nguzo Saba says our purpose must be the rebuilding of our people to their traditional greatness. One reason for the stress on history, if you do not even know of your traditional greatness, then you will not aspire to anything but dry-rock white "radicalism" (like some 1930's vampire re-risen from the grave to suck back peoples' blood) as some kind of alternative to the maggoty pork that exists. But neither is our shot, brother. Initially our purpose is *Nation building*. To raise black people to "our traditional greatness." National Liberation as Malcolm called it.

Karenga stresses cultural nation for the same reasons that Mao continues his cultural revolution on a continuous basis in China even after his political revolution has been realized. It is a constant process. The minds of the people are the most important factor of any movement; without them you can have nothing else. And we do not have to settle for maggoty pork or renewed draculism (a white "radical"). We can have and be ourselves.

But you must have the cultural revolution, i.e., you must get the mind before you move fuhtha. There is no violent revolution except as a result of the black mind expanding, trying to take control of its own space. Our armies are not yet formed as armies. We cannot fight a war, an actual physical war, with the forces of evil just because we are angry. We can begin to build. We must build black institutions. In all the different aspects of culture. Political, religious, social, economic, ethical, creative, historical institutions, all based on a value system that is beneficial to black people.

All these institutions will be alternatives to the Euro-American or Negro institutions that exist, but will exist in their own right as expressions of the black sensibility and not merely as reactions to an alien sensibility. If Mao does not control the minds of the Chinese, his political victories are lost, his military is hostile, Maoism is another name for what was. Ghana should have had a continuous cultural revolution. To maintain the consciousness of the people. So that they could not be taken off by the criminal sickness of the white-led Negro mentality that re-invaded Ghana. If the chief of state of Biafra names as his country's national anthem "Finlandia," then we know where his politics are right off. The internalization of a white value system will always militate for white decisions about the way things should be. Whether it is a national anthem or an economic system.

Black creativity, *Kuumba*, is the sixth principle. Which tells us how we must devise a way out of our predicament. How we must build, with what methodology. In what emotionalism, the fire of blackness. So that even Ujamaa is Kuumba in regard to the distribution of wealth among men. For the European, Ujamaa, like jazz, is a saying, a pretending illusion, rather than a being. And we are not racists when we say this; we are merely recognizing the traits of different peoples.

When we call white people evil it is based on empiricism, not theory. Do you remember how you Africans got here to the Western

Hemisphere in the first place? (I mean as slaves, not as Egyptians and Moorish explorers and settlers.) The recital of the horrors black people have suffered at the hands of the white makes us racists? Only to the white, or the *white committed*. Herodotus came up with the Teutonic Origins theory of why white was best and how the rest were not, on a descending xenophobic scale all the way down to us. A theory, not a fact. The lynching and oppression and enslavement of black people by European, and the capacity for such cruelty by the European mind is fact, not theory. It is empirical, we have witnessed and lived through it, are still living through it. And just because some dude wants to sleep with a white woman, let him not call those of us who do not racists. These are facts to which any honest man had better bear witness.

When we said Black Art, we meant Kuumba. The spiritual characteristic of revelation through the creative. The artist is respected in Bantu philosophy because he could capture some of the divinity. Because it flowed through his fingers or out of his mouth, and because he would lend this divinity to the whole people to raise them in its image, building great nations reared in the image of righteousness. What is soul (like the one sun the sole solar force, in this system)? Our connection, our relation with the infinite. And it is feeling, like inner revelation, that is the connection, the force of the uncreated, which we constantly make reference to, bringing into creation. Yehh! we scream, bearing witness to the power of Kuumba.

But black creativity is what will save us—not just "artists" but all of us—after all is said and done—nothing else. An antidote to birth or mind control! The Ngnzo Saba itself is one of the strongest examples of Kuumba. And each idea or act that animates our lives must be measured against the Nguzo Saba in each of its components. You must ask of each new idea or dissociation that comes to mind, what does this have to do with bringing about unity for black people, what does it contribute to black people's self-determination —does it have anything to do with Ujima, collective work and responsibility, and so on. So for instance a "black" TV program with a straight-haired sister dancing a Martha Graham—Merce Cunninghamesque tribute to the ghetto (?) is not Kuumba—neither the dance nor the program.

A nation coming into being is a new creation. It must be willed into existence by itself. It is new—it is literally something other than what exists.

Imani is faith—Faith in your leaders, teachers, parents,—but first faith in *blackness*—that it will win. Faith in Nationalism, that *we* can build *ourselves* into a conscious nation once again—that we can free ourselves from the chain of white commitment—this is all that binds us to slavery—*the fact that we are emotionally committed to it* —to being slaves.

Imani is the supra-rational aspect of Nationalism, but the aspect that we cannot survive without. We must believe past 2 + 2 or 180 vs 40 that the number we want is the one we can achieve.

Simple faith, like church people say: that's what we want— hardrock emotional faith in what we're doing. The same way your grandmamma used to weep and wring her hands believing in Jeez-us, that deep deep connection with the purest energy, this is what the Nationalist must have. Can you understand this? That we must believe past any bullshit "rationale" that we may or may not achieve, based on 7 million subjective-objective variables. We must believe in Nationalism. We must believe in the justness of our struggle and the certainty of our victory. *No matter how long this might take.* There is no time. Only change.

Nationalism must be the basis for our entire lives. It must always be the content and initiator of anything we do. The formulator of any act must be the need to see that act contribute to the building of a Nation. That is our purpose, Nationalism our direction. Black is our identity. The totality of these as a life focus is simple faith, even before it exists as spirituality. But that is what faith is, if it is directed toward grace—spirituality.

We say spirituality because the spiritual is the blessing of life. It is what all life points toward. Complete consciousness and Nationalism, at this point, is the definer and director of our people toward that goal of absolute, yes, absolute consciousness.

So the seventh principle, Faith, is actually at one with the first—to create the whole, the one (it's what Umoja means).

There is nothing anyone can do about the fact of the Nguzo Saba. It does—they do—exist. Now it is only for the studying or aspiring Nationalist to accept these principles as the clearest statement of the badly needed new value system.

It is spiritual without being religious. That is, it moves to the higher levels of human aspiration but describes no ritual dogma. The Nguzo Saba would organize the morality of the would-be Nationalist, give him a new and more relevant morality, to begin to build Blackness anew.

As long as we are committed to old ways and ideas, to paraphrase Touré, we will never move from where we are. A value system is a describer of your life on the planet, how you lived, in what manner and for what reasons, i.e., to what purpose. If you do not consciously create a new value system, one that is quite different from the rest of crazy America's—you will be exactly what crazy America is and die the way she dies.

But we want to survive. We want life. We want to build and create. We do not want a modified version of what exists, we want the totally new—newly claimed but as the eastern, the traditional, the African, the black—i.e., we want a whole different version of men's life on earth. We do not want what Marx wanted or what Abbie Hoffman wants. We want our new black selves as absolute masters of our own space. Can you dig it—*space*, and I repeat it for all these simple "black" cryptohippies who believe in Malcolm solely *because he is dead*—*space* is what we are fighting for. And it manifests itself as anything or everything. Institutional space, living, i.e. human space, thinking space or the actual planet-room una fahamu? Like they say, land. It is all space. CAN YOU UNDERSTAND??

But the point, man, is Malcolm never had a *doctrine*—we learned from him because he was straight and true, but he made no doctrines, no real *organization*, and we must face this. This is *our* work now, today, to organize better than Malcolm did. Can you understand? Malcolm's teachings must now be analyzed, formalized, and a structure and program issued out of them.

Elijah had a formal teaching, something close to a doctrine, and Malcolm sprang from it but made some other decisions. But he, Malcolm, made no doctrine. But now a doctrine has been made, formalized around a black value system, and this is what we need. How you live is how you project and how you will project. Your progeny, your creations are products of life, manifestations of your way, scenes from your path. The Nguzo Saba is the key to the new Nationalism. It is the key to the new learning. And that learning is the complete doctrine of Maulana Karenga.

The Nguzo Saba is the first, the basic, primary teaching. The rest of the doctrine, covering the completeness of modern experience is a black ideology in toto. A path itself to blackness and nationhood.

The doctrine now is mostly in the head and hands of organization people and a few key organizers and student leaders around the country. (*The Quotable Karenga* is a light sampling of some of the doctrine's content.) But soon it will be published and available to most of us. It is the central ingredient of the new nationalist organization. It will transform black people, and by doing this will transform yes, America.

You better get ready for it.

6

A Study of the
Black Fighter

NATHAN HARE

Fighters occupy a peculiar position within the realm of the professional athlete. They emerge from the most oppressed strata within the major cities and excite widespread attention as the most exploited group within the athletic world. Currently, most (more than 70 per cent) are black, and the "white hope" syndrome is so intense as to enter into fights between two blacks.

When the late Sonny Liston was preparing to fight Floyd Patterson, the NAACP and Ralph Bunche both made public statements that victory for Liston would strike a serious blow for the black struggle for equality.[1] When Muhammad Ali joined the the black muslims, Martin Luther King remarked that he had become "a champion of racial segregation." Ali responded that he was "an example for the youth of the whole world."[2] Today, when Ali fights, blacks and whites of a variety of political persuasions will regard him and his fight as a political force.

Fighters as a group are:

NATHAN HARE, publisher of *The Black Scholar*, is author of *The Black Anglo-Saxons* and more than eighty articles in *Newsweek, Negro Digest, Saturday Review, The Times of London, Social Education* and *The Black Scholar*. A graduate of Langston University and the University of Chicago, where he received a Ph.D. in sociology, Hare has written biographies for *American Men of Science, Who's Who in American Education,* and *Dictionary of International Biographies*. The first coordinator of a black studies program in the U.S.A., Hare has taught at Howard University and San Francisco State College. His forthcoming book, *Guidelines for Black Studies,* will be published in September, 1973.

1. Barry Gottenhrer, "How Great Is Sonny Liston?" *Boxing Yearbook,* 1964, p. 11.
2. Jose Torres, *Sting Like a Bee,* New York: Abelard-Schuman, 1971, pp. 138-139.

. . . set apart in the public mind by the fact that the object of their sport is to inflict bodily injury. Thus to some people they represent brutality and degradation; to others, virility and courage . . . They are very human individuals, equipped with all the human reactions and emotions. Most fighters know the natural fear of getting hurt. Most of them do not enjoy hurting their opponents and feel a compulsion to rationalize this as a business necessity. Although they are all looking for finanical reward, the greatest number are impelled even more by the desire for recognition and prestige. They long for the approval of the fans and for public understanding and acceptance. In their private lives they have a number of special problems, and when they retire they find it difficult to adjust to routine life.[3]

For the black fighter, these and other problems are intensified. I know this to be true for two main reasons. One is that I was a boxer myself.[4] Although I boxed mainly as an avocation and never attained great heights as a fighter, I did have thirty-six fights, both amateur and professional. In my last professional fight on December 5, 1967 in the Washington, D.C. Coliseum, I knocked out my opponent in two minutes and twenty-two seconds of the first round. In all, I won twenty-eight and lost eight and was never knocked down or badly beaten.

In the process, I came to know personally hundreds of fighters and retired fighters, including Muhammad Ali and Bobby Foster, the light-heavyweight champion, with whom I frequently sparred in the days when he was still an up-and-coming fighter.

However, my observations on professional fighters go beyond my daily contacts with them. For my master's thesis at the University of Chicago, I conducted a systematic study of fifty-eight professional fighters, some active, some retired, and nearly all of them black. I sought to discover what forces lured them into the boxing ring and what happened to them after retirement.

During months of canvassing gymnasiums, I witnessed the interethnic conflict, rivalries and other private emotions the fighters expressed. I saw ethnic groups stealing the towels of another group and listened to their hostile racial jokes. I saw that it was a particular comedown for a black fighter to lose to a white fighter. Many black fighters relieve racial hostility in their fights with white fighters. Whenever a black fighter has a fight scheduled with a white fighter, his comrades kid him with the query as to whether he is

3. Nathan Hare, "What Makes a Man a Fighter?" W. C. Heinz (ed.) *Saturday Evening Post*, March 8, 1958, p. 27.

4. "Dr. Nathan Hare: Black Power Professor with a Punch." *Sepia*, April, 1968, pp. 50-54. Bernard Garrett, "Fired Howard University Teacher Returns to Boxing Career." *Jet*, October 26, 1967, pp. 16-21.

"afraid of white folks," a fear which had been said to motivate even
Muhammad Ali in part.

A Louisville friend who had known Ali since childhood once
observed:

Even when he's talking about race—when he says, "I don't want to be
bombed, I don't want to be set on fire, I don't want to be lynched or
have no dogs chase me"—he's expressing more of a general fright than he
is a real racial attitude. I think he finds it safer to be with Negroes, his
own kind. It allays his fear of all those things his father used to tell him
the whites'd do to him. He keeps this tight little Negro group around
him and he's scared to death to venture away from it.[5]

Fighters are products of the racial hostilities and socio-economic
conflicts in which they live. Professor Kirson Weinberg, of Chicago's
Roosevelt University, has found that professional boxers reflect
changes in the ethnic composition of the lower strata of the urban
slums. In the early part of the century the Irish predominated. By
1928 Jewish fighters had replaced them; by 1936 the Italians succeeded them. Since 1948 the blacks have dominated.[6] Currently
seven of the eleven best heavyweights in the world are black Americans.[7] Except for the four years Rocky Marciano was champion,
and the year Ingemar Johansson borrowed the title briefly from
Floyd Patterson, blacks have held the heavyweight championship
since 1936. In recent years Tampa, Florida barred professional
boxing because, the commission's report read in part, "boxers no
longer represent a cross-section of America." [8]

A "natural" to the fight mob connotes any fight which pits a white man
against a Negro, although the Madison Avenue boys who have moved
into the promotional forefront of the sport would seek a euphemistic
definition. By any definition it brings loot . . . It has been traditional that
any "white hope" is matched against a colored champion, a natural is in
the making. It appeals to all that is primitive and basic in this most primitive and basic of all sports.[9]

Because of this premium placed on white fighters, black fighters
feel that they must fight them harder in order to get ahead. Black
fighters especially are forced to seek in boxing the financial security
and the social esteem denied them outside the ring, not to mention

5. Jack Olsen, *Black Is Best: The Riddle of Cassius Clay.* New York: Dell,
1967, p. 93.

6. S. Kirson Weinberg and Henry Arond, "The Occupational Culture of the
Boxer." *American Journal of Sociology,* March, 1952, p. 460.

7. "Boxing Illustrated's World Boxing Ratings." *Boxing Illustrated,* August,
1971, p. 16.

8. Nathan Hare, "White Supremacy Backfires in Boxing." *Flamingo,* September, 1962, p. 42.

9. Jack Zanger, "Here Comes Ingo . . . Again." *Boxing Annual,* 1963, p. 10.

the gnawing resentments built up from a lifetime of abuse suffered at the hands of white supremacists. Joe Louis was so enraged by Max Schmeling's pre-bout boasts that Germans are superior to blacks that he attacked the Nordic with a fury that left him hospitalized. In this reaction, Louis was not unique.

Most black persons do not become fighters, however. To find out why some turn to boxing, I went to the origins of the fighters in my sample. From the Illinois State Athletic Commission I obtained the address from which each fighter applied for his first professional license. I visited each dwelling and noted the economic need of their family origins. Only 35 per cent had had working fathers at home when they turned professional. All the working fathers were laborers, except one who operated a small laundry. Twenty-nine per cent said their fathers had deserted the family, and five per cent said their fathers had died.

Since most poor boys do not become fighters either, I sought out the specific reasons why those in my group had entered the ring. Thirty-one said they first became interested in boxing because a relative, friend or neighbor (a role model) was a fighter. Thirteen traced their interest to natural ability discovered in street fights. Fourteen gave other reasons, such as childhood membership in an organization sponsoring boxing or a fondness for sports in general and boxing in particular.

One interesting point was that only five per cent of the scientific boxers attributed their initial interest to street fighting, whereas 48 per cent of the sluggers gave this reason. My survey findings are borne out by the cases of various well-known fighters. Sluggers such as Sonny Liston and Henry Hank had much success in street fights. It was different with scientific boxers like Ray Robinson and Ezzard Charles.

Robinson, who used to run from street fights as a child, started to box because he lived in the same Detroit neighborhood as Joe Louis and often carried Louis' bag to the gym. Charles first became interested when, near his home in Cincinnati one day, he saw Kid Chocolate, the featherweight champion, in an expensive car and heard Chocolate tell of his sizeable wardrobe.

Boys in the black slums take note of these and other benefits a boxing career can offer and are moved to use this means of escaping slum deprivation. Joe Louis, after he humiliated Max Schmeling, became a hero for blacks all over the nation; and nonwhites throughout the world also were able to take him for a model.

Many boxers, far from being "born" fighters, had to learn it to get by as boys in their tough slum environments. Professor Weinberg even found fighters who took up fighting because as boys they had suffered insults to their manliness.[10] The girlish name of one, for instance, attracted the jeers of playmates. The boy eventually altered his name to make it manly-sounding and set out to learn boxing to back up his new name. He was soon able to convince his jesters that he was at least as manly as they.

This problem also has plagued well-known fighters. At the weighing-in ceremonies before the bout in which champion Benny Kid Paret was fatally injured a few years ago, Paret called Griffith a "woman," apparently because Griffith used to be a choirboy and is now a designer of ladies' hats. Paret's widow, Lucy, blames this insult for the "bad blood" between the fighters and the savage fury of Griffith's punches.[11]

Although almost all fighters start with the idea of making money, 45 per cent in my sample told me that after three or more years they liked the recognition and prestige even more than the financial rewards. Joe Law, a lightweight, expressed it this way: "A guy knocks you down. You get up and put up a good fight and the crowd cheers you. Drop into a night club and people recognize you. The emcee says, 'We got a celebrity in the house,' and shines the spotlight on you. I'm telling you, it makes you feel good."

Sonny Liston explained:

I never had a dime to my name before I became a fighter. I never had friends before, or respect. Now when people see me on the street, they turn around and say, "Ain't that Sonny Liston, the fighter?" [12]

Muhammad Ali has said: "I started boxing because I thought this was the fastest way for a black person to make it in this country." [13]

Most fighters begin with an exaggerated idea of the prestige and money to be made. They read about the huge purses received by the Alis and Louises and Robinsons and have little understanding of how much must be deducted for taxes, expenses and manager's share. Of the forty-eight retired fighters I questioned, none said they had saved most of the money they earned in fighting. Two out of three had saved little, and 25 per cent had saved none at all.

"My manager was like a father to me," said a lightweight who won forty-six of his sixty-three fights, "but you've still got expenses and a lot of friends. Everybody wants to have a good time off your money. Once I made $5,000 in a fight in California, but by the time I got home I only had about $500."

10. Arond and Weinberg, *op. cit.*, p. 461.

11. Hare, *op. cit.*, p. 44.

12. Alexander Berger, "Best Bet for the Big Title." *Boxing Illustrated*, August, 1959, p. 35.

13. Torres, *op. cit.*, p. 83.

"The higher a fighter goes in the fight game, the higher the class of people he runs around with," another fighter told me. "He's got to spend money to keep up with the crowd. His manager won't let him keep on livin' on State Street, payin' cheap rent, because it won't look right. A boxer comes from the bottom. He ain't been used to nothin' or he wouldn't be fighting in the first place."

In the effort to squeeze the most from the fighter as a commodity, managers must seek to extract a viciousness and disdain for suffering in the fighter. Trainers assist them in conditioning the fighter to taking and giving punishment. "This ain't no baby game. You got to be mean. You got to be tough," trainers repeatedly tell their fighters. "You got to try to kill that guy; he's going to try to knock your head off. Try to kill him. Try to knock his eye out. He's going to knock yours out if he can."

The fighter who succeeds best is thus able to suppress his emotions sufficiently to sustain a "killer instinct" and take advantage of his opponent. Questioned after his fatal injury of then featherweight champion Davey Moore, Sugar Ramos remarked: "As long as ε ιan keeps hitting me I know I have to hit him back." After fatally injuring Art Doyle, Sugar Ray Robinson said simply that "hurting people is my business."

To force him to fight harder, Johnny Bratton's manager used to bet his fighter's purse on the outcome of his fights, leaving Bratton broke and wanting whenever he lost.[14] In the exploitation of the boxer by his handlers, it is necessary to exercise intensive control and constraint over the fighter's thinking and behavior, to dominate the fighter and his total mood. Manager Cus D'Amato was said to feel a "sadistic delight in keeping Floyd Patterson under his hypnotic spell." He would tell Floyd over and over again: "The entire world is against you, trust no one but me."[15]

At the same time, a fighter cannot always count on his manager's good intentions. While most fighters are black, almost all managers are white. One manager I know bet against his boxer, then secured a woman for him shortly before the fight to weaken him for defeat.

Beyond this, many fighters feel resentful that their success depends too little on what they know and too much on whom their managers know. "You have to be in a clique," a former fighter insisted to me. "You take some guys that are fighting in the preliminaries, and if they had the right backing they could get somewhere.

14. George Puscas, "Child of Tragedy." *Negro Digest*, April 1962, p. 42.
15. Wendell Smith, "Patterson—The Recluse." *Boxing and Wrestling*, January, 1962, p. 41.

It used to be that when you lost three or four fights you dropped in the ratings. Now some fighters lose three or four and then fight for the title."

Further evidence of the exploitation and racism of promoters is that today, when most fighters are black, most fight clubs still pay their preliminary fighters what they paid them thirty years ago when prices and tickets were cheaper.

The financial exploitation of the fighter compounds the special strain which his career places upon marriage. Forty of the fifty-eight I talked to were or had been married. Among the forty-eight retired fighters in the group, twenty-five were still married, but the wives of ten others had deserted them.

The glamor of boxing and, in the case of successful fighters, the huge sums of money they make, frequently enable boxers to marry women from higher social classes. Joe Louis, for instance, who did not complete high school, was married to a prominent attorney. Thus many fighters encounter class conflict in their marriages.

"A fighter starts at the bottom," one told me. "Every notch you move up in boxing, you move up a notch with the big shots. That's how come a lot of fighters marry women too high for them. Or if they don't do that, they get their wives too used to luxury and prestige. Then after you quit and can't keep it up, she gets where she can't stand you and leaves."

I found this fighter in his room in a third-class hotel. He had missed a previous appointment with me because, he explained, he had been drunk. He told me that he had taken to alcohol after his wife had left him. "I'd be the happiest man in the world," he said, "if I could just find her and get her back."

Another fighter, who had become close enough as a friend to invite me to be the best man in his wedding to a Washington, D.C. schoolteacher, told me that some individuals were telling him that to continue fighting would degrade his wife's profession.

"No wife, I mean no wife, approves," one fighter told me. "All wives like the glory, but they also got to see you come in with your face all beat in—see you nursing your face at night."

Many wives grow impatient with a fighter's financial progress. "I'm like you," I once heard a young fighter confide to another in a Chicago dressing room. "My wife's getting tired of me not being able to keep a job more'n six months at a time. I get money from a fight and I give it to her, but I don't get that too regular, so all the time she's buying the groceries. She just bought nineteen dollars' worth of food last Saturday, and that's all gone. I made the mistake of asking her for a dollar—I caught hell before I got that dollar. She's tired of it," he said. "You know, living with her people and they know whenever we get in an argument, and I ain't fucking her or nothing trying to get in shape for a fight."

A common reason for marriage failure among fighters is the enforced separation that their training rules demand. Managers and trainers caution fighters to limit their sexual relations as much as possible. But many fighters find it hard to "hold out" against their women, wanting to end long sexual vacations before a fight. Some trainers will go so far as to sleep with their fighters before an important bout in order to keep them out of trouble with their wives. Sixty-two per cent of the fighters in my sample told me, however, that they often broke one rule or another in their relationships with women. In general, fighters feel that about two weeks of celibate living before a fight is sufficient—three said only one day—but all who had experienced marriage named this as a major problem.

"You got to keep up your homework," a middleweight told me one night in a Chicago tavern frequented by fighters and ex-fighters. "If you don't, somebody else'll be doing it for you. A fighter fights in so many different cities it's best for him not to have a wife, because she'll cheat on him. It's a mental disturbance to leave, knowing she'll cheat. You can't box if your mind is split on something else."

In spite of all this, only ten of thirty-four who had an opinion on the subject thought marriage was bad for a fighter. Managers and trainers, on the other hand, are almost unanimous in believing that fighters should not burden themselves with marital responsibilities.

"It's better to leave your wife at home," a trainer told me in Washington, D.C. "Of course, if she was rooting for you, she'd come unbeknownst to you. But it's better to leave her home." Later, he told a young fighter not to bring any of his relatives, because he might try to "show off" and end up doing worse than ever.

Most of the fighters I studied had launched their careers with the approval of their families. Only about one-sixth of the fathers disapproved, and only two-fifths of the mothers. A fighter's relations with his family generally change, however, during his career and immediately following it. His family's admiration for him fluctuates with his success and usually wanes when his career is ended.

One of the most pathetic examples was a former welterweight—now in his thirties and unemployed—who said he had made enough money during his career to send his sister through college. I found him living with his mother in a third-floor walk-up apartment on Chicago's South Side. He was dressed in a shirt and old slacks. I suggested that we go out for a beer.

"My sister's a schoolteacher. My brother's got a good government job," he told me in the tavern. "I'm the bum in the family. My mother wouldn't allow my youngest brother to become a fighter, and he was a natural. I wasn't—I had to develop my skill. My mother can't stand the sight of a fighter, especially me. I had a birthday last month, and I didn't get one present from my family."

At that point he fell silent, and a friend of his entered the bar and walked over to him. "Your mother wants you to come home and clean out the cellar," he said. "I got to get out of this," the former fighter said to me.

Another put his brother into business, but they soon fell into periodic fights in which he beat his brother. Finally his brother took out a warrant for his arrest and won't speak to him or give him money now that he is broke.

Such factors lead most fighters to long to return to the ring. Almost 70 per cent of the retired fighters at one time or another got the urge to resume, and 40 per cent actually did make one or more comeback attempts. This indicates the difficulty most fighters experience in trying to adjust occupationally and otherwise after their ring careers end. The problems of physically and mentally impaired ex-boxers have been widely publicized, but it seems to me that too little attention has been paid to the more common problem of maladjustment.

Fighters come mostly from urban slum areas where there is a lower standard of living and a higher prevalence of mental and physical disease. Professional boxing fails to equip its graduates for other work. In fact, it tends to prejudice them against it. Managers and trainers are opposed to having their fighters learn other trades or work at other jobs during their careers. They want a fighter to devote himself completely to boxing. They also feel that a fighter who has no other means of support and no other skills will train harder and, when the going in the ring gets rough, fight harder.

There is no way in which a fighter can use his special skills after retirement, unless he becomes a trainer of fighters. He finds it hard to accept the routine, time-clock nature of most jobs, and he has become used to receiving his pay in comparatively large lump sums, rather than in small, fixed amounts at regular intervals. In the partnership of boxer, manager and trainer, the fighter rightfully is the important party. He loses and misses this sense of importance when he embarks upon another line of work.

"I ain't going to do no hard work," an ex-fighter who had tried nine jobs in six months told me. "Look. Feel my hands. I never had a callus in my life. When I was boxin' I wasn't used to havin' a boss and workin' all day. Oh, before I'd steal I'd work for a while, but I'd do it where nobody could see me. I'd die if somebody saw me."

White boxers typically do better in post-career life because of greater benevolence on the part of their managers (c.f. Rocky Marciano and Joe Louis). Also, for small-time fighters (by far the majority) there are better jobs available to whites after retirement.

Thirty-seven of the forty-eight retired fighters I visited did have steady jobs, but 60 per cent of those said they would be happier in different work. Most of them were unskilled or semi-skilled laborers. Four operated small taverns or restaurants, one was a jazz musician, and one ran a dry-cleaning establishment.

I found that scientific boxers adjusted to post-career life slightly better than the sluggers. The unsuccessful scientific boxers adjusted best of all, and the successful sluggers experienced the most difficulty. Half of all the retired fighters, however, told me that they would need more than an additional $100 a week to live the way they wanted.

We may conclude, then, that boxing does not leave all its scars on a fighter's face. The tragedy of the fighter's life is that when his career comes to an end in his late twenties or early thirties—an age at which most young men are just approaching their prime—he feels that the best years of his life are already behind him. For too many this is the unfortunate truth.

In the gyms I watched the active fighters working and waiting for the lucky break which, they believed, would take them to the wealth and glory of a championship. In the taverns and poolrooms I listened to the former fighters reliving their own fighting careers, boasting to sustain their pride, dissatisfied now with their present lot and trying to call back in conversation the youth and skills that had once been theirs.

Three years after winning the welterweight championship, Johnny Saxton was charged with two burglaries and held in a New Jersey jail. There he tried to take his own life and had to be confined for a while in the New Jersey State Mental Hospital. "I used to be somebody," the ex-champ explained, "but now I'm nobody. I wish the police had shot me."

I have seen ex-fighters trying to borrow carfare to no avail, and I have seen a blind ex-fighter doing calisthenics and shadowboxing nightly in his hotel room. One night I found a fighter who retired about thirty years ago after sixteen years in the ring, whose name still evokes memories for fight fans who go back that far. I found him living with his wife in a transient hotel room in a slum area, reminiscing about the days when he was the National Boxing

Association middleweight champion, boxing throughout this country and in Paris, and she was a professional dancer.

Boxing is good for some black men, allowing them to escape the deprivation of the slums, but for most, it merely reflects and aggravates their basic oppression.

7

The Sources of the Black Athlete's Superiority

HARRY EDWARDS

In 1967 and 1968, America was shocked into a new consciousness regarding the totality of black people's commitment to achieving liberation from racism, injustice and inhumanity. During a sixteen-month period ending in October of 1968 at the Olympic Game in Mexico City, a number of dedicated black athletes had taken the struggle of human dignity into the sacred empire of American sports, shattering long-standing myths, exposing countless hypocrisies, and laying bare the fact that the sports establishment is nothing more nor less than racist, authoritaran, vulturistic white America functioning in microcosm. Not since the days of Paul Leroy Robeson (the Rutgers University All-American who turned his back on the recognition derived from playing the role of the "responsible Negro athlete") has white society in general and the sports world in particular exhibited such anger over the refusal of black men to entertain a decadent social order by performing as uni-dimensional twentieth-century gladiators.

Since 1968 the countless rebellions, boycotts and strikes carried out by black athletes and others have made it quite clear that the revolt in sports is a good deal more than a passing fad or political gesture. It has even spread to the ranks of white athletes, a fact attested to in recent books by Dave Meggyesy and Jim Bouton, who point out and denounce numerous characteristic examples of racism, fascism and inhumane exploitation in both amateur and professional athletics.

HARRY EDWARDS is Assistant Professor of Sociology, University of California at Berkeley. Edwards received his Ph.D. from Cornell University. He is the leading spokesman of the black athlete in this country and led the 1968 Olympic Boycott. The 28-year-old scholar and athlete is author of *Revolt of the Black Athlete*, *Black Students* and the forthcoming *Sports: Its Myths and Realities*.

Since the onset of the revolt of the black athlete there have been numerous occurrences which many interpret as indicative of improvement in the overall racial situation in the sports arena:

- The hiring of unprecedented numbers of black coaches and administrative assistants at predominantly white educational institutions which have traditionally depended heavily upon black athletic talent for sports success;
- The naming of a black manager to a minor league or farm club subsidiary of a major league professional baseball team;
- The naming of three black player-coaches in the National Basketball Association;
- The establishment of athletic boards and committees at many institutions to handle the grievances of black athletes;
- The nomination of pre-1947 baseball stars to a "special" baseball hall of fame roster;
- A highly visible increase in the number of black athletes doing paid television commercials.

There have also been several positive intangibles which have emerged from the black revolt in sports. One of the most important of these has been the development of a heightened consciousness among actual and aspiring black athletes as to their political responsibilities and potentials in the worldwide black liberation struggle. Another intangible result has been a partial dissolution of the black athlete's image as the purely physical and apolitical automaton, the unquestioningly obedient Uncle Tom. These were images well-established and legitimated by a long line of Negroes who were only too happy to fulfill their assigned roles for money, a few sports trinkets, or a few sentences in the newspaper.

Finally, there is the fact that the black athlete has achieved new prestige and respect among the black masses, not because of his athletic excellence, but because, despite his relatively high status, he has at long last begun to speak out on the social and political issues affecting the lives and destinies of all Afro-American athletes and non-athletes alike. Only time will disclose whether or not these accomplishments of the revolt will have any impact toward positively altering the oppressed and degrading conditions of black people, inside and outside the sports world.

Widespread publicity in recent months has been given yet another "accomplishment." Many view it as a concession by the white-controlled sports world—nonrecognition of the new spirit of pride, political awareness, and cultural identity among black athletes. This would-be accomplishment is embodied in the fact that diverse and highly influential persons and publications (usually considered part of the "sports establishment" in America) have finally admitted

what every objective observer of the sports scene already knew—
to wit, that the performance of black athletes, on the average, is
significantly superior to that of whites in all sports participated in
by both groups in numbers. This admission has not been put forth
grudgingly; rather it has been enthusiastically presented and echoed,
even by sports commentators and coaches, usually considered conservative or right-wing in their orientation toward the thrust for
black dignity in sports.

While there can be little argument with the obvious fact that
black performances in sports have been and continue to be superior
on the whole to those of whites, there is room for considerable debate over the identity and character of the factors which have determined that superiority and contributed to its perpetuation.

The world of the athlete is one dominated by competition, where
the value of one's performance is never absolute but always relative
to both the past and the present performances of others. In his
newly established role as one of the most visible manifestations of
black pride and competence, the black athlete often feels increased
pressures to conquer "whitey" in the sports arena. Thus, in their
hasty grasp for long-overdue recognition of the general superiority
of blacks over whites in athletics, it was perhaps to be expected that
many well-meaning black athletes would inadvertently substantiate
not only the fact of that superiority itself, but also the prevailing
arguments put forth regarding the causal factors underlying that
situation. Apparently, few paused before making their comments
to give serious consideration to the broader implications of these
arguments for either black athletes or the black population at large.

The central concern of this essay is to analyze these arguments
and their implications. Further, what is considered to be a scientifically defensible postulation of the causal factors underlying black
superiority will be presented.

The myth of the black male's racially determined inherent physical and athletic superiority over the white male rivals the myth of
black sexual superiority in antiquity. While both are well fixed in
the Negro lore and folk-beliefs of American society, in recent years
the former has been subject to increasing emphasis due to the overwhelmingly disproportionate representation of black athletes on all-
star rosters, on Olympic teams, in the various "most valuable player"
categories, and due to the black athletes' overall domination of the
highly publicized or so-called "major sports"—basketball, football,
baseball, track and field. But seldom in recent times has the myth
of racially linked black athletic prowess been subject to so explicit a
formulation and presentation as in the January 18, 1971 issue of
Sports Illustrated magazine. In an article entitled "An Assessment

of 'Black Is Best' " by Martin Kane, one of the magazine's senior editors, several arguments are detailed, discussed, and affirmed by a number of widely known medical scientists, athletic researchers, coaches, and black athletes. In essence, the article constitutes an attempt to develop a logical and scientifically defensible foundation for the assertion that black athletic superiority in sports is due to racial characteristics indigenous to the black population in America but not generally found within the white population.

Kane cites the following as evidence of the black athletes' superior abilities:

1—In basketball three of the five players named to the 1969–70 All-NBA team were black, as were all five of the athletes named to the all-rookie team. Blacks have won the league's Most Valuable Player award twelve times in the past thirteen seasons;

2—In professional football, all four of the 1969 Rookie of the Year awards for the offense and defense were won by blacks;

3—In baseball, black men have won the National League's Most Valuable Player awards sixteen times in the past twenty-two seasons;

4—Today there are 150 blacks out of 600 players in major league baseball, 330 blacks out of 1,040 athletes in professional football, and 153 players out of 280 in basketball are black. Of the athletes in professional sports in 1969–70 All-Star teams, 36% in baseball were black, 44% in football were black, and blacks comprised 63% of the All-Star talent in basketball.

Clearly there is no argument that black society is contributing more than its eleven per cent share of athletes and star-status performers to professional sports. And where blatant racism and discrimination do not keep blacks from participation almost completely—such as in the Southeastern Conference—a similar pattern of black domination prevails in colleges and at other amateur levels where major sports endeavors are pursued.

Attempting to explain this disproportionate representation, Kane mentions, almost in passing, the probable influences of contemporary societal conditions and then launches into a delineation and discussion of the major factors giving rise to black athletic superiority. They are as follows:

Racially linked physical and psychological characteristics

1—Proportionately longer leg lengths, narrower hips, wider calf bones, and greater arm circumference among black athletes than among whites.

2—A greater ratio of tendon to muscle among blacks, giving rise to a condition typically termed "double jointedness," and a relatively dense bone structure.

3—A basically elongated body structure among black athletes enabling them to function as more efficient heat dissipaters than whites.

Race-related psychological factors
1—The black athlete's greater capacity for relaxation under pressure than that of the white athlete.

Racially specific historical occurrences
1—The selectivity of American slavery in weeding out the hereditarily and congenitally weak from among those who came to be the forbears of today's black population.

Let us now turn to a general consideration of these major factors.

Racially Linked Physical and Physiological Characteristics

Kane's attempt to establish the legitimacy of this category of factors as major contributions to the emergence of black athletic superiority suffers from two basic maladies—one methodological, the other arising from a dependence upon scientifically debatable assumptions and presumptions concerning differences between the "races" of men and the impact of these differences upon capacity for physical achievement.

Simply stated, one grossly indefensible methodological tactic is obvious in virtually every case of "scientific" evidence presented in support of a physical or physiological basis for black athletic superiority. *In no case was the presented evidence gathered from a random sample of subjects selected from the black population at large in America.* Thus, supporting data, for the most part, were taken from black athletes of already proven excellence or from blacks who were available due to other circumstances, reflective of some degree of uncontrolled social, political, or otherwise continued selectivity. Therefore, the generalization of the research findings on these subjects to the black population as a whole—even assuming the findings to be valid—constitutes a scientific blunder of the highest magnitude and invalidates the would-be scientific foundations of this component of the author's argument.

But there are still other considerations which give doubt as to the credibility of Kane's presentation. There is first of all the problem of justifying the posing of his argument within a context which assumes the biological and genetic validity of delineating human populations into "races." The use of such an approach in an attempt to discover athletically meaningful patterns of differences between the defined groups does not take complete consideration of the fact that human breeding populations are determined to a great extent by cultural circumstances and social and political conditions, as well as the factors of opportunity, propinquity, and convenience, not merely by the factor of similarity in morphological characteristics. Thus, to

assume a biological and genetic validity to the concept of race implies that, as a population, Afro-Americans have bred endogamously
and have maintained their original genotypical and anatomical traits
—excepting for an occasional mutation brought about by natural or
environmental selectivity.

This of course is nonsense. Virtually every attempt to define or
pose problems within a context which either assumes or explicitly
postulates the validity of a biological and/or genetic concept of
race has resulted in a troublesome issue of defensibility for the
scientist involved, not to speak of the social and political problems
that have emerged. This accounts for such widespread disagree-
ment among human biologists and anthropologists concerning the
definitions of race and the identification of the races of man. These
definitions range all the way from the denial that genetically and
biologically discernible races exist at all to those which delineate
specific "races" of man numbering from two or three categories to
classifications totaling in the hundreds. Invariably, once a biologist
or anthropologist has settled upon a definition which suits him, he
discovers there is little that he can do with his "races" other than
list them. For typically they have defied any effort at deriving consistent patterns of valid relationships between racial heritage and
meaningful social, intellectual, or physical capabilities. Hence, Kane
treads upon ground of dubious solidity from the moment he couches
his argument within the assumption that scientifically valid delinea-
tions of racial groupings exist at all.

A more specific analysis of the major points incorporated into this
aspect of the author's overall argument only furthers the above assertions. With regard to the alleged physical traits supposedly characteristic of black athletes, the question can justifiably be posed, "What
two outstanding black athletes look alike or have identical builds?"
One of Kane's resource persons answers this question:

"Floyd C. 'Bud' Winter makes it quite obvious that black athletes
differ from each other physically quite as much as whites do. He
notes that Ray Norton, a sprinter, was tall and slender with scarcely
discernible hips; that Bobby Painter, a sprinter, was squat and
dumpy with a sway back and a big butt; that Denis Johnson was
short and wiry; that Tommy Smith was tall and wiry and so on."
Further evidence is plentiful: "What physical characteristics does
Lew Alcindor have in common with Elgin Baylor, or Wilt Chamberlain with Al Attles, etc.? The point is simply that Wilt Chamberlain
and Lew Alcindor have more in common physically with Mel
Counts and Henry Finkel, two seven-foot white athletes, than with
most of their fellow black athletes."

Even excepting the hyperbolic illustrations just documented, what emerges from any objective analysis of supposed physical differences between so-called races is the undeniable fact that there exist more differences between individual members of any one racial group than between any two groups as a whole. So a fabricated "average" of the differences between racial groupings, even if it is scientifically generated, may serve certain heuristic purposes but provides a woefully inadequate basis for explaining specific cases of athletic excellence or superior ability. No black athlete conforms to that artificial average. As a matter of scientific fact, black athletes, as is true with the black population as a whole, manifest a wide range of physical builds, body proportions, and other highly diverse anatomical, physiological, and biological features, as do other groups including the so-called white race.

Recognition of this essential fact precludes the type of incredible qualification that Kane is forced to make when faced with exceptions which do not fit the framework which he has developed. A case in point is his assertion that the physical differences between white and black racial groupings predisposes blacks to dominate the sports requiring speed and strength, while whites, due to racially linked physical traits, are predestined to prevail in those sporting events requiring endurance. When confronted with the fact that black Kenyans won distance races and defeated highly touted and capable whites in the 1968 Olympic Games, the author makes the ridiculous post hoc assertion that (the Kenyans) Keino and Bikila have black skin but many white features.

Directly pertinent to Kane's presentation of would-be evidence that physiological differences underly black athletic superiority are the facts concerning efficient heat dissipation. In essence, the author attempts to present a case for the notion that due to an elongation of the body, black athletes are more efficient heat dissipaters than are whites and thus excel over whites in sports. First of all, either tall or short individuals may have body builds which enable them to function as relatively efficient heat dissipaters. The efficiency with which one's body dissipates heat is only incidentally related to the factor of height; it is directly related to the proportion of body surface to body mass. Therefore, one way to maximize heat-dissipating efficiency is to present a proportionately greater amount of body surface to the air by stretching a given body mass into an elongated shape. Another way of changing the gross mass to surface ratio is to change the overall size of the body. Hence, a decrease in size will decrease the mass (proportional to the cube root of any linear dimension) in relation to the surface area, the end product being the accomplishment of the same thing that body elongation can do.

Substantiation for the accuracy of this formulation is evidenced simply by the Nilotic African or Watusi who is normal in body mass but elongated in shape. Thus, the factor of elongated body proportions becomes neutralized by the fact that a small white athlete could be as efficient a heat dissipater as an elongated black athlete. In sports where the small athlete can function effectively against other athletes, one would expect at least occasionally to see small and elongated black and white athletes performing at comparable levels of excellence. Evidence of the invalidity of Kane's argument in this regard is the fact that black athletes of a variety of sizes and shapes have dominated sports such as track and field over white athletes who themselves embodied a variety of shapes and sizes and thus body mass to body surface ratio. One last point: given the complexity of variables which determine athletic excellence, even where physical differences exist between individuals, one proceeds on dangerous ground when he assumes that these observable or measurable differences are the major factors determining differences in demonstrated athletic excellence.

Race-Related Psychological Factors

Here the incredibility of Kane's presentation and the supporting statements of those who attempt to substantiate it are almost beyond belief. The academic belief in the existence of a national or a racial "character" was supposedly disposed of by scholars decades ago. Their persistence among the ranks of coaches and other segments of the American population only indicates the difficulty with which racial stereotypes and caricatures are destroyed or altered to comply with prevailing knowledge. Kane and his resource persons, mostly coaches, re-create a portrait of the black athlete as the happy-go-lucky, casual, "what—me worry?" Negro made so familiar to Americans through history books, Stepin Fetchit movies, and other societal outlets. But beside the fact that the overall portrayal itself is inappropriate, not even the specific psychological traits attributed to black athletes are substantiated by contemporary knowledge.

Kane quotes Lloyd C. Winter, former coach of a long line of successful black track and field athletes, as stating: "A limber athlete has body control, and body control is part of skill. It is obvious that many black people have some sort of head-start motor in them, but for now I can only theorize that their great advantage is relaxation under stress. As a class, the black athletes who have trained under me are far ahead of whites in that one factor—relaxation under pressure. It's their secret."

In data collected by Bruce C. Ogolvie and Thomas A. Tutko, two athletic psychologists whose work was ironically featured in the same issue of *Sports Illustrated* in which Kane's article appears, a strong case is made for the fact that black athletes are significantly less relaxed than white athletes in the competitive situation. (I am intimately familiar with this data as a result of my Ph.D. dissertation.) Using a test which has been found to have a high degree of reliability in both cross-cultural and simple comparative investigations, the following findings emerged when the psychological orientations of successful black and white athletes were compared:

1—On the I.P.A.T., successful black athletes showed themselves to be considerably more serious, concerned and "uptight" than their white counterparts as indicated by their relative scores on the item "Sober—happy-go-lucky." Blacks had a mean stern score of 5.1 as compared to a mean score for whites of 5.5 (level of significance of differences is .01; N = 396 whites, 136 blacks).

2—On the I.P.A.T. item of "Casual-Controlled" successful black athletes, indicating a more controlled orientation, blacks had a mean stern score of 6.6 as compared with the whites' mean score of 6.2 (level of significance of differences is .01; N = 396 whites, 136 blacks).

Sociologically, this pattern of differences given black athletes is expected, as they are aware that they operate at a decided disadvantage competing against whites for highly valued positions and rewards in an admittedly white racist society. Furthermore, sports hold the only promise of escape from the material degradation of oppressed black society. Thus, the assertion that black athletes are more "relaxed" than whites not only lacks scientific foundation but is ludicrous as even a common sense assumption.

Racially Specific Historical Occurrences

This is perhaps the most odious part of Kane's presentation, perhaps because he enlists the opinions of undoubtedly well-meaning but uninformed and unthinking black athletes to support his assertions. Kane cites the remarks of Yale University graduate Calvin Hill who now plays football for the Dallas Cowboys professional football team:

I have a theory about why so many pro stars are black. I think it boils down to the survival of the fittest. Think of what the African slaves were forced to endure in this country merely to survive. Well, black athletes are their descendants. They are the offspring of those who are physically and mentally tough enough to survive. . . . We were simply bred for physical qualities.

Continuing, Kane himself states that "it might be that without special breeding the African has a superior physique." The statements of Kane and his resource persons evidence confusion as to the scope of characteristics involved in the selectivity process as it has affected mankind. Natural selection or "the survival of the fittest" has been predicated upon relative strength and physical attributes to a lesser degree in mankind than in any other forms of animal life. This has been due largely to man's tremendously developed mental capabilities. The same would have held for the slave. While some may have survived as a result of greater physical strength and toughness, many undoubtedly also survived due to their shrewdness and thinking abilities.

Secondly, Kane and his informants speak as if blacks in American society have somehow remained "pure" as a racial stock. The fact of the matter is that our best sociological, genetic, and demographical knowledge indicates that the genetic make-up of blacks in America is at least thirty-five per cent white, not counting genetic influences from various other so-called racial groupings. Therefore, to assert that Afro-Americans are superior athletes due to the genetic make-up or physical prowess of the original slaves would be naive and ridiculous.

Finally, Kane's argument is that for blacks, demonstration of physical ability alone is all that is required to become a successful athlete. Anyone who is even vaguely familiar with the internal dynamics of organized sports at either the amateur or professional level in America knows that physical ability will *maybe* open that door, but before one reaches the level of a Bill Russell or a Gale Sayers, there are a great number of political, psychological and racial hurdles to conquer. Hence, perhaps the most vaguely related influence on the determination of black athletic superiority is the genetic or biological heritage of the black population as a racial group. Undoubtedly of much more importance as a determining factor is the facility with which the black athlete surmounts arbitrary political, psychological, and racial barriers, reflective of the contemporary sickness of American society. For the black athlete, the implications of Kane's article and similar perspectives on black athletic superiority are the following:

1—These arguments imply that the accomplishments of the black athlete in sports are as natural to him as flight is to an eagle, and thus the facts of a lifetime of dedication, effort, sweat, blood, and tears are ignored. What Kane is essentially telling black athletes is that "you would have been a superior athlete despite yourself." Perhaps it is coincidental, but such a stance allows racist whites in American society to affirm the undeniable superiority of the black athlete on the one hand and maintain their definitions of black people as lazy, shiftless and irresponsible on the other.

2—The notion that black athletes are by racial heritage physically superior to white athletes provides a basis for maintaining a white monopoly on certain key positions in sports which ostensibly require greater thinking and organizational ability—e.g., quarterback in football, manager in baseball, and head coach in most sports. Thus no matter how excellent an athlete a black player might be, a white player always gets the nod over him for these "intellectual" positions, since the black athlete excels on inborn physical superiority alone. Since the white athlete, under these conditions, would have to work harder toward mastering any given sport, he would probably know the dynamics of the sport better than the black athlete who "naturally" sails through the requirements of the endeavor, and hence the white athlete would make a better coach or manager.

The major implication of Kane's argument for the black population at large is that it opens the door for at least an informal acceptance of the idea that whites are *intellectually* superior to blacks. Blacks, whether athletes or non-athletes, must not give even passing credence to the possibility of white intellectual superiority. By a tempered or even enthusiastic admission of black physical superiority, the white population of this racist society loses nothing. For it is a simple fact that a multitude of even lower animals are physically superior, not only to whites, but to mankind as a whole: gorillas are physically superior to whites, leopards are physically superior to whites, as are lions, walruses, and elephants. So by asserting that blacks are physically superior, whites at best reinforce some old stereotypes long held about Afro-Americans—to wit, that they are little removed from the apes in their evolutionary development.

On the other hand, intellectual capability is the highest priced commodity on the world market today. If in a fit of black identity or simple stupidity, we accept the myth of innate black physical superiority, we could be inadvertently recognizing and accepting an ideology which has been used as the justification for black slavery, segregation and general oppression. Further, it was just such an ideology which led to genocide against native Americans in this country and against the Jews in Nazi Germany.

To those black athletes who have spoken out in support of the ideas expressed in Kane's article, I say only that it is a wise warrior who proceeds with caution and discretion when an enemy tosses bouquets in his direction. The argument that blacks are physically superior to whites as athletes or as a people is merely a racist ideology camouflaged to appeal to the ignorant, the unthinking, and the unaware in a period heightened by black identity. If it is accepted by blacks, whites will be relieved of the pressure to come up with a white hope in sports year after year, and they can also maintain their gut beliefs in white supremacy—unchallenged. The sacrifice of black human dignity and respect, born of almost 400 years of struggle and despair, is too high a price to pay for white recognition of black athletic prowess. The black athlete has worked hard and diligently to achieve his present status in the athletic world—perhaps harder than his white counterpart, who has fewer obstacles facing him.

What then are the major factors underlying black athletic superiority? These factors emerge from a complex of societal conditions. These conditions instill a heightened motivation among black male youths to achieve success in sports; thus they channel a proportionately greater number of talented black people than whites into sports participation. Our best sociological evidence indicates that capacity for physical achievement (like other common human traits such as intelligence, artistic ability, etc.) are evenly distributed throughout any population. Thus it cuts across class, religious, and, more particularly, racial lines. For race, like class and religion, is primarily a culturally determined classification. *The simple fact of the matter is that the scientific concept of race has no proven biological or genetic validity.* As a cultural delineation, however, it does have a social and political reality. This social and political reality of race is the primary basis of stratification in this society and the key means of determining the priority of who shall have access to means—valued goods and services.

Blacks are relegates in this country, having the lowest priority to claiming valued goods and services. This fact, however, does not negate the equal and proportionate distribution of talent across both black and white populations. Hence, a situation arises wherein whites, being the dominant group in the society, have access to *all* means toward achieving desirable valuables defined by the society. Blacks on the other hand are channeled into the one or two endeavors open to them—sports and, to a lesser degree, entertainment.

Bill Russell once stated that he had to work as hard to achieve his status as the greatest basketball player of the last decade, as the president of General Motors had to work to achieve his position. The evidence tends to indicate that Russell is quite correct. In short, it takes just as much talent, perseverance, dedication and earnest effort to succeed in sports as it does to become a leading financier, business executive, attorney or doctor. Few occupations (music and art being perhaps the exceptions) demand more time and dedication than sports. A world-class athlete will usually have spent a good deal of his youth practicing the skills and techniques of his chosen sports endeavor.

The competition for the few positions is extremely keen, and if he is fortunate he will survive in that competition long enough to become a professional athlete or an outstanding figure in one of the amateur sports. For as he moves up through the various levels of competition, fewer and fewer slots or positions are available, and the competition for these becomes increasingly intense because the rewards are greater. (Since the talents of 25 million Afro-Americans have a disproportionately higher concentration in sports, the number of highly gifted whites in sports is proportionately less than the number of blacks.) Under such circumstances, black athletes naturally predominate. Further, the white athletes who do participate in sports operate at a psychological disadvantage (relative to their black counterparts), because they believe blacks to be inherently superior as athletes. Thus the white man has become the chief victim of his own lie.

Therefore, white racism in American society seems to be responsible for black athletic superiority to whites. That being the case, the real question is perhaps not "Why is the number of black athletes so disproportionately high?" The basic factor determining that the number of blacks in sports does not soar still higher is white racism in the sports sphere itself. Sports aggregations at all levels of athletic participation operate under informal quotas as to the number of blacks allowed to make the roster. This is particularly true in the college and professional ranks where the rewards of participation are relatively higher. Also, as we mentioned earlier, certain positions in sports—such as quarterback—are the monopoly of white players.

Each year white America publicizes a "white hope" in sports: in 1968, it was Jim Ryun at the Olympic games; in 1970 it was Jerry Quarry in his fight against Muhammed Ali; in 1971 it was Pete Maravich. If this society is ever to realize its fondest dream in the sports realm—the development of at least relative parity between black and white athletes with regard to sports excellence—it must give Afro-Americans an opportunity for achievement in high status endeavors outside of sports participation.

It is well known that all the great quarterbacks are white because blacks have never, en masse, had an opportunity to play that position. All the great professional football coaches and baseball managers are white, because blacks have never had an opportunity to be professional head football coaches or major league baseball managers. So even these "great" white sports figures are contrived phonies, as are the so-called greats in the many other sports closed to blacks. This is due to racism, which leads to de facto denial of opportunity to blacks who have potential for excellence in these activities. The latter is particularly true of sports such as golf, tennis, swimming and auto racing.

The necessity for white America to generate a white hope year after year, and to attempt to justify far-flung and irrational myths (as postulated in Kane's article), will all decrease proportionately to the degree that American society divests itself of the racist restrictions that limit opportunity for blacks across the occupational spectrum. As long as sports provide the only visible high-status occupational role model for the masses of black male youths, black superiority over whites shall go unchallenged.

II

FAMILY

1

Guidelines for Black Psychologists

JOSEPH WHITE

At the present time, black psychologists are still operating with a lot of assumptions and machinery that have been developed by white psychologists primarily for white people. For us to begin to develop a viable black psychology, it is important that we first assess some of the premises of white psychology, its various schools, and how those premises operate when black people are the object of their scrutiny.

As an example, let us take the white educational psychologist looking at the black home. He might observe that many of the standard cultural trappings of the middle class white home are missing: the collected works of Shakespeare might not be there; James Brown will be there instead of Brahms; *Jet, Ebony* and maybe *Sepia* are there instead of *Harper's* or *The Atlantic Monthly*. Not seeing the familiar white cultural trappings and seeing some that he does not understand, the tendency of the psychologist has been to assume that the child is deprived in some way.

As a psychologist, he thus enters the observational net of the black home or client with a deficit or weakness hypothesis, so that his recommended programs are based upon some concept of enrichment for the child, family or client. It is enrichment defined by the dominant culture—from Head Start to Upward Bound to language enrichment programs, etc. Somehow the analysis is always corrective; implied is always some deficit that the child brings to the situa-

JOSEPH WHITE is Director of Black Studies at the University of California, Irvine. He was formerly Dean of Undergraduate Studies at San Francisco State College and was one of five black administrators who resigned in protest against that college's policy toward blacks. Prior to that Dr. White was Director of Special Admissions at Long Beach State College. He received the Ph.D. in child psychology from the University of Michigan (East Lansing) in 1961.

tion from his home. This analysis has pre-psychological origins, and it is a clear carryover from slavery and Reconstruction days—that there is something inferior about the black child, and therefore with the black man.

One psychologist, Jensen, just out and out states that it is a genetic thing, that blacks are inferior by birth. But the more liberated type of white psychologist wants to move under the cultural deprivation, cultural deficit, psychological deficit type of hypothesis. Besides the cognitive school of psychology, the practice of which I outlined briefly, we also have many psychologists who have been touched by Freudian and psychoanalytic kinds of thinking.

Such psychologists observe the black home and conclude that there is not a male figure present with the same frequency that there is in the dominant culture's home. From this premise, the neo-Freudian begins to develop all kinds of theories about the atypical attachment of black youth—especially male children—to their mothers. There is central emphasis on the Oedipus complex. Psychologists' perceptions of relationships between black males and black females lead them to conclude that we are a matriarchal culture and that, therefore, the mother must translate to the male child a kind of negation of the male role and that she also does this to the female child.

Such an analysis is just another more sophisticated example of the deprivation hypothesis: either there is something wrong with us cognitively (we don't develop right and therefore we need school enrichment), or at a depth level, we have psycho-sexual problems which we act out through our adult life in the male-female relationship and in the parent-child relationship.

What black psychologists must try to do is enter a theory building net about black children that does not draw primarily from either the psychoanalytic hypothesis or the cognitive deprivation hypothesis. Instead, they must try to develop the kind of psychological model that accounts for the strengths in our children. Many children growing up in the black community learn a certain kind of mental toughness. They learn survival skills. They know how to deal with the credit man; they know how to deal with the cat at the corner market; they know how to deal with hypes and pimps. They know how to jive the school principal, and they show a lot of psychological cleverness and originality in the particular style they emerge with. But most institutions have not yet learned how to appreciate and capitalize upon this particular kind of style.

As black psychologists, we might establish this hypothesis: that the psychology the black child has developed is a very positive and healthy kind of thing. It shows his recognition that he exists in a complicated and hostile environment, that he has an objective awareness of this environment and makes behaviors in terms of that awareness. I would also continue to stress that as we analyze the psychological make-up of white institutions, we find that the institution itself tends to negate the authenticity of the black child's existence. For example, if he comes to school popping his fingers and talking about another youngster's mama or being loud, the institution begins to negate the style as improper, bad and otherwise worthless.

White psychologists further find it very difficult to understand the apparent contradictions in black culture, the fact that these apparent contradictions do not mean the same thing that they would mean in white culture. For example, I remember one white psychology student who wanted to interview and observe a black nationalist student club. The brothers wouldn't let him come inside, but they did allow him to view the meeting from a window. A particular brother whom we both knew went to the black nationalist meeting where the brothers laid down a typical 1968 type of black power set. The brother was a very active participant in the meeting: right on, the whole bit. Subsequently, this brother left the meeting and went kitty-corner across the street to a store-front type of church, grabbed a tambourine, entered the ceremony and rocked with the sisters for about an hour and shouted a bit. Then he left there and went down the street a block to a bar and began to drink a little gin and dig on Aretha Franklin.

So when the white boy interviewed him in the bar, he asked him, "Well, don't you see a contradiction between black nationalist ideology, the store-front church and you sitting in this bar drinking gin?" The brother said he didn't see any contradiction because he did it every Sunday and all the sets were part of him. He just dug on it.

While it might have represented for the white psychologist a logical contradiction, it meant nothing to the brother. Black people could see the church as an organ of strength on the part of their community and as an escapist movement at the same time without one negating the other.

Closely related to black ease with seeming contradictions is the fact that black people have a greater tolerance for ambiguity and ambivalence than the white culture, and the white psychologist does not recognize this fact sufficiently. Instead, assuming that black people are lower-class, he therefore assumes that blacks are impulsive. One of the things impulsive people have is little tolerance for stress and contradiction. Seeing us as being more impulsive, the white psychologist assumes that we have less ability to handle contradictions. I would turn it the other way around.

Furthermore, as Price Cobbs points out, it is good for black people to have a "healthy paranoia." A black person who is not suspicious of this culture is tied up in using a lot of very pathological mechanisms, like the denial of certain basic realities. The sociologist E. Franklin Frazier touched on this very well in *Black Bourgeoisie*. Part of the objective situation of black persons in this society is a paranoid condition: there is a persecution, an irrational persecution at that. Moreover, it is systematic. We have therefore developed a set of tools to deal with it.

On the other hand, if a white dude were to sit down and tell a psychologist that he's being persecuted, that he's got some people who have been systematically persecuting him everywhere from his front door to the White House, the psychologist might say, "Well, man, you'd better take a little ride down to Fairview, and we'll help you out." Black psychologists and white psychologists who have dealings with black people must bear this distinction in mind—that what can be seen as illness for the white man can be health for the black man, attitudinally, as it bears on his relationships to the white power structure in this country.

Black and white people operate from different frames of reference. When black people confront white people, what they primarily want is, first, a legitimate acknowledgement of their point of view and needs, and second, the appropriate actions to be taken. But when a white person is pushed up against the wall, the worst thing he can do is admit that the party who pushed him up there has a valid point of view. So, in a conference situation, when black people escalate the tempo of their language and their gestural style and get into verbal fireworks, the white reaction is to feel angry, threatened and alienated. Were whites to drop their defensiveness and acknowledge the legitimacy of the black point of view, they might be able to go from there to a more cooperative relationship. But this culture is so deeply entrenched in the whole concept of sin and atonement, and paying up for that sin, that it expects retaliation in the Old Testament style once it admits "sin"; it expects a retribution, a punishment.

The question of image and hero emerges here. This culture is steeped in the tradition of a white hero who is infallible and rigid, who scores his triumphs with inhuman skill and retires undefeated. The whole psychology of the hero in the black and white cultures is different. In the black culture the hero is by and large the brother who messes with the system and gets away with it. Black people on the whole could care less about certain political figures going off to the Caribbean and spending a little dough. They can dig it and can identify with it. Whereas this same hero, to the white psychologist, appears to be the villain. This comes together in literature. In John O. Killens' *And Then We Heard the Thunder*, Solly, the so-called Noble Savage, is a black college graduate who has had Officer's Candidate School. He's got this goof-off in his outfit, this brother who battles the officers, etc. But finally, over the course of the book, it's the bad nigger who becomes the hero. Nowadays, the bad nigger is very much in vogue as the hero in the black community, and yet white people continue to perceive this person as the villain.

Such was true in the case of Eldridge Cleaver. Eldridge became a kind of culture hero in the United States; a lot of white people were disappointed because he didn't stand trial. He had let down his responsibilities to his people and he wasn't "a credit to his race." But anybody who had heard Eldridge or read his books or knew anything about his life knew where he had been and knew he wasn't going to go there again.

What we black psychologists are getting at is a set of objective or factual recognitions that might help black people recognize that psychology is social as well as personal and help them develop a social psychology of blackness. Most of the white psychological theory that we have is personal, either some kind of cognitive approach or psychoanalytic approach. It further assumes that there is a regular social order which is satisfactory. These theories are not valid with respect to the needs of black people. If one looks at the work of black psychiatrist Frantz Fanon, for example, he finds the opposite emphasis: that black psychological strains have social origins and that the present social order is not satisfactory for blacks but oppressive.

One type of psychological theory that we can possibly modify and use is that of the Gestalt psychologists, such as Carl Rogers, who view people as having a frame of reference and an individual phenomenal field which is legitimate. In this theory, people come from certain experiential pools, and those pools determine who they are. Its primary ingredients are the home, the family and the immediate neighborhood. We have got to work to make these frames legitimate and then allow our children extension of them, in role models that they can associate with.

It's very important that these role models be realistic. Again, white psychologists and educators tend to miss the boat here. For example, a couple of weeks ago I was looking at some new children's books. Now all publishers have got the idea that you have to have something black in children's literature so that black youngsters can identify with the pictures. One of these had a story of some white boys playing baseball. At the beginning of the ball game a brother was standing at the side, just standing there. One of the players had to go home, and then the white boys allowed the brother to play. Well, he hit four home runs and struck out six people in a row and saved the game. But what the book was projecting is an image of another Willie Mays, that "super-niggers" are okay in ones and twos. Whereas, the average everyday, typical white boy is projected *all over* the culture—radio, television, books, periodicals and films. So from the black psychological standpoint we have to work to make a kind of breakthrough that puts black children into typical situations rather than into omniscient and omnipotent kinds of roles. As individual people, we have to trust our own kind of perception and not absorb white expectations of black super-heroes and villains.

One very valuable thing about the black consciousness movement is that it begins to psychologically legitimatize being black. But we must not equate the imagery of that consciousness with the actualities of social progress. We cannot have a black and proud community with no jobs, no transportation, no way of feeding the kids, no control of the police force, schools and other institutions. It must be a two-stage kind of operation, consciousness and action. Perhaps as we develop black cultural anthropologists or whatever would be the black equivalent, we can get some greater insights to guide us.

One of the very different things about the black culture and the black psyche of America is that it is an oral culture—the blues, the gospel songs, the heavy rap, the sermon and traditions are carried orally, and people are going to have to examine that oral expression in order to make new insights into the psychological functioning of black people. For example, in black idioms—what we call black English or whatever—we do things that are unique in terms of syntax. I think this might have had its roots in an oral existence which still has some Africanisms, but also in our social need to use language to simultaneously reveal and conceal. Black language is very deep in subtle meaning and nuances. For example, if you take a poem like the "Signifying Monkey," there are a lot of psychological processes tied up in there and there is a heavy amount of deception. Or take the old song ". . . steal away, steal away, steal away, Jesus, steal away home . . . I ain't got long to stay here . . ." The slavemaster perceived in the antebellum South that the brothers were thinking about heaven and religion when the cats were really laying out a message that the Underground Railway is coming through and you better jump on board.

This would probably mean—and I don't know if we can ever develop the instruments to test this out—that people who grow up in the black community tend to be much more intuitive in terms of their response to signs and gestures than they are in relating to the concrete syntax. In the attempt to translate black English into the standard vernacular, some of its quality and meaning may be lost. For example, a youngster might say, "Well the cat was rappin' on my rib," and we try to translate it, "He was flirting with my girl-friend," or, "He was being unduly solicitous toward a young woman whom I was dating," and something is lost. It's amazing that this is only now being talked about, because many of us have always recognized that things get lost when they are translated from one language or style into another. Yet it is a daily black experience.

A consideration of black sensitivity training is in order. I think we have to develop some kind of psychological process by which black agents of change who are continuously on the firing line can blow their minds out from time to time—go through some inner cleansing. Because I'm sensing around the country that a lot of brothers are beginning to suffer from some combat fatigue and entropy. It is very difficult in such a state of mind to see clearly both the goal that one is striving for and the relevance of the tactic to the particular goal in the immediate situation. In that frame of mind, one begins to use words in a very global kind of way. Words like revolution, liberation, offing, Tomming, and so on. We may need to identify a network of black psychologists who can help brothers in groups work through the renewal, self-regeneration process. And there are probably some things we can utilize through standard sensitivity models, but they would probably need certain alterations.

For while aggression, affection and sexuality may be the kinds of encounters that white people need to work through within them-selves, I think that as I see brothers in 1970, we need to work out in our local situations a clarity of direction, given where we are. We must work through the kinds of problems that we get into when we mix image and rhetoric with the process of change itself. We may need the kinds of sets that have brothers examine what they are really saying. I can conceive of a set where we put some brothers together for a couple of hours and let them rap on closed circuit television as intensely as they want to about where they are rela-tive to change. We could then have each of those brothers watch the set together and individually and see the whole process at work, and then try to get back together and tell each other what they thought they were saying, what they then observed about them-selves and the group, and then what the difference was between the intended message and the actual message.

As to black-white encounters, one of the things I saw on television recently that fascinated me was the forcing of each group to take the role of the other, but not a typical role-playing session. The sensitivity trainers put white masks on the black people and black masks on the white people and forced them to interchange positions. If one talks about psychologists having difficulty because they enter the communication net with different frames of reference, one way of helping them learn the other frame of reference is by forcing them to act it through—not for a fifteen-minute period but over a long 30-hour encounter.

A lot of sensitivity and T-group work can be a useful thing for blacks who are involved in the movement and leadership roles, to clean out their pipes once in a while.

With such sessions, the trainer or psychologist should be a black from another location who does not have any built-in emotional reaction and/or commitments to any member of the group. We could also interchange black personnel—some of the brothers from the East might come here and work with us and some of us might go back there and work with them.

Another value I see to the group process type of model is that with all that has happened in the Movement in the last ten years, there is a lot of confusion as we move from one pattern to another, just in the people in the community itself. We may need some type of store-front in the ghetto itself, where brothers can drop in in groups, rap about child rearing, rap about hash, and rap about the revolution and so on. For we don't seem to have a vehicle through which the standard citizen can involve himself except when we call a mass meeting. That mass meeting, more often than not, is related to a particular crisis in the community. We don't have a place where, like on Monday night, there will be certain trained black personnel available who will work with any group that drops in from seven to nine o'clock.

Former group nets are being broken up. For example, the church used to involve itself in a lot of activities in groups. They may not have been sensitivity groups, but you could drop down, and on Tuesday night there was choir rehearsal, Wednesday night young people's meeting, but that's breaking up now. Brothers also don't play the bar set the way they used to, going out on Saturday night, taking a chick, meeting his boys certain places, dancing, carrying on. That set doesn't seem to be as prevalent anymore. Brothers don't have a place to go to plug in—even barber shops, even clubs and joints are fading out.

A good sensitivity model, then, could pick up the communication lag that has occurred as the churches, the barber shops, the bars, and the joints lose that sanction.

These are the concerns that black psychologists must address themselves to. We must begin to develop a model of black psychology which is free from the built-in assumptions and values of the dominant culture. We cannot, by rote, employ the psychoanalytic model nor the cognitive model. Real gains might come from the model of Gestalt psychology, with its sense of experiential pools, of field and subject. We must develop a kind of psychological jui-jitsu and recognize that what the dominant culture deems deviant or anti-social behavior might indeed be the functioning of a healthy black psyche which objectively recognizes the antagonisms of the white culture and develops machinery for coping with them.

We should also recognize that black people have a great tolerance for ambiguity and uncertainty, for living with seemingly contradictory alternatives. As practitioners, then, we must eliminate the tendency to think in either-or terms with respect to the black experience. Finally, we need to develop dynamic models of a group nature, to help support and restore and refresh our leadership and to renew communication within all levels of the black community.

2

The Black Movement and Women's Liberation

LINDA LA RUE

Let us first discuss what common literature addresses as the "common oppression" of blacks and women. This is a tasty abstraction designed purposely or inadvertently to draw validity and seriousness to the women's movement through a universality of plight. Every movement worth its "revolutionary salt" makes these headliner generalities about "common oppression" with others—but let us state unequivocally that, with few exceptions, the American white woman has had a better opportunity to live a free and fulfilling life, both mentally and physically, than any other group in the United States, with the exception of her white husband. Thus, any attempt to analogize black oppression with the plight of the American white woman has the validity of comparing the neck of a hanging man with the hands of an amateur mountain climber with rope burns.

"Common oppression" is fine for rhetoric, but it does not reflect the actual distance between the oppression of the black man and woman who are unemployed, and the "oppression" of the American white woman who is "sick and tired" of *Playboy* fold-outs, or of Christian Dior lowering hemlines or adding ruffles, or of Miss Clairol telling her that blondes have more fun.

Is there any logical comparison between the oppression of the black woman on welfare who has difficulty feeding her children and the discontent of the suburban mother who has the luxury to protest the washing of the dishes on which her family's full meal was consumed?

The surge of "common oppression" rhetoric and propaganda may

LINDA LA RUE is a graduate student in political science at Purdue University, Lafayette, Indiana. She was one of twenty-four students to be awarded the coveted Marshall Fellowship for study in England in 1969. She plans to do further study at Cornell in Asian and Third World Studies.

lure the unsuspecting into an intellectual alliance with the goals of women's liberation, but it is not a wise alliance. It is not that women ought not to be liberated from the shackles of their present unfulfillment, but the depth, the extent, the intensity, the importance—indeed, the suffering and depravity of the *real* oppression blacks have experienced—can only be minimized in an alliance with women who heretofore have suffered little more than boredom, genteel repression and dishpan hands.

For all the similarities and analogies drawn between the liberation of women and the liberation of blacks, the point remains that when white women received their voting rights, most blacks, male and female, had been systematically disenfranchised since Reconstruction. And even in 1970, when women's right of franchise is rarely questioned, it is still a less than common occurrence for blacks to vote in some areas of the South.

Tasteless analogies like abortion for oppressed middle-class and poor women idealistically assert that all women have the right to decide if and when they want children and thus fail to catch the flavor of the actual circumstances. Actual circumstances boil down to middle-class women deciding when it is convenient to have children, while poor women decide the prudence of bringing into a world of already scarce resources another mouth to feed. Neither their motives nor their objectives are the same. But current literature leads one to lumping the decisions of these two women under one generalization, when in fact the difference between the plights of these two women is as clear as the difference between being hungry and out of work, and skipping lunch and taking a day off.

If we are realistically candid with ourselves, we will accept the fact that despite our beloved rhetoric of Pan-Africanism, our vision of third world liberation, and perhaps our dreams of a world state of multi-racial humanism, most blacks and a good many who generally exempt themselves from categories still want the proverbial "piece of cake." American values are difficult to discard, for, unlike what more militant "brothers" would have us believe, Americanism does not end with the adoption of Afro hairstyles on pregnant women covered in long African robes.

Indeed, the fact that the independent black capitalism demonstrated by the black Muslims and illustrated in Nixon's speeches appeared for many blacks as the way out of the ghetto into the light, lends a truthful vengeance to the maxim that perhaps blacks are nothing more than black anglo-saxons. Upon the rebirth of the liberation struggle in the sixties, a whole genre of "women's place" advocates immediately relegated black women to home and babies, which is almost as ugly an expression of black anglo-saxonism as is Nixon's concept of "black capitalism."

The study of many developing areas and countries reflects at least an attempt to allow freedom of education and opportunity to women. Yet black Americans have not adopted developing areas' "new role" paradigm, but rather the Puritan-American status of "home and babies" which is advocated by the capitalist Muslims. This reflects either ingrained Americanism or the lack of the simplest imagination.

Several weeks ago, women's lib advocates demanded that a local women's magazine be "manned" by a woman editor. Other segments of the women's movement have carried on smaller campaigns in industry and business.

If white women have heretofore remained silent while white men maintained the better position and monopolized the opportunities by excluding blacks, can we really expect that white women, when put in direct competition for employment, will be any more open-minded than their male counterparts when it comes to the hiring of black males and females in the same positions for which they are competing? From the standpoint of previous American social inter-action, it does not seem logical that white females will not be tempted to take advantage of the fact that they are white in an economy that favors whites. It is entirely possible that women's liberation has developed a sudden attachment to the black liberation movement as a ploy to share the attention that it has taken blacks 400 years to generate. In short, it can be argued that women's liberation not only attached itself to the black movement, but did so with only marginal concern for black women and black liberation and with functional concern for the rights of white women.

The industrial demands of two world wars temporarily offset the racial limitations to mobility and allowed the possibility of blacks entering industry, as an important labor force, to be actualized. Similarly women have benefited from an expanded science and industrialization. Their biological limitation, successfully curbed by the pill and by automation, which makes stressing physical labor more the exception than the rule, has created an impressively large and available labor force of women.

The black labor force, never fully employed and always representing a substantial percentage of the unemployed in the American economy, will now be driven into greater unemployment as white women converge at every level on an already dwindling job market.

Ideally, we chanced to think of women's liberation as a promising beginning of the "oppressed rising everywhere" in the typically Marxian fashion that many blacks seem drawn to. Instead, the spectre of racism and inadequate education, job discrimination, and even greater unequal opportunity will be, more than ever before, a function of neither maleness nor femaleness, but of blackness.

This discussion has been primarily to ward off any unintelligent alliance of black people with white women in this new liberation movement. Rhetoric and anathema hurled at the right industrial complex, idealism which speaks of a final humanism, and denunciation of the system which makes competition a fact of life, do not mean that women's liberation has as its goal anyone else's liberation except its own.

It is time that definitions be made clear. Blacks are *oppressed,* and that means unreasonably burdened, unjustly, severely, rigorously, cruelly and harshly fettered by white authority. White women, on the other hand, are only *suppressed,* and that means checked, restrained, excluded from conscious and overt activity. And there is a difference.

For some, the dangers of an unintelligent alliance with women's liberation will suggest female suppression as the only protection against a new economic threat. For others, a greater answer is needed, and required, before women's liberation can be seen in perspective.

To say that black women must be freed before the black movement can attain full revolutionary consciousness is meaningless because of its malleability. To say that black women must be freed from the unsatisfactory male-female role relationship which we adopted from whites as the paradigm of the good family has more meaning because it indicates the incompatibility of white role models with the goal of black liberation. If there is anything to be learned from the current women's lib agitation, it is that roles are not ascribed and inherent, but adopted and interchangeable in every respect except pregnancy, breastfeeding and the system generally employed to bring the two former into existence.

Role integration, which I will elaborate upon as the goal and the strength of the black family, is substantially different from the role "usurpation" of men by women. The fact that the roles of man and woman are deemed in American society as natural and divine leads to false ego attachments to these roles. During slavery and following Reconstruction, black men felt inferior for a great number of reasons, among them that they were unable to work in positions comparable to the ones to which black women were assigned. With these positions often went fringe benefits of extra food, clothes, and perhaps elementary reading and writing skills. Black women were in turn jealous of white women and felt inadequate and inferior, because paraded in front of them constantly was the white woman of luxury who had no need for work, who could, as Sojourner Truth pointed out, "be helped into carriages and lifted over ditches and . . . have the best place everywhere."

The resulting "respect" for women and the acceptance of the dominating role for men encouraged the myth of the immutability of these roles. The term "matriarchy" Frazier employed and Moynihan exploited was used to indicate a dastardly, unnatural role alteration which could be blamed for inequality of opportunity, discrimination in hiring and sundry other ills. It was as if "matriarchy" were transgression of divine law or natural law and thus would be punished until the proper hierarchy of man over woman was restored.

Black people have an obligation, as do white women, to recognize that the designation of "mother-head" and "father-head" does not imply inferiority of one and the superiority of the other. They are merely arbitrary role distinctions which vary from culture to culture and circumstance to circumstance.

Thus to quip, as has been popularly done, that the only place in the black movement for black women is prone is actually supporting a white role ideal, and it is a compliment neither to men nor to women to advocate sexual capitalism or sexual colonialism.

It seems incongruous that the black movement has sanctioned the involvement of women in the Algerian revolution, even though its revolutionary circumstances modified and often altered the common role models, but they have been duped into hating even their own slave grandmothers, who in not so admirable yet equally frightening and demanding circumstances also modified and altered the common role models of the black family. Fanon wrote in glorious terms about this role change:

The unveiled Algerian woman, who assumed an increasingly important place in revolutionary action, developed her personality, discovered the exalting realm of responsibility. . . . This woman who, in the avenues of Algiers or of Constantine, would carry the grenades or the submachine gun charges, the woman who tomorrow would be outraged, violated, tortured, could not put herself back into her former state of mind and relive her behavior of the past. . . .[1]

Can it not be said that in slavery black women assumed an increasingly important place in the survival action and thus developed their personalities and sense of responsibility? And after being outraged, violated and tortured, could she be expected to put herself back into her former state of mind and relive her behavior of the past?

1. Frantz Fanon, A Dying Colonialism. New York: Grove Press, 1965, p. 107.

The crux of this argument is essentially that blacks, since slavery and throughout their entire existence in America, have also been living in revolutionary circumstances and under revolutionary pressures. Simply because the black liberation struggle has taken 400 years to come to fruition does not mean that it is not every bit as dangerous or psychologically exhausting as the Algerian struggle. Any revolution calls upon the best in both its men and its women. This is why Moynihan's statements that "matriarchy" is a root *cause* of black problems is as unfounded as it is inane. He does not recognize the liberation struggle and the demands that it has made on the black family.

How unfortunate that blacks and whites have allowed the most trying and bitter experience in the history of black people to be interpreted as the beginning of an "unashamed plot" to usurp the very manhood of black men. But the myth was perpetuated, and thus what brought the alteration of roles in Algeria was distorted and systematically employed to separate black men and women in America.

Black women take kindness for weakness. Leave them the least little opening and they will put you on the cross. . . . It would be like trying to pamper a cobra. . . .[2]

Unless we realize how thoroughly the American value of male superiority and female inferiority has permeated our relationships with one another, we can never appreciate the role it plays in perpetuating racism and keeping black people divided.

Most, but not all, American relationships are based on some type of "exclusive competition of the superior and the exclusive competition of the inferior." This means essentially that the poor, the uneducated, the deprived and the minorities of the aforementioned groups, compete among themselves for the same scarce resources and inferior opportunities, while the privileged, middle-class, educated, and select white minorities compete with one another for rather plentiful resources and superior opportunities for prestige and power. Competition among groups is rare, due to the fact that elements who qualify are almost invariably absorbed to some extent (note the black middle class) by the group to which they seek entry. We may well understand that there is only one equal relationship between man and woman, black and white, in America, and this equality is based on whether or not you can force your way into qualifying for the same resources.

But instead of attempting to modify this competitive definition within the black movement, many black males have affirmed it as a

2. Eldridge Cleaver, *Soul on Ice*. New York: McGraw-Hill, 1968, p. 158.

way of maintaining the closure of male monopolization of scarce benefits and making the "dominion of males" impenetrable to black females. This is, of course, very much the American way of exploitation.

The order of logic which makes it possible to pronounce, as did Dr. Robert Staples, that "Black women cannot be free qua women until all blacks attain their liberation," [3] maintains, whether purposely or not, that black women will be able to separate their femaleness from their blackness, and thus they will be able to be free as blacks, if not free as women; or, that male freedom ought to come first; or, finally, that the freedom of black women and men and the freedom of black people as a whole are not one and the same.

Only with the concept of role integration can we hope to rise above the petty demarcations of human freedom that America is noted for and that are unfortunately inherent in Dr. Staples' remark. Role integration is the realization that:

- ego attachments to particular activities or traits must be abolished as a method of determining malehood and femalehood; that instead, ego attachments must be distributed to a wider variety of tasks and traits in order to weaken the power of one activity in determining self-worth, and
- the flexibility of a people in effecting role alternation and role integration has been an historically proven asset to the survival of any people—witness Israel, China and Algeria.

Thus, the unwitting adoption and the knowing perpetuation of this American value reflects three interrelated situations:

- black people's growing sense of security and well-being and their failure to recognize the expanse of black problems;
- black people's over-identification with the dominant group, even though the survival of blacks in America is not assured and
- black people's belief in the myth of "matriarchy" and their subsequent rejection of role integration as unnatural and unnecessary.

While the rhetoric of black power and the advocates of cultural nationalism laud black people for their ability to struggle under oppressive odds, they simultaneously seek to strip away or incapacitate the phenomenon of role integration—the very means by which blacks were able to survive! They seek to replace it with a weak, intractable role separation which would completely sap the strength of the black movement because it would inhibit the mobilization of

3. Robert Staples, "The Myth of the Black Matriarchy." *The Black Scholar*, Jan.-Feb. 1970, p. 16.

both women and men. It was this ability to mobilize black men and black women that guaranteed survival during slavery.

The strength of role integration is sorely overlooked as blacks throw away the hot comb, the bleach cream, the lye, and yet insist on maintaining the worst of American values by placing the strength of black women in the traction of the white female status.

I would think black men would want a better status for their sister black women; indeed, black women would want a better status for themselves, rather than a warmed-over throne of women's inferiority, which white women are beginning to abandon.

Though most white women's lib advocates fail to realize the possibility, their subsequent liberation may spell a strengthening of the status quo values from which they sought liberation. Since more and more women will be participating in the decision-making process, those few women participating in the "struggle" will be outnumbered by the more traditional middle-class women. This means that the traditional women will be in a position to take advantage of new opportunities which radical women's liberation has struggled to win. Voting studies now reflect that the traditional women, middle-class and above, tend to vote the same way as their husbands. Because blacks have dealt with these husbands in the effort to secure jobs, housing and education, it does not seem likely that blacks will gain significantly from the open mobility of less tolerant women whose viewpoints differ little from those of their husbands.

If white radical thought has called upon the strength of all women to take a position of responsibility and power, can blacks afford to relegate black women to "home and babies" while white women reinforce the status quo?

The cry of black women's liberation is a cry against chaining very much needed labor and agitating forces to a role that once belonged to impotent, apolitical white women. Blacks speak lovingly of the vanguard and the importance of women in the struggle and yet fail to recognize that women have been assigned a new place, based on white-ascribed characteristics of women, rather than on their actual potential. The black movement needs its women in a position of struggle, not prone. The struggle blacks face is not taking place between knives and forks, at the washboard, or in the diaper pail. It is taking place on the labor market, at the polls, in government, in the protection of black communities, in local neighborhood power struggles, in housing and in education.

Can blacks afford to be so unobservant of current events as to send their women to fight a nonexistent battle in a dishpan?

Even now, the black adoption of the white values of women has

begun to show its effects on black women in distinctive ways. The
black liberation movement has created a politicized, unliberated
copy of white womanhood. Black women who participated in the
struggle have failed to recognize, for the most part, the unique contradiction between renunciation of capitalistic competition and the
acceptance of sexual colonialism. The failure of the black movement
to resolve and deal with this dilemma has perpetuated the following attitudes in American politicized black women:

- The belief in the myth of matriarchy. The black woman has been
  made to feel ashamed of her strength, and so to redeem herself she
  has adopted from whites the belief that superiority and dominance
  of the male is the most "natural" and "normal" relationship. She consequently believes that black women ought to be suppressed in order
  to attain that "natural balance."
- Because the white woman's role has been held up as an example to
  all black women, many black women feel inadequate and so ardently
  compete in "femininity" with white females for black males' attention.
  She further competes with black females in an attempt to be the
  "blackest and the most feminine," thereby superior to her fellow
  black sisters in appealing to black politicized men. She competes
  also with the apolitical black female in an attempt to keep black
  males from "regressing" back to females whom she feels have had
  more "practice" in the traditional role of white woman than has she.
- Finally, she emphasizes the traditional roles of women, such as
  housekeeping, children, supportive roles, and self-maintenance, but
  she politicizes these roles by calling them the roles of black women.
  She then adopts the attitude that her job and her life is to have more
  children which can be used in the vanguard of the black struggle.
- Black women, as the song "Black Pearl" relates, have been put up
  where they belong, but by American standards. Is it so incon-
  ceivable that the American value of respect and human relationships
  is distorted? It has taken the birth of women's liberation to bring the
  black movement back to its senses.
- The black woman is demanding a new set of female definitions and
  a recognition of herself as a citizen, companion and confidante, not a
  matriarchal villain or a stepstool baby-maker. Role integration advocates the complementary recognition of man and woman, not the
  competitive recognition of same.

The recent unabated controversy over the use of birth control in
the black community is of grave importance here. Black people,
even the "most liberated of mind," are still infused with ascribed
inferiority of females and the natural superiority of males. These
same values foster the idea of "good blood" in children. If indeed
there can be any black liberation, it must start with the recognition
of contradictions like the following.

It gives a great many black males pride to speak, as Dr. Robert Staples does, of ". . . the role of the black woman in the black liberation struggle is an important one and cannot be forgotten. From her womb have come the revolutionary warriors of our time." [4]

How many potential revolutionary warriors stand abandoned in orphanages while blacks rhetorize disdain for birth control as a "trick of The Man" to halt the growth of black population? Why are there not more revolutionary couples adopting black children? Could it be that the American concept of "bastard," which is equivalent to inferior in our society, reflects black anglo-saxonism? Do blacks, like whites, discriminate against black babies because they do not represent "our own personal" image? Or do blacks, like the most racist of whites, require that a child be of their own blood before they can love that child or feed it? Does the vanguard of which Dr. Staples so reverently speaks recognize the existence of the term "bastard"?

Someone once suggested that the word "bastard" be deleted from the values of black people. Would it not be more revolutionary for blacks to advocate a five-year moratorium on black births until every black baby in an American orphange was adopted by one or more black parents? Then blacks could really have a valid reason for continuing to give birth. Children would mean more than simply a role for black women to play or fuel for the legendary vanguard. Indeed, blacks would be able to tap the potential of the existing children and could sensibly add more potential to the black struggle for liberation. To do this would be to do something no other civilization, modern of course, has ever done, and blacks would be allowing every black child to have a home and not just a plot in some understaffed children's penal farm.

What makes a healthy black baby in an orphanage different from "our own flesh and blood"? Except for the American value of inferiority-superiority and the concept of "bastard" that accompanies it, there is nothing "wrong" with the orphaned child save what white society has taught us to perceive.

We can conclude that black women's liberation and black men's liberation is what we mean when we speak of the liberation of black people. I maintain that the true liberation of black people depends on their rejection of the inferiority of women, the rejection of competition as the only viable relationship between men, and their reaffirmation of respect for general human potential in whatever form —man, child or woman—it is conceived.

4. *Ibid.*

3

The Myth of the
Impotent Black Male

ROBERT STAPLES

In White America there is a cultural belief that the Black community is dominated by its female members, its men having been emasculated by the historical vicissitudes of slavery and contemporary economic forces. This cultural belief contains a duality of meaning: that black men have been deprived of their masculinity and that black women participated in the emasculinization process. The myth of the black matriarchy has been exploded elsewhere.[1] Black female dominance is a cultural illusion that disguises the triple oppression of black women in this society. They are discriminated against on the basis of their sex role affiliation, their race and their location in the working-class strata of this upper-class dominated country.

The assumption that black men have been socially castrated has yet to be challenged. Before examining the fallacies of black male castration, it is important to understand the function of these cultural images of black men and women for maintaining the status quo level of black deprivation and white privilege. Most of these theories of black life come from the field of social science, a discipline ostensibly dedicated to the pursuit of truth. It would be more realistic to view social science research as a form of ideology,

ROBERT STAPLES, Ph.D., is a member of the faculty in the Department of Sociology at Howard University. He is the author of numerous articles in both popular and professional periodicals and has edited a book entitled *The Black Family: Essays and Studies* published by Wadsworth Publishing Company. He is a contributing editor for *The Black Scholar* and Associate Editor of the *Journal of Marriage and the Family*.

1. Robert Staples, "The Myth of the Black Matriarchy." *The Black Scholar*, February, 1970, pp. 9-16.

a propaganda apparatus which serves to justify racist institutions and practices. Social science as ideology is a means of social control exercised by white America to retain its privileges in a society partially sustained by this ideology. As one observer noted:

Social scientists and journalists in America generally operate under an ideology-laden code of professional conduct that requires objectivity . . . But this objectivity is in effect a commitment to the ruling class.[2]

Stereotypes of the black male as psychologically impotent and castrated have been perpetuated not only by social scientists but through the mass media, and they have been accepted by both blacks and whites alike. This assault on black masculinity is made *precisely because black males are men*, not because they are impotent, and that is an important distinction to make. As one sociologist candidly admits, "Negro men have been more feared, sexually and occupationally, than Negro women."[3] She further admits that the Negro man had to be destroyed as a man to "protect" the white world.[4] It should be added that the attempt to destroy him failed, but the myth of his demasculinization lingers on. One can see in this myth an unmitigated fear of black male power, an unrelenting determination on the part of white America to create in fiction what it has been unable to accomplish in the empirical world.

From a historical perspective, the black male's role has changed as he has traversed from the African continent to the shores of North America. This span of time has introduced the forces of slavery, racism and wage exploitation in the determination of his masculine expressions. In Africa, he resided in a male-dominated society. Although women had an important place in African society, most important decisions were made by male members of the community.[5]

Taken forcibly from his African roots, the black man experienced radical changes in his status. In the beginning of the period of slavery, black men greatly outnumbered black women. It was not until 1840 that there was an equal sex ratio among blacks.[6] As a result of this low sex ratio, there were numerous cases of sex relations between black slaves and indentured white women. The intermarriage rate between black men and white women increased to the extent that interracial marriages were prohibited. Previously, black

2. William Ellis, *White Ethics and Black Power*. Chicago: Aldine Publishing Company, 1969, p. xiii.
3. Jessie Bernard, *Marriage and Family Among Negroes*. Englewood Cliffs, New Jersey: Prentice-Hall, Inc., 1966, p. 69.
4. *Ibid.*, p. 73.
5. John Hope Franklin, *From Slavery to Freedom*. New York: Random House, 1947.
6. *Ibid.*

men were encouraged to marry white women in order to augment the human capital of the slave-owning class.[7]

After black women were brought over to the New World, they served as breeders of children who were treated as property, and as the gratifiers of white plantation owners' carnal desires. More importantly, they became the central figure in black family life. The black man's only crucial function within the family was that of siring the children. The mother's role was far more important than the father's. She cleaned the house, prepared the food, made clothes and raised the children. The husband was at most his wife's assistant, her companion and her sex partner. He was often thought of as her possession, as was the cabin in which they lived. It was common for a mother and her children to be considered a family without reference to the father.[8]

Under slavery the role of father was, in essence, institutionally obliterated. Not only was the slave father deprived of his sociological and economic functions in the family, but the very etiquette of plantation life eliminated even the honorific attributes of fatherhood from the black male, who was addressed as boy—until, when the vigorous years of his prime were past, he was permitted to assume the title of uncle. If he lived with a woman, "married," he was known as her husband (e.g. Sally's John), again denying him a position as head of the household.[9]

That black men were reduced to a subordinate status in the family is quite true. That they abdicated their responsibility to their families probably highlights the unusual—not the prosaic—behavior of black men. Although somewhat unusual, for example, there was the case of a black slave who, when his wife complained of the beating she had taken from the overseer, took her to a cave away from harm. He fixed it up for her to live in; he brought her food; he protected her. Three children were born in the cave, and only with emancipation did the family come out to join him.[10]

There are those who say that slavery prevented black men from coming to emotional maturity, that they were childlike, docile creatures who were viewed not as objects of fear or hatred but as a

7. E. Franklin Frazier, *The Negro Family in the United States*. Chicago: University of Chicago Press, 1939.

8. Maurice Davie, *Negroes in American Society*. New York: McGraw-Hill, 1949, p. 207.

9. Stanley M. Elkins, *Slavery: A Problem in American Institutional and Intellectual Life*. New York: Grosset and Dunlap, Inc., 1963, p. 130.

10. B. A. Botkin, *Lay My Burden Down*. Chicago: The University of Chicago Press, 1945, pp. 179-80.

source of amusement.[11] In conflict with this view is the observation that:

In spite of all attempts to crush it, the slave had a will of his own which was actively as well as passively opposed to the master's. And it is this stubborn and rebellious will—tragic, heroic, defeated or triumphant —that, more than all else . . . haunted the master, frustrating his designs by a ceaseless though perhaps invisible countermining . . . The slave expressed his hatred of enslavement and his contempt for his enslaver in less subtle and more open ways, such as taking what belonged to him, escaping or assisting others to escape, secretly learning or teaching others to read and write, secret meetings, suicide, infanticide, homicide, and the like.[12]

In addition to this covert resistance, the so-called "docile" slave put together a number of elaborate conspiracies and insurrections. According to Aptheker, over 250 slave revolts were planned.[13] After slavery, however, the black male continued to encounter assaults on his manhood. White America has tried to subjugate him in every aspect of his life. The historical literature, for instance, suggests that Jim Crow was directed more at the black male than at the black female.[14] Black women, in a very limited way, were allowed more freedom, suffered less discrimination and were provided more opportunities than black men.

The structural barriers to black manhood were great. In a capitalistic society, being able to provide basic life satisfactions is inextricably interwoven with manhood. It is the opportunity to provide for his family, both individually and collectively, which has been denied the black man. After emancipation the economic role of the black woman was strengthened as blacks left the rural areas and migrated to the cities where it was difficult for black men to obtain employment. Although they had previously held jobs as skilled craftsmen, carpenters, etc., they were forced out of these occupations by a coalition of white workers and capitalists. In some instances they found employment only as strikebreakers.[15]

Through this systematic denial of an opportunity for black men to work, white America thrust the black woman into the role of family provider. This pattern of female-headed families was reinforced by the marginal economic position of the black male. The

11. Elkins, *op. cit.*, p. 128.

12. Botkin, *op. cit.*, pp. 137-38.

13. Herbert Aptheker, *American Negro Slave Revolts*. New York: International Publishers, 1963.

14. C. Vann Woodward, *The Strange Career of Jim Crow*. New York: Oxford University Press, 1966.

15. C. F. Pierre Van Der Berghe, *Race and Racism*. New York: John Wiley, 1967.

jobs available to him lacked the security and level of income necessary to maintain a household and in some cases were simply not
available. Additionally, certain jobs performed by black men (e.g.
waiter, cook, dishwasher, teacher, social worker, etc.) often carry
a connotation in American society as being woman's work.[16]

Economically destitute black families may be forced into a welfare system where it makes "sense" in terms of daily economic
security for black men to leave their families. An example of this is
a black woman who refused to permit her husband back into the
family after he got a job. She said:

Not me! With him away I've got security. I know when my welfare
check is coming, and I know I can take him to court if he doesn't pay me
child support. But as soon as he comes back in, then I don't know if he's
going to keep his job or if he's going to start acting up and staying out
drinking and spending his pay away from home. This way I might be
poor, but at least I know how much I got.[17]

White society has placed the black man in a tenuous position
where manhood has been difficult to achieve. Black men have been
lynched and brutalized in their attempts to retain their manhood.
They have suffered from the cruelest assault on mankind that the
world has ever known. For black men in this society it is not so
much a matter of acquiring manhood as a struggle to feel it their
own. As a pair of black psychiatrists comment:

Whereas the white man regards his manhood as an ordained right,
the black man is engaged in a never ending battle for its possession. For
the black man, attaining any portion of manhood is an active process. He
must penetrate barriers and overcome opposition in order to assume a
masculine posture. For the inner psychological obstacles to manhood are
never so formidable as the impediments woven into American society.[18]

After placing these obstacles to manhood in the black man's way,
white America then has its ideological bearers, the social scientists,
falsely indict him for his lack of manhood. There are various sociological and psychological studies which purport to show how black
males are demasculinized, how in fact they may be latent homosexuals. The reason cited is that black males reared in female-cen-
tered households are more likely to acquire feminine characteristics
because there is no consistent adult male model or image to shape

16. Harold Proshansky and Peggy Newton, "The Nature and Meaning of
Negro Self-Identity," in Social Class, Race and Psychological Development,
Martin Deutsch, et al., eds. New York: Holt, Rinehart and Winston, 1968.
17. William Yancey, Vanderbilt University, personal communication, 1971.
18. William H. Grier and Price M. Cobbs, Black Rage. New York: Basic
Books, 1968, p. 49.

their personalities.[19] One sociologist stated that since black males are unable to enact the masculine role, they tend to cultivate their personalities. In this respect they resemble women who use their personalities to compensate for their inferior status in relation to men.[20]

If the above reasoning seems weak and unsubstantiated, the other studies of black emasculation are equally feeble. Much of this supposition of the effeminate character of black men is based on their scores on the Minnesota Multiphasic Inventory Test (MMPI), a psychological instrument that asks the subject the applicability to himself of over five hundred simple statements. Black males score higher than white males on a measure of femininity. As an indicator of their femininity, the researchers cite the fact that black men more often agreed with such feminine choices as "I would like to be a singer" and "I think I feel more intensely than most people do." [21]

This is the kind of evidence that white society has marshaled to prove the feminization of the black male. The only thing this demonstrates is that white standards cannot always be used in evaluating black behavior. Black people live in another environment, with different ways of thinking, acting and believing than those of the white middle-class world. Singers such as James Brown and others represent successful role models in the black community. Black male youth aspire to be singers because this appears to be an observable means for obtaining success in this country, not because they are more feminine than white males. Additionally, music is an integral part of black culture.

One can easily challenge the theory that black males cannot learn the masculine role in father-absent homes. Black people are aware—if whites are not—that even in female-headed households in the black comunity, there is seldom one where adult males are totally absent. A man of some kind is usually around. He may be a boyfriend, an uncle or just the neighborhood bookie. Even if these men do not assume a central family role, the black child may use them as source material for the identification of masculine behavior.[22]

Furthermore, men are not the only ones who teach boys about masculinity. Sex roles can also be learned by internalizing the culturally determined expectations of these roles. Consequently, black

19. Thomas Pettigrew, *A Profile of the Negro American*. Princeton, New Jersey: D. Van Nostrand Company, 1964, pp. 17-22.

20. E. Franklin Frazier, *Black Bourgeoisie*. New York: Crowell-Collier Publishing Co., 1962, p. 182.

21. J. E. Hollanson and G. Calder, "Negro-White Differences on the MMPI." *Journal of Chemical Psychology*, 1960, pp. 32-33.

22. Ulf Hannerz, "The Roots of Black Manhood." *Transaction*, October, 1969, p. 16.

mothers can spell out the role requirements for their fatherless sons. She can symbolically communicate to him the way that men act. He will be shown the way men cross their legs, how they carry their books, the way they walk, etc. Through the culture's highly developed system of rewards for typical male behavior and punishment for signs of femininity, the black male child learns to identify with the culturally defined, stereotyped role of male.[23]

Black males are put in the psychological trick-bag of being "damned if they do, damned if they don't." If they acted effeminate they would be considered effeminate. Because they act like real men, they are charged with an exaggeration of normal masculine behavior to compensate for, or disguise, their femininity. The psychologists ignore one of their own tenets in this case: If men define situations as real, then they are real in their consequences.[24] If men define their behavior as masculine, for all practical purposes it becomes masculine to them. For black men, masculinity is the way they act. White America's definition of masculinity is of little importance, or validity, to them.

The myth of black matriarchy is accompanied by the falsehood that the model black father has abdicated his paternal responsibilities. That this is untrue was confirmed in a study by Schulz which found that most black men assume a very responsible quasi-father role vis-à-vis their women and her children. Black men, however, have to spend a large part of their lives bargaining for a familial relationship, the major impediment being a limited income that cannot equal the combined resources of their present job plus their woman's welfare check. These men, who are not officially father or husband, play a more supportive role than is generally acknowledged.[25]

While some black men obviously relinquish their paternal role functions, most black men perform ably in that role, considering the circumstances under which black families must live. Typical of the black father's concern for his children is this man's statement:

My youngest boy is seven. All my kids are in school. I try to instill in their minds that the only sound way to succeed is by laying a good foundation of learning and then to get actual experience. I hope to be able to see them all through college. I own property where I live and have

23. David Lynn, "The Process of Learning Parental and Sex Role Identification." *Marriage and Family Living*, 28, November, 1966, pp. 466-570.

24. C. F. W. I. Thomas and Florence Znaniecki, *The Polish Peasant in Europe and America*. New York: Alfred A. Knopf, 1927.

25. David Schulz, "The Role of the Boyfriend in Lower Class Negro Life." *The Family Life of Black People*, Charles V. Willie, ed., Columbus, Ohio: Charles E. Merrill, 1970, pp. 231-246.

a few dollars in the bank. I own a car, too. My greatest ambition is to see my children come along and keep this cleaning and pressing business of mine going, or else get into something they like better.[26]

That many black fathers never realize their aspirations for their children can be attributed to America's racist social structure. Instead, black women are charged with complicity with white men to subordinate the black male to his lowly position. Contrary to this assumption, one finds that when the Afro-American male was subjected to such abject oppression, the black woman was left without protection and was used—and is still being used—as a scapegoat for all the oppression that the system of white racism has perpetrated on black men. The system found it functional to enslave and exploit them and did so without the consent, tacit or otherwise, of black women. Moreover, while black men may be subjected to all sorts of dehumanizing practices, they still have someone who is below them—black women.[27]

Nevertheless, black women have had a variety of responses to the plight of black men. Some black women accepted the prevailing image of manhood and womanhood that depicted black men as shiftless and lazy if they did not secure employment and support their families as they ought to. There are reported instances of the black male ceasing to provide any economic support for the family and having his wife withdraw her commitment from him and from the marriage.[28] Other black women have ambivalent feelings about black men and remember painful experiences with them. They believe that black men do not fully appreciate the role of black women in the survival of the black race. Some even internalize white society's low regard for black men but are bothered by their appraisals.[29]

These attitudes on the part of black women are understandable. There are many black male-female conflicts which are a result of the psychological problems generated by their oppressed condition. Under a system of domestic colonialism, the oppressed peoples turn their frustrations and wrath toward each other rather than toward their oppressor.[30] Being constantly confronted with problems of

26. St. Clair Drake and Horace Cayton, *Black Metropolis*. Chicago: University of Chicago Press, 1945, p. 665.

27. Frances Beal, "Double Jeopardy: To Be Black and Female." *New Generation*, 51, Fall 1969, pp. 23-28.

28. Lee Rainwater, "Crucible of Identity: The Negro Lower Class Family." *Daedalus*, 95, Winter 1966, pp. 251-255.

29. Nathan and Julia Hare, "Black Women 1970." *Transaction*, 8, November, 1970, pp. 66-67.

30. C. F. Frantz Fanon, *The Wretched of the Earth*. New York: Grove Press, 1966.

survival, blacks become more psychologically abusive toward their spouses than perhaps they would under other circumstances.

On the other hand some black women are very supportive of their men. As Hare notes, the black woman realizes that she must encourage the black man and lay as much groundwork for black liberation as he will let her. She realizes that it is necessary to be patient with black men whenever they engage in symbolic assertions of manliness. Her role is to assist strongly but not dominate.[31] Black women, however, may not realize the contradiction between their desire for a comfortable standard of living and wanting the black man to exercise his masculinity. The expression of black masculinity can frequently be met with the harshest punishment white society can muster. Physical punishment and economic deprivation are frequently the white response to expressions of black manliness.

Whatever the role of the black woman, she realizes that the mythical castrated black male can rarely be dominated. In the dating situation, he has the upper hand because of the shortage of black men in the society. Black women, if they want a black man, frequently have to accept the relationship on male terms. If she does not give into his demands, there are always other women who will. The henpecked black husband is usually a mythical figure. The fact that black wives carry a slightly larger share of the housework than white wives [32]—while not a particularly desirable situation—effectively dispels any notion of the black husband in the role of a domestic servant.

It was mentioned earlier that the attempt to emasculate the black male was motivated by the fear of his sexual power. As Bernard has stated, "the white world's insistence on keeping Negro men walled up in the 'concentration camp' was motivated in large part by its fear of their sexuality." [33] One needs a deep understanding of the importance of sex in the United States in order to see the interrelationship of sex and racism in American society. In a society where white sexuality has been repressed, the imagined sexual power of the black male poses a serious threat. According to Hernton:

There is in the psyche of the racist an inordinate disposition for sexual atrocity. He sees in the Negro the essence of his own sexuality; that is, those qualities that he wishes for but fears he does not possess. Symbolically, the Negro at once affirms and negates the white man's sense of

31. Hare, *loc. cit.*

32. Robert O. Blood, Jr. and Donald M. Wofe, "Negro-White Difference in Blue Collar Marriages in a Northern Metropolis." *Social Forces*, 48, September, 1969, pp. 59-63.

33. Bernard, *op. cit.*, p. 75.

sexual security . . . Contrary to what is claimed, it is not the white woman who is dear to the racist. It is not even the black woman toward whom his real sexual rage is directed. It is the black man who is sacred to the racist. And this is why he must castrate him.[34]

Whether the white woman is dear to the racist is debatable. It certainly appears that he is concerned about preserving the purity of white womanhood. Since 1698 social censure and severe penalties were reserved for the association of black men and white women.[35] The evidence for these suppositions is voluminous, ranging from the accusations by lynch mobs that the black man raped or threatened to rape the white woman, the white South's obsession with the purity of white womanhood, the literal castration of black men for centuries, and in the death of an Emmet Till, who was killed for looking at a white woman. As Fanon comments, the white man fears that the black man will "introduce his daughter into a sexual universe for which the father does not have the key, the weapons, or the attributes." [36]

The question might be posed: What is the empirical basis of black male sexual superiority? Contrary to prevailing folklore, it is not the size of his genitalia. According to the Kinsey Institute, the majority of both white and black penises measured in their sample were less than or equal to four and a half inches in the flaccid state and less than or equal to seven inches in their erect state.[37] However, three times as many black males had penises larger than seven inches in length. The Masters and Johnson report indicates no particular relationship between penis size and sexual satisfaction except that induced by the psychological state of the female.[38]

What, then, can be said about the sexual abilities of white men and black men? First, it must be acknowledged that sexual attitudes and behavior are culturally determined—not inherent traits of a particular group. But sex relations have a different nature and meaning to black people. Their sexual expression derives from the emphasis in the black culture on feeling, of releasing the natural functions of the body without artificiality or mechanical movements. In some circles this is called "soul" and may be found among peoples of African descent throughout the world.

34. Calvin Hernton, *Sex and Racism in America*. Garden City, New York: Doubleday, 1965, pp. 111-112.

35. Frazier, *The Negro Family in the United States, op. cit.*, pp. 50-51.

36. Frantz Fanon, *Black Skin, White Mask*. New York: Grove Press, 1967. p. 163.

37. Allan Bell, *Black Sexuality, Fact and Fancy*, a paper, Black America Series, Indiana University, Bloomington, Indiana, 1968.

38. William Masters and Virginia Johnson, *Human Sexual Response*. Boston: Little, Brown and Co., 1966.

In a concrete sense, this means that black men do not moderate their enthusiasm for sex relations as white men do. They do not have a history of suppressing the sexual expression of the majority of their women while singling out a segment of the female population for premarital and extramarital adventures. This lack of a double standard of sexual conduct has also unleashed the sexual expression of black women. Those black women who have sexual hang-ups acquired them by their acculturation of the puritanical moral values of white society.

The difference between black men and white men in sexual responses may be explained by realizing that for white men sex has to be fitted into time not devoted to building the technological society, whereas for black men it is a natural function, a way of life. An example of this is that white men when confronted with their woman's state of sexual readiness may say business first, pleasure later. The black man when shown the black woman's state of sexual excitation manages to take care of both the business and pleasure task. If one task is left unfinished, it is unlikely that the black woman is left wanting.

It is this trait of the black male that white society would prefer to label sexual immorality. The historical evidence reveals, however, that the white man's moral code has seldom been consistent with his actual behavior. The real issue here is one of power. In a society where women are regarded as a kind of sexual property, the white male tries to insure that he will not have to compete with black men on an equal basis for any woman. Not only may the white male experience guilt over his possession of black womanhood, but he fears that as the black man attains a bedroom equality he will gain a political and economic equality as well.

Sexual fears, however, do not totally explain the attemped castration of black men. White society realizes quite well that it is the men of an oppressed group that form the vanguard, the bulwark, of any liberation struggle. By perpetrating the myth of the impotent black male on the consciousness of black and white people, they are engaging in wishful thinking. It is patently clear that men such as Nat Turner, Denmark Vesey, Frederick Douglass and Malcolm X were not impotent eunuchs. The task of black liberation has been carried out by black men from time immemorial. While black women have been magnificently supportive, it is black men who have joined the battle.

White America will continue to perpetuate the myth of the impotent black male as long as it serves its purpose. Meanwhile, the task of black liberation is at hand. It will continue to be in the hands of black men. While racists fantasize about the impotency of the black man—his childlike status—the liberation struggle will proceed, with one uncompromising goal: total freedom for all black people, men and women alike.

4

Reflections on the Black Woman's Role in the Community of Slaves

ANGELA DAVIS

I was immensely pleased to learn of *The Black Scholar's* plans to devote an entire issue to the black woman.

The paucity of literature on the black woman is outrageous on its face. But we must also contend with the fact that too many of these rare studies must claim as their signal achievement the reinforcement of fictitious cliches. They have given credence to grossly distorted categories through which the black woman continues to be perceived. In the words of Nathan and Julia Hare, ". . . she has been labeled 'aggressive' or 'matriarchal' by white scholars and 'castrating female' by [some] blacks." (*Transaction,* Nov.-Dec., 1970) Many have recently sought to remedy this situation. But for the time being, at least, we are still confronted with these reified images of

ANGELA DAVIS was acquitted in 1972 of three capital charges of murder, kidnapping and conspiracy. The charges stemmed from an abortive escape attempt by black prisoners from the Marin County Courthouse in San Rafael, California. Prior to her arrest, Sister Davis was teaching in the philosophy department at the University of California in Los Angeles. She was fired twice by the university's regents: once because she was a member of the Communist party and the second time for her speeches and other activities on behalf of the Soledad brother and other political prisoners. Her book, *If They Come in the Morning: Voices of Resistance,* edited by Angela Davis and Bettina Aptheker, was published in October 1971 by Third Press, New York, New York. Containing a number of fundamental essays by Angela Davis, it includes articles by Bettina Aptheker, James Baldwin, Margaret Burnham, Ericka Huggins, Ruchell Magee, Howard Moore, Huey P. Newton, Bobby Seale and the Soledad brothers.

ourselves. And for now, we must still assume the responsibility of shattering them.

Initially, I did not envision this paper as strictly confined to the era of slavery. Yet, as I began to think through the issue of the black matriarch, I came to the conclusion that it had to be refuted at its presumed historical inception.

The chief problem I encountered stemmed from the conditions of my incarceration: opportunities for researching the issue I wanted to explore were extremely limited. I chose, therefore, to entitle this piece "Reflections . . ." It does not pretend to be more than a collection of ideas which would constitute a starting point—a framework within which to conduct a rigorous reinvestigation of the black woman as she interacted with her people and with her oppressive environment during slavery.

I would like to dedicate these reflections to one of the most admirable black leaders to emerge from the ranks of our liberation movement—George Jackson, whom I loved and respected in every way. As I came to know and love him, I saw him developing an acute sensitivity to the real problems facing black women and thus refining his ability to distinguish these from their mythical transpositions. George was uniquely aware of the need to extricate himself and other black men from the remnants of divisive and destructive myths purporting to represent the black woman. If his life had not been so precipitously and savagely extinguished, he would surely have accomplished a task he had already outlined some time ago: a systematic critique of his past misconceptions about black women and of their roots in the ideology of the established order. He wanted to appeal to other black men, still similarly disoriented, to likewise correct themselves through self-criticism. George viewed this obligation as a revolutionary duty, but also, and equally important, as an expression of his boundless love for all black women.

The matriarchal black woman has been repeatedly invoked as one of the fatal by-products of slavery. When the Moynihan Report consecrated this myth with Washington's stamp of approval, its spurious content and propagandistic mission should have become apparent. Yet even outside the established ideological apparatus, and also among black people, unfortunate references to the matriarchate can still be encountered. Occasionally, there is even acknowledgement of the "tangle of pathology" it supposedly engendered. (This black matriarchate, according to Moynihan et al., defines the roots of our oppression as a people.) An accurate portrait of the African woman in bondage must debunk the myth of the matriarchate. Such a portrait must simultaneously attempt to il-

luminate the historical matrix of her oppression and must evoke her
varied, often heroic, responses to the slaveholder's domination.

Lingering beneath the notion of the black matriarch is an unspoken indictment of our female forebears as having actively as-
sented to slavery. The notorious cliche, the "emasculating female,"
has its roots in the fallacious inference that in playing a central part
in the slave "family," the black woman related to the slaveholding
class as collaborator. Nothing could be further from the truth. In the
most fundamental sense, the slave system did not—and could not—
engender and recognize a matriarchal family structure. Inherent in
the very concept of the matriarchy is "power." It would have been
exceedingly risky for the slaveholding class to openly acknowledge
symbols of authority—female symbols no less than male. Such legiti-
mized concentrations of authority might eventually unleash their
"power" against the slave system itself.

The American brand of slavery strove toward a rigidified disorganization in family life, just as it had to proscribe all potential
social structures within which black people might forge a collective
and conscious existence.[1] Mothers and fathers were brutally sep-
arated; children, when they became of age, were branded and
frequently severed from their mothers. That the mother was "the
only legitimate parent of her child" did not therefore mean that
she was even permitted to guide it to maturity.

Those who lived under a common roof were often unrelated
through blood. Frederick Douglass, for instance, had no recollec-
tion of his father. He only vaguely recalled having seen his mother
—and then on extremely rare occasions. Moreover, at the age of
seven, he was forced to abandon the dwelling of his grandmother,
of whom he would later say: "She was to me a mother and a
father." [1a] The strong personal bonds between immediate family
members which oftentimes persisted despite coerced separation
bore witness to the remarkable capacity of black people for resisting the disorder so violently imposed on their lives.

Where families were allowed to thrive, they were, for the most
part, external fabrications serving the designs of an avaricious,
profit-seeking slaveholder.

1. It is interesting to note a parallel in Nazi Germany: with all its ranting
and raving about motherhood and the family, Hitler's regime made a conscious
attempt to strip the family of virtually all its social functions. The thrust of their
unspoken program for the family was to reduce it to a biological unit and to
force its members to relate in an unmediated fashion to the fascist bureaucracy.
Clearly the Nazis endeavored to crush the family in order to ensure that it
could not become a center from which oppositional activity might originate.

1a. Herbert Aptheker, ed., *A Documentary History of the Negro People in
the United States.* New York: The Citadel Press, 1969 (1st ed., 1c   p. 272.

The strong hand of the slave owner dominated the Negro family, which existed at his mercy and often at his own personal instigation. An ex-slave has told of getting married on one plantation: "When you married, you had to jump over a broom three times." [2]

This slave went on to describe the various ways in which his master forcibly coupled men and women with the aim of producing the maximum number of healthy child-slaves. In the words of John Henrik Clarke,

The family as a functional entity was outlawed and permitted to exist only when it benefited the slave master. Maintenance of the slave family as a family unit benefited the slave owners only when and to the extent that such unions created new slaves who could be exploited. [3]

The designation of the black woman as a matriarch is a cruel misnomer. It is a misnomer because it implies stable kinship structures within which the mother exercises decisive authority. It is cruel because it ignores the profound traumas the black woman must have experienced when she had to surrender her child-bearing to alien and predatory economic interests.

Even the broadest construction of the matriarch concept would not render it applicable to the black slave woman. But it should not be inferred that she therefore played no significant role in the community of slaves. Her indispensable efforts to ensure the survival of her people can hardly be contested. Even if she had done no more, her deeds would still be laudable. But her concern and struggles for physical survival, while clearly important, did not constitute her most outstanding contributions. It will be submitted that by virtue of the brutal force of circumstances, the black woman was assigned the mission of promoting the consciousness and practice of resistance. A great deal has been said about the black *man* and resistance, but very little about the unique relationship black women bore to the resistance struggles during slavery. To understand the part she played in developing and sharpening the thrust towards freedom, the broader meaning of slavery and of American slavery in particular must be explored.

Slavery is an ancient human institution. Of slave labor in its traditional form and of serfdom as well, Karl Marx had the following to say:

The slave stands in absolutely no relation to the objective conditions of his labor; it is rather the *labor* itself, in the form of the slave as of the

2. Andrew Billingsley, *Black Families in White America*. Englewood, New Jersey: Prentice-Hall, Inc., 1968, p. 61.
3. John Henrik Clarke, "The Black Woman: A Figure in World History," Part III. *Essence*, New York, July, 1971.

serf, which is placed in the category of *inorganic condition* of production alongside the other natural beings, *e.g.* cattle, or regarded as an appendage of the earth.[4]

The bondsman's existence as a natural condition of production is complemented and reinforced, according to Marx, by his membership in a social grouping which he perceives to be an extension of nature. Enmeshed in what appears to be a natural state of affairs, the attitude of the slave, to a greater or lesser degree, would be an acquiescence in his subjugation. Engels points out that in Athens, the state could depend on a police force consisting entirely of slaves.[5]

The fabric of American slavery differed significantly from ancient slavery and feudalism. True, black people were forced to act as if they were "inorganic conditions of production." For slavery was "personality swallowed up in the sordid idea of property—manhood lost in chattelhood." [6] But there were no pre-existent social structures or cultural dictates which might induce reconciliation to the circumstances of their bondage. On the contrary, Africans had been uprooted from their natural environment, their social relations, their culture. No legitimate sociocultural surroundings would be permitted to develop and flourish, for, in all likelihood, they would be utterly incompatible with the demands of slavery.

Yet another fact would militate against harmony and equilibrium in the slave's relation to his bondage: slavery was enclosed in a society otherwise characterized by "free" wage-labor. Black men and women could always contrast their chains with the nominally free status of white working people. This was quite literally true in such cases where, like Frederick Douglass, they were contracted out as wage-laborers. Unlike the "free" white men alongside whom they worked, they had no right to the meager wages they earned. Such were some of the many contradictions unleashed by the effort to forcibly inject slavery into the early stages of American capitalism.

The combination of a historically superseded slave labor system based almost exclusively on race and the drive to strip black people of all their social and cultural bonds would create a fateful rupture at the heart of the slave system itself. The slaves would not readily adopt fatalistic attitudes towards the conditions surrounding and ensnaring their lives. They were a people who had been violently

4. Karl Marx, *Grundrisse der Kritik der Politischen Oekonomie*. Berlin: Dietz Verlag, 1953, p. 389.

5. Frederick Engels, *Origin of the Family, Private Property and The State*. New York: International Publishers, 1942, p. 107.

6. Frederick Douglass, *Life and Times of Frederick Douglass*. New York: Collier Books, 1962, p. 96.

thrust into a patently "unnatural" subjugation. If the slaveholders had not maintained an absolute monopoly of violence, if they had not been able to rely on large numbers of their fellow white men— indeed the entire ruling class as well as misled working people—to assist them in their terrorist machinations, slavery would have been far less feasible than it acually proved to be.

The magnitude and effects of the black people's defiant rejection of slavery has not yet been fully documented and illuminated. But there is more than ample evidence that they consistently refused to succumb to the all-encompassing dehumanization objectively de- manded by the slave system. Comparatively recent studies have demonstrated that the few slave uprisings—too spectacular to be relegated to oblivion by the racism of ruling class historians—were not isolated occurrences, as the latter would have had us believe. The reality, we know now, was that these open rebellions erupted with such a frequency that they were as much a part of the texture of slavery as the conditions of servitude themselves. And these re- volts were only the tip of an iceberg: resistance expressed itself in other grand modes and also in the seemingly trivial forms of feigned illness and studied indolence.

If resistance was an organic ingredient of slave life, it had to be directly nurtured by the social organization which the slaves them- selves improvised. The consciousness of their oppression, the con- scious thrust towards its abolition, could not have been sustained without impetus from the community they pulled together through the sheer force of their own strength. Of necessity, this community would revolve around the realm which was furthermost removed from the immediate arena of domination. It could only be located in and around the living quarters, the area where the basic needs of physical life were met.

In the area of production, the slaves—pressed into the mold of beasts of burden—were forcibly deprived of their humanity. (And a human being thoroughly dehumanized has no desire for freedom.) But the community gravitating around the domestic quarters might possibly permit a retrieval of the man and the woman in their funda- mental humanity. We can assume that, in a very real material sense, it was only in domestic life—away from the eyes and whip of the overseer—that the slaves could attempt to assert the modicum of freedom they still retained. It was only there that they might be inspired to project techniques of expanding it further by leveling what few weapons they had against the slaveholding class whose unmitigated drive for profit was the source of their misery.

Via this path, we return to the African slave woman: in the living quarters, the major responsibilities "naturally" fell to her. It was the woman who was charged with keeping the "home" in order. This role was dictated by the male supremacist ideology of white society in America; it was also woven into the patriarchal traditions of Africa. As her biological destiny, the woman bore the fruits of pro-creation; as her social destiny, she cooked, sewed, washed, cleaned house, raised the children. Traditionally the labor of females, do-mestic work is supposed to complement and confirm their inferiority.

But with the black slave woman, there is a strange twist of af-fairs: in the infinite anguish of ministering to the needs of the men and children around her (who were not necessarily members of her immediate family), she was performing the *only* labor of the slave community which could not be directly and immediately claimed by the oppressor. There was no compensation for work in the fields; it served no useful purpose for the slaves. Domestic labor was the only meaningful labor for the slave community as a whole (dis-counting as negligible the exceptional situations where slaves re-ceived some pay for their work).

Precisely through performing the drudgery which has long been a central expression of the socially conditioned inferiority of women, the black women in chains could help to lay the foundation for some degree of autonomy, both for herself and for her men. Even as she was suffering under her unique oppression as female, she was thrust by the force of circumstances into the center of the slave com-munity. She was, therefore, essential to the *survival* of the com-munity. Not all people have survived enslavement; hence her sur-vival-oriented activities were themselves a form of resistance. Survival, moreover, was the prerequisite of all higher levels of struggle.

But much more remains to be said of the black woman during slavery. The dialectics of her oppression will become far more com-plex. It is true that she was a victim of the myth that only the woman, with her diminished capacity for mental and physical labor, should do degrading household work. Yet, the alleged benefits of the ideology of femininity did not accrue to her. She was not sheltered or protected; she would not remain oblivious to the desperate strug-gle for existence unfolding outside the "home." She was also there in the fields, alongside the man, toiling under the lash from sunup to sundown.

This was one of the supreme ironies of slavery: in order to ap-proach its strategic goal—to extract the greatest possible surplus from the labor of the slaves—the black woman had to be released from the chains of the myth of femininity. In the words of W.E.B. DuBois, ". . . our women in black had freedom contemptuously thrust upon them." [7] In order to function as slave, the black woman had to be annulled as woman; that is, as woman in her historical stance of wardship under the entire male hierarchy. The sheer force of things rendered her equal to her man.

Excepting the woman's role as caretaker of the household, male supremacist structures could not become deeply embedded in the internal workings of the slave system. Though the ruling class was male and rabidly chauvinistic, the slave system could not confer upon the black man the appearance of a privileged position vis-a-vis the black woman. The man-slave could not be the unquestioned superior within the "family" or community, for there was no such thing as the "family provider" among the slaves. The attainment of slavery's intrinsic goals was contingent upon the fullest and most brutal utilization of the productive capacities of every man, woman and child. They all had to "provide" for the master. The black woman was therefore wholly integrated into the productive force.

The bell rings at four o'clock in the morning and they have half an hour to get ready. Men and women start together, and the women must work as steadily as the men and perform the same tasks as the men.[8]

Even in the posture of motherhood—otherwise the occasion for hypocritical adoration—the black woman was treated with no greater compassion and with no less severity than her man. As one slave related in a narrative of his life:

. . . . women who had sucking children suffered much from their breasts becoming full of milk, the infants being left at home; they therefore could not keep up with the other hands: I have seen the overseer beat them with raw hide so that the blood and the milk flew mingled from their breasts.[9]

Moses Grandy, ex-slave, continues his description with an account of a typical form of field punishment reserved for the black woman with child:

She is compelled to lie down over a hole made to receive her corpulency and is flogged with the whip, or beat with a paddle which has holes in it; at every stroke comes a blister.[10]

7. W. E. B. DuBois, *Darkwater, Voices from Within the Veil.* New York: AMS Press, 1969, p. 185.
8. Lewis Clarke, *Narrative of the Sufferings of Lewis and Milton Clarke, Sons of a Soldier of the Revolution.* Boston: 1846, p. 127 [Quoted by E. Franklin Frazier, *The Negro Family in the United States*].
9. Moses Grandy, *Narrative of the Life of Moses Grandy; Late a Slave in the United States of America.* Boston: 1844, p. 18 [quoted by Frazier].
10. *Ibid.*

The unbridled cruelty of this leveling process whereby the black woman was forced into equality with the black man requires no further explanation. She shared in the deformed equality of equal oppression.

But out of this deformed equality was forged quite undeliberately, yet inexorably, a state of affairs which could unharness an immense potential in the black woman. Expending indispensable labor for the enrichment of her oppressor, she could attain a practical awareness of the oppressor's utter dependence on her—for the master needs the slave far more than the slave needs the master. At the same time she could realize that while her productive activity was wholly subordinated to the will of the master, it was nevertheless proof of her ability to transform things. For "labor is the living, shaping fire; it represents the impermanence of things, their temporality . . ." [11]

The black woman's consciousness of the oppression suffered by her people was honed in the bestial realities of daily experience. It would not be the stunted awareness of a woman confined to the home. She would be prepared to ascend to the same levels of resistance which were accessible to her men. Even as she performed her housework, the black woman's role in the slave community could not be identical to the historically evolved female role. Stripped of the palliative feminine veneer which might have encouraged a passive performance of domestic tasks, she was now uniquely capable of weaving into the warp and woof of domestic life a profound consciousness of resistance.

With the contributions of strong black women, the slave community as a whole could achieve heights unscalable within the families of the white oppressed or even within the patriarchal kinship groups of Africa. Latently or actively, it was always a community of resistance. It frequently erupted in insurgency, but it was daily animated by the minor acts of sabotage which harassed the slavemaster to no end. Had the black woman failed to rise to the occasion, the community of slaves could not have fully developed in this direction. The slave system would have to deal with the black woman as the custodian of a house of resistance.

The oppression of black women during the era of slavery, therefore, had to be buttressed by a level of overt ruling-class repression. Her routine oppression had to assume an unconcealed dimension of outright counter-insurgency.

*   *   *

11. Marx, *Grundrisse*, p. 266.

To say that the oppression of black slave women necessarily incorporated open forms of counter-insurgency is not as extravagant as it might initially appear. The penetration of counter-insurgency into the day to day routine of the slavemaster's domination will be considered toward the end of this paper. First, the participation of black women in the overt and explosive upheavals which constantly rocked the slave system must be confirmed. This will be an indication of the magnitude of her role as caretaker of a household of resistance—of the degree to which she could concretely encourage those around her to keep their eyes on freedom. It will also confirm the objective circumstances to which the slavemaster's counter-insurgency was a response.

With the sole exceptions of Harriet Tubman and Sojourner Truth, black women of the slave era remain more or less enshrouded in unrevealed history. And, as Earl Conrad has demonstrated, even "General Tubman's" role has been consistently and grossly minimized. She was a far greater warrior against slavery than is suggested by the prevalent misconception that her only outstanding contribution was to make nineteen trips into the South, bringing over 300 slaves to their freedom.

[She] was head of the Intelligence Service in the Department of the South throughout the Civil War; she is the only American woman to have led troops black and white on the field of battle, as she did in the Department of the South . . . She was a compelling and stirring orator in the councils of the abolitionists and the anti-slavers, a favorite of the anti-slavery conferences. She was the fellow planner with Douglass, Martin Delany, Wendell Phillips, Gerrit Smith and other leaders of the anti-slavery movement.[12]

No extensive and systematic study of the role of black women in resisting slavery has come to my attention. It has been noted that large numbers of freed black women worked towards the purchase of their relatives' and friends' freedom. About the participation of women in both the well-known and more obscure slave revolts, only casual remarks have been made. It has been observed, for instance, that Gabriel's wife was active in planning the rebellion spearheaded by her husband, but little else has been said about her.

The sketch which follows is based in its entirety on the works of Herbert Aptheker, the only resources available to me at the time of this writing.[13] These facts, gleaned from Aptheker's works on slave

12. Earl Conrad, "I Bring You General Tubman." *The Black Scholar*, Vol. 1, No. 3-4, Jan.-Feb., 1970, p. 4.

13. In February, 1949, Herbert Aptheker published an essay in *Masses and Mainstream* entitled "The Negro Woman." As yet I have been unable to obtain it.

revolts and other forms of resistance, should signal the urgency to undertake a thorough study of the black woman as anti-slavery rebel. In 1971 this work is far overdue.

Aptheker's research has disclosed the widespread existence of communities of blacks who were neither free nor in bondage. Throughout the South (in South and North Carolina, Virginia, Louisiana, Florida, Georgia, Mississippi and Alabama), maroon communities consisting of fugitive slaves and their descendants were "an ever present feature"—from 1642 to 1864—of slavery. They provided ". . . havens for fugitives, served as bases for marauding expeditions against nearby plantations and, at times, supplied leadership to planned uprisings." [14]

Every detail of these communities was invariably determined by and steeped in resistance, for their *raison d'être* emanated from their perpetual assault on slavery. Only in a fighting stance could the maroons hope to secure their constantly imperiled freedom. As a matter of necessity, the women of those communities were compelled to define themselves—no less than the men—through their many acts of resistance. Hence, throughout this brief survey the counter-attacks and heroic efforts at defense assisted by maroon women will be a recurring motif.

As will be seen, black women often poisoned the food and set fire to the houses of their masters. For those who were also employed as domestics, these particular overt forms of resistance were especially available.

The vast majority of the incidents to be related involve either tactically unsuccessful assaults or eventually thwarted attempts at defense. In all likelihood, numerous successes were achieved, even against the formidable obstacles posed by the slave system. Many of these were probably unpublicized even at the time of their occurrence, lest they provide encouragement to the rebellious proclivities of other slaves and, for other slaveholders, an occasion for fear and despair.

During the early years of the slave era (1708) a rebellion broke out in New York. Among its participants were surely many women, for one, along with three men, was executed in retaliation for the killing of seven whites. It may not be entirely insignificant that while the men were hanged, she was heinously burned alive.[15] In the same colony women played an active role in a 1712 uprising in the course

14. Herbert Aptheker, "Slave Guerrilla Warfare" in *To Be Free, Studies in American Negro History*. New York: International Publishers, 1969 (1st ed., 1948), p. 11.

15. Herbert Aptheker, *American Negro Slave Revolts*. New York: International Publishers, 1970 (1st ed., 1943), p. 169.

of which slaves, with their guns, clubs and knives, killed members of the slaveholding class and managed to wound others. While some of the insurgents—among them a pregnant woman—were captured, others—including a woman—committed suicide rather than surrender.[16]

"In New Orleans one day in 1730 a woman slave received 'a violent blow from a French soldier for refusing to obey him' and in her anger shouted 'that the French should not long insult Negroes.'"[17] As was later disclosed, she and undoubtedly many other women had joined in a vast plan to destroy slaveholders. Along with eight men, this dauntless woman was executed. Two years later, Louisiana indicted a woman and four men as leaders of a planned rebellion. They were all executed, and in a typically savage gesture their heads were publicly displayed on poles.[18]

Charleston, South Carolina condemned a black woman to die in 1740 for arson,[19] a form of sabotage, as earlier noted, frequently carried out by women. In Maryland, for instance, a slave woman was executed in 1776 for having destroyed by fire her master's house, his outhouses and tobacco house.[20]

In the thick of the Colonies' war with England, a group of defiant slave women and men were arrested in Saint Andrew's Parish, Georgia in 1774. But before they were captured, they had already brought a number of slave owners to their death.[21]

The maroon communities have been briefly described; from 1782 to 1784, Louisiana was a constant target of maroon attacks. When twenty-five of this community's members were finally taken prisoner, men and women alike were all severely punished.[22]

As can be inferred from previous example, the North did not escape the tremendous impact of fighting black women. In Albany, New York, two women were among three slaves executed for antislavery activities in 1794.[23] The respect and admiration accorded the black woman fighter by her people is strikingly illustrated by an incident which transpired in York, Pennsylvania, when, during the early months of 1803, Margaret Bradley was convicted of attempting to poison two white people, causing the black inhabitants of the area to revolt en masse.

16. *Ibid.*, p. 173.
17. *Ibid.*, p. 181.
18. *Ibid.*, p. 182.
19. *Ibid.*, p. 190.
20. *Ibid.*, p. 145.
21. *Ibid.*, p. 201.
22. *Ibid.*, p. 207.
23. *Ibid.*, p. 215.

They made several attempts to destroy the town by fire and succeeded, within a period of three weeks, in burning eleven buildings. Patrols were established, strong guards set up, the militia dispatched to the scene of the unrest . . . and a reward of three hundred dollars offered for the capture of the insurrectionists.[24]

A successful elimination by poisoning of several "of our respectable men" (said a letter to the governor of North Carolina) was met by the execution of four or five slaves. One was a woman who was burned alive.[25] In 1810, two women and a man were accused of arson in Virginia.[26]

In 1811 North Carolina was the scene of a confrontation between a maroon community and a slave-catching posse. Local newspapers reported that its members "had bid defiance to any force whatever and were resolved to stand their ground." Of the entire community, two were killed, one wounded and two—both women—were captured.[27]

Aptheker's *Documentary History of the Negro People in the United States* contains a portion of the transcript of an 1812 confession of a slave rebel in Virginia. The latter divulged the information that a black woman brought him into a plan to kill their master and that yet another black woman had been charged with concealing him after the killing occurred.[28]

In 1816 it was discovered that a community of three hundred escaped slaves—men, women, children—had occupied a fort in Florida. After the U.S. Army was dispatched with instructions to destroy the community, a ten day siege terminated with all but forty of the three hundred dead. All the slaves fought to the very end.[29] In the course of a similar though smaller confrontation between maroons and a militia group (in South Carolina, 1826), a woman and a child were killed.[30] Still another maroon community was attacked in Mobile, Alabama in 1837. Its inhabitants, men and women alike, resisted fiercely—according to local newspapers, "fighting like Spartans." [31]

Convicted of having been among those who, in 1829, had caused a devastating fire in Augusta, Georgia, a black woman was "executed, dissected, and exposed" (according to an English visitor). More-

24. *Ibid.*, p. 239.
25. *Ibid.*, pp. 241-242.
26. *Ibid.*, p. 247.
27. *Ibid.*, p. 251.
28. Aptheker, *Documentary History*, pp. 55-57.
29. Aptheker, *Slave Revolts*, p. 259.
30. *Ibid.*, p. 277.
31. *Ibid.*, p. 259.

over, the execution of yet another woman, about to give birth, was imminent.[32] During the same year, a group of slaves, being led from Maryland to be sold in the South, had apparently planned to kill the traders and make their way to freedom. One of the traders was successfully done away with, but eventually a posse captured all the slaves. Of the six leaders sentenced to death, one was a woman. She was first permitted, for reasons of economy, to give birth to her child.[33] Afterwards, she was publicly hanged.

The slave class in Louisiana, as noted earlier, was not unaware of the formidable threat posed by the black woman who chose to fight. It responded accordingly: in 1846 a posse of slave owners ambushed a community of maroons, killing one woman and wounding two others. A black man was also assassinated.[34] Neither could the border states escape the recognition that slave women were eager to battle for their freedom. In 1850 in the state of Missouri "about thirty slaves, men and women, of four different owners, had armed themselves with knives, clubs and three guns and set out for a free state." Their pursuers, who could unleash a far more powerful violence than they, eventually thwarted their plans.[35]

This factual survey of but a few of the open acts of resistance in which black women played major roles will close with two further events. When a maroon camp in Mississippi was destroyed in 1857, four of its members did not manage to elude capture, one of whom was a fugitive slave woman.[36] All of them, women as well as men, must have waged a valiant fight. Finally, there occurred in October 1862 a skirmish between maroons and a scouting party of Confederate soldiers in the state of Virginia.[37] This time, however, the maroons were the victors, and it may well have been that some of the many women helped to put the soldiers to death.

*   *   *

The oppression of slave women had to assume dimensions of open counter-insurgency. Against the background of the facts presented above, it would be difficult indeed to refute this contention. As for those who engaged in open battle, they were no less ruthlessly punished than slave men. It would even appear that in many cases they may have suffered penalties which were more excessive than those meted out to the men. On occasion, when men were hanged, the women were burned alive. If such practices were widespread,

32. *Ibid.*, p. 281.
33. *Ibid.*, p. 487.
34. Aptheker, "Guerrilla Warfare," p. 27.
35. Aptheker, *Slave Revolts*, p. 342.
36. Aptheker, "Guerrilla Warfare," p. 28.
37. *Ibid.*, p. 29.

their logic would be clear. They would be terrorist methods designed to dissuade other black women from following the examples
of their fighting sisters. If all black women had risen up alongside
their men, the institution of slavery would have been in difficult
straits.

It is against the backdrop of her role as fighter that the routine
oppression of the slave woman must be explored once more. If she
was burned, hanged, broken on the wheel, her head paraded on
poles before her oppressed brothers and sisters, she must have also
felt the edge of this counter-insurgency as a fact of her daily existence. The slave system would not only have to make conscious
efforts to stifle the tendencies towards acts of the kind described
above; it would be no less necessary to stave off escape attempts
(escapes to maroon country!) and all the various forms of sabotage
within the system. Feigning illness was also resistance as were work
slowdowns and actions destructive to the crops. The more extensive
these acts, the more the slaveholder's profits would tend to diminish.

While a detailed study of the myriad modes in which this counter-
insurgency was manifested can and should be conducted, the following reflections will focus on a single aspect of the slave woman's
oppression, particularly prominent in its brutality.

Much has been said about the sexual abuses to which the black
woman was forced to submit. They are generally explained as an
outgrowth of the male supremacy of Southern culture: the purity,
of white womanhood could not be violated by the aggressive sexual
activity desired by the white male. His instinctual urges would find
expression in his relationships with his property—the black slave
woman, who would have to become his unwilling concubine. No
doubt there is an element of truth in these statements, but it is
equally important to unearth the meaning of these sexual abuses
from the vantage point of the woman who was assaulted.

In keeping with the theme of these reflections, it will be submitted
that the slavemaster's sexual domination of the black woman contained an unveiled element of counter-insurgency. To understand
the basis for this assertion, the dialectical moment of the slave
woman's oppression must be restated and their movement recap-
tured. The prime factor, it has been said, was the total and violent
expropriation of her labor with no compensation save the pittance
necessary for bare existence.

Secondly, as female, she was the housekeeper of the living quarters. In this sense, she was already doubly oppressed. However,
having been wrested from passive "feminine" existence by the sheer
force of things—literally by forced labor—confining domestic tasks
were incommensurable with what she had become. That is to say,

by virtue of her participation in production, she would not act the part of the passive female, but could experience the same need as her men to challenge the conditions of her subjugation. As the center of domestic life, the only life at all removed from the arena of exploitation, and thus as an important source of survival, the black woman could play a pivotal role in nurturing the thrust towards freedom.

The slavemaster would attempt to thwart this process. He knew that as a female, this slave woman could be particularly vulnerable in her sexual existence. Although he would not pet her and deck her out in frills, the white master could endeavor to reestablish her femaleness by reducing her to the level of her *biological* being. Aspiring with his sexual assaults to establish her as a female *animal*, he would be striving to destroy her proclivities towards resistance. Of the sexual relations of animals, taken at their abstract biological level (and not in terms of their quite different social potential for human beings), Simone de Beauvoir says the following:

> It is unquestionably the male who *takes* the female—she is *taken*. Often the word applies literally, for whether by means of special organs or through superior strength, the male seizes her and holds her in place; he performs the copulatory movements; and, among insects, birds, and mammals, he penetrates. . . . Her body becomes a resistance to be broken through . . .[38]

The act of copulation, reduced by the white man to an animal-like act, would be symbolic of the effort to conquer the resistance the black woman could unleash.

In confronting the black woman as adversary in a sexual contest, the master would be subjecting her to the most elemental form of terrorism distinctively suited for the female: rape. Given the already terroristic texture of plantation life, it would be as a potential victim of rape that the slave woman would be most unguarded. Further, she might be most conveniently manipulable if the master contrived a ransom system of sorts, forcing her to pay with her body for food, diminished severity in treatment, the safety of her children, etc.

The integration of rape into the sparsely furnished legitimate social life of the slaves harks back to the feudal "right of the first night," the *jus primae noctis*. The feudal lord manifested and reinforced his domination over the serfs by asserting his authority to have sexual intercourse with all the females. The right itself referred specifically to all freshly married women. But while the right to the

38. Simone de Beauvoir, *The Second Sex*. New York: Bantam Books, 1961, pp. 18-19.

first night eventually evolved into the institutionalized "virgin tax," [39] the American slaveholder's sexual domination never lost its openly terroristic character.

As a direct attack on the black female as potential insurgent, this sexual repression finds its parallels in virtually every historical situation where the woman actively challenges oppression. Thus, Frantz Fanon could say of the Algerian woman: "A woman led away by soldiers who comes back a week later—it is not necessary to question her to understand that she has been violated dozens of times." [40]

In its political contours, the rape of the black woman was not exclusively an attack upon her. Indirectly, its target was also the slave community as a whole. In launching the sexual war on the woman, the master would not only assert his sovereignty over a critically important figure of the slave community; he would also be aiming a blow against the black man. The latter's instinct to protect his female relations and comrades (now stripped of its male supremacist implications) would be frustrated and violated to the extreme. Placing the white male's sexual barbarity in bold relief, Du Bois cries out in a rhetorical vein:

I shall forgive the South much in its final judgement day: I shall forgive its slavery, for slavery is a world-old habit; I shall forgive its fighting for a well-lost cause, and for remembering that struggle with tender tears; I shall forgive its so-called 'pride of race,' the passion of its hot blood, and even its dear, old, laughable strutting and posing; but one thing I shall never forgive, neither in this world nor the world to come: its wanton and continued and persistent insulting of the black womanhood which it sought and seeks to prostitute to its lust.[41]

The retaliatory import of the rape for the black man would be entrapment in an untenable situation. Clearly the master hoped that once the black man was struck by his manifest inability to rescue his women from sexual assaults of the master, he would begin to experience deep-seated doubts about his ability to resist at all.

Certainly the wholesale rape of slave women must have had a profound impact on the slave community. Yet it could not succeed in its intrinsic aim of stifling the impetus towards struggle. Countless black women did not passively submit to these abuses, as the slaves in general refused to passively accept their bondage. The struggles of the slave woman in the sexual realm were a continuation

39. August Bebel, *Women and Socialism*. New York: Socialist Literature Co., 1910, pp. 66-69.

40. Frantz Fanon, *A Dying Colonialism*. New York: Grove Press, 1967, p. 119.

41. Du Bois, *Darkwater*, p. 172.

of the resistance interlaced in the slave's daily existence. As such, this was yet another form of insurgency, a response to a politically tinged sexual repression.

Even E. Franklin Frazier (who goes out of his way to defend the thesis that "the master in his mansion and his colored mistress in her special house nearby represented the final triumph of social ritual in the presence of the deepest feelings of human solidarity" [42]) could not entirely ignore the black woman who fought back. He notes: "That physical compulsion was necessary at times to secure submission on the part of black women . . . is supported by historical evidence and has been preserved in the tradition of Negro families." [43]

The sexual contest was one of many arenas in which the black woman had to prove herself as a warrior against oppression. What Frazier unwillingly concedes would mean that countless children brutally fathered by whites were conceived in the thick of battle. Frazier himself cites the story of a black woman whose great grandmother, a former slave, would describe with great zest the battles behind all her numerous scars—that is, all save one. In response to questions concerning the unexplained scar, she had always simply said: "White men are as low as dogs, child, stay away from them." The mystery was not unveiled until after the death of this brave woman: "She received that scar at the hands of her master's youngest son, a boy of about eighteen years at the time she conceived their child, my grandmother Ellen." [44]

* * *

An intricate and savage web of oppression intruded at every moment into the black woman's life during slavery. Yet a single theme appears at every juncture: the woman transcending, refusing, fighting back, asserting herself over and against terrifying obstacles. It was not her comrade brother against whom her incredible strength was directed. She fought alongside her man, accepting or providing guidance according to her talents and the nature of their tasks. She was in no sense an authoritarian figure; neither her domestic role nor her acts of resistance could relegate the man to the shadows. On the contrary, she herself had just been forced to leave behind the shadowy realm of female passivity in order to assume her rightful place beside the insurgent male.

42. E. Franklin Frazier, *The Negro Family in the United States.* Chicago: University of Chicago Press, 1966 (1st ed., 1939), p. 69.

43. *Ibid.*, p. 53.

44. *Ibid.*, pp. 53-54.

This portrait cannot, of course, presume to represent every individual slave woman. It is rather a portrait of the potentials and possibilities inherent in the situation to which slave women were anchored. Invariably there were those who did not realize this potential. There were those who were indifferent and a few who were outright traitors. But certainly they were not the vast majority. The image of black women enchaining their men, cultivating relationships with the oppressor, is a cruel fabrication which must be called by its right name. It is a dastardly ideological weapon designed to impair our capacity for resistance today by foisting upon us the ideal of male supremacy.

According to a time-honored principle, advanced by Marx, Lenin, Fanon and numerous other theorists, the status of women in any given society is a barometer measuring the overall level of social development. As Fanon has masterfully shown, the strength and efficacy of social struggles—and especially revolutionary movements—bear an immediate relationship to the range and quality of female participation.

The meaning of this principle is strikingly illustrated by the role of the black woman during slavery. Attendant to the indiscriminate brutal pursuit of profit, the slave woman attained a correspondingly brutal status of equality. But in practice, she could work up a fresh content for this deformed equality by inspiring and participating in acts of resistance of every form and color. She could turn the weapon of equality in struggle against the avaricious slave system which had engendered the mere caricature of equality in oppression. The black woman's activities increased the total incidence of anti-slavery assaults. But most important, without consciously rebellious black women, the theme of resistance could not have become so thoroughly intertwined in the fabric of daily existence. The status of black women within the community of slaves was definitely a barometer indicating the overall potential for resistance.

This process did not end with the formal dissolution of slavery. Under the impact of racism, the black woman has been continually constrained to inject herself into the desperate struggle for existence. She—like her man—has been compelled to work for wages, providing for her family as she was previously forced to provide for the slaveholding class. The infinitely onerous nature of this equality should never be overlooked. For the black woman has always also remained harnessed to the chores of the household. Yet, she could never be exhaustively defined by her uniquely "female" responsibilities.

As a result, black women have made significant contributions to struggles against the racism and the dehumanizing exploitation of a wrongly organized society. In fact, it would appear that the intense levels of resistance historically maintained by black people, and thus the historical function of the black liberation struggle as harbinger of change throughout the society, are due in part to the greater *objective* equality between the black man and the black woman. DuBois put it this way:

> In the great rank and file of our five million women, we have the upworking of new revolutionary ideals, which must in time have vast influence on the thought and action of this land.[45]

Official and unofficial attempts to blunt the effects of the egalitarian tendencies as between the black man and woman should come as no surprise. The matriarch concept, embracing the cliched "female castrator," is, in the last instance, an open weapon of ideological warfare. Black men and women alike remain its potential victims—men unconsciously lunging at the woman, equating her with the myth; women sinking back into the shadows, lest an aggressive posture resurrect the myth in themselves.

The myth must be consciously repudiated as myth, and the black woman in her true historical contours must be resurrected. We, the black women of today, must accept the full weight of a legacy wrought in blood by our mothers in chains. Our fight, while identical in spirit, reflects different conditions and thus implies different paths of struggle. But as heirs to a tradition of supreme perseverance and heroic resistance, we must hasten to take our place wherever our people are forging on towards freedom.

45. DuBois, *Darkwater*, p. 185.

5

But Where Are the Men?

JACQUELYNE J. JACKSON

In comparison with black males and white males and females, black women yet constitute the most disadvantaged group in the United States, as evidenced especially by their largely unenviable educational, occupational, employment, and income levels, and availability of marital partners.[1] My examination of relevant data, largely culled from census records over the past fifty or more years, clearly revealed significant inequities confronting black women, who can, of course, be viewed as being even more victimized than can black men by virtue of both racism and sexism, as opposed to racism only in this context for black males.

Before proceeding further, let us examine some of the myths which assert that black women have special privilege in comparison to black men in terms of superior education, occupation, employment and income. It is especially important to examine these myths, for they have been the basis for two cruel and erroneous theories with reference to the black woman, her mate and her family—that she is a matriarch and that she emasculates her man. The black

JACQUELYNE J. JACKSON is Associate Professor of Medical Sociology at Duke University Medical Center in Durham, North Carolina. A John Hay Whitney and National Science Foundation scholar, she earned a Ph.D. degree from Ohio State University and has previously taught at Southern University, Jackson State College and Howard University. Miss Jackson is secretary and member of the executive committee of the Caucus of Black Sociology of the American Sociology Association and on the Advisory Council to the United States Senate on aging and aged blacks. Frequently published in anthologies and journals, she is the author of *These Rights They Seek*.

1. For more detailed discussion on the issues raised, see especially Jacquelyne J. Jackson, "Black Women in a Racist Society," in Charles Willie, Bertram Brown, and Bernard Cramer (eds.), *Racism and Mental Health* (forthcoming, University of Pittsburgh Press, Pittsburgh, 1972) and Jacquelyne J. Jackson, "Black Women and Higher Education," in Ralph Hines and Richard Robbins (eds.), *Black Colleges in Transition* (forthcoming, Temple University Press, Philadelphia, 1972).

woman has become "the black widow of modern sociology" and this notion must be dispelled.

The Myth of the Black Female's Education

The data examined showed quite clearly that while the median number of years of formal education obtained by black women had exceeded that of black males, for example, that that quantitative difference was really quite insignificant, particularly if education were regarded principally as a means to an end. Consequently, it is really nonsensical to even speak of black females as being "better educated" than black males. For those 25 years or more of age in 1940, the quantitative difference between the median educational level of black females (6.1 years) and black males (5.3 years) was 0.8, or less than one year of schooling. By 1960, respective data were 8.4 years for the females and 7.7 years for the males, or a difference of 0.7. By 1970, the difference between the females (10.2 years) and the males (9.6 years) was 0.6. Such minute differences in educational attainment failed to provide black females with any significant "headstart" in the labor force.

Even if the data were narrowed to focus only on higher education, it still remains that black females have, in fact, been severely disadvantaged. In 1940, a slightly larger (but highly insignificant) proportion of black males, 25+ years of age, were more likely to complete four or more years of college than their black female counterparts (1.3 to 1.2%). Twenty years later, of course, the pattern had reversed, and 3.3 percent of black females in the age-specified group had completed higher education, as opposed to 2.8 percent of the black males. However, in 1970, for those 21 or more years of age, another reversal had occurred: 4.5 percent of the black males, as compared with 4.4 percent of black females, had completed or gone beyond a college education.

It is also significant to note that, for blacks 25 to 34 years of age, fairly interesting educational fluctuations have been occurring within the past five years. Quite specifically, 6.1 percent of the females had completed four or more years of college in 1966, but by 1969 the percentage had dropped to 5.6, rising again to 6.4 percent in 1970. For the males, 5.2 percent had completed four or more years of college in 1966, rising to 7.6 percent in 1969, but dropping to 5.8 percent in 1970, a phenomenon needing investigation to determine the specific factors inducing that decline and requiring action to reverse this unwarranted trend.

The critical comparisons, however, should not be between black females and males, but a comparison of both black females and black males with that group most likely to receive higher education in the United States, namely white males. When such comparisons are made, it is readily apparent that the greatest educational gains made during the 1960's were not those made by blacks at all, but those made especially by white males. Between 1960 and 1970, 1.8 percent more black females were likely to have received at least a bachelor's degree at the close of that decade than at the beginning. Corresponding data were 1.9 percent for black males, 4.9 percent for white females, and, highest of all, 5.2 percent for white males.

Another criterion which may be employed in examining black female higher education is that of the prestige ratings of the institutions which they attended. In the main, a larger proportion of black male college graduates have obtained degrees from the more prestigious institutions, even among the black institutions only, than have the females. That is, black females have had less access to the more prestigious institutions of higher education than have black males or white females and males. A corollary of this point is that black females receiving higher education have been educated largely at the traditional teacher-training institutions, which, of course, has affected greatly their occupational patterns.

Finally, it should be noted that, of the aforementioned groups, black females have been most disadvantaged with respect to receipt of graduate and professional education. Thus, based upon this and other criteria, the entire issue of "black female educational superiority" is far more complicated than generally assumed. Vast improvements are yet needed in the educational levels of black women, particularly when the vast majority of this population, 21 or more years of age, is yet denied higher education.

The Myth of Black Female Employment

When occupational comparisons are made, it becomes quite clear that black women have usually had the greatest access to only the worst jobs at the lowest earnings. Contrary to opinions commonly expressed, black males historically have outnumbered black females in the employed labor market. In 1910 black males comprised 61.2 percent of all employed blacks. In 1920, they were 67.4 percent of employed blacks; in 1930, 66.6 percent; in 1940, 65.6 percent; and, among nonwhites, 65.2 percent in 1950, 60.2 percent in 1960, and 57.0 percent in 1969. In short, black males have continued to outnumber black females in the labor market, and, in general, unemployment rates have been higher among black females than among black males.

Not only have black males generally had greater access to employment than has been true of black females, but, excepting public school teaching and certain limited service jobs, black men and women have usually not been in competition for the same jobs. Moreover, even if the comparison were restricted only to professional categories, it is quite apparent that black females have been far more restricted to the highly traditional occupations (i.e., public school teaching, nursing and social work) than have black males. As a matter of fact, black females were not even more numerous proportionately among black professionals until 1940, for in 1910 black males constituted 56.5 percent of all black professionals, 52.1 percent in 1920, and 53.6 percent in 1930. The 1940 census combined professional and semi-professional data, and black females then become more numerous. Nevertheless, throughout the years prior to and subsequent to 1940, black females have been in the minority among black physicians, dentists, college presidents, attorneys, architects, college professors, scientists and other professional occupations commonly ranked higher in status than public school teaching, nursing, and social work.

Hence, just as the commonly held belief that black women have been "better educated" needs considerable examination, it is also the case that the myths about black female employment, and especially about its impact upon black male employment, stand in need of considerable reexamination. In short, black women have not been responsible for black male unemployment. It should be remembered, e.g., that when black male unemployment rates were severe during the economic depression of the 1930's, black female unemployment rates were even higher. It should also be remembered that, even in 1969, one out of every five employed black females was a private household worker. Finally, it may simply be noted that occupational heterogeneity has been far greater among black males than among black females, a pattern persisting into the present.

When one examines income data, one is immediately struck by the fact that black women "have been had." Again on the average, the income levels of black women have been considerably lower than those of our remaining comparison groups. In 1969, for persons 25 or more years of age, the black female median income was $2,078, $435 lower than that of the average white female, $2,670 less than that of the average black male, and $5,812 less than that of the average white male. Even when controls are established for education, the black female still earns less money than does the black or white male. For example, the median 1969 income for white males with four or more years of college education was $12,437, and for the black male, $8,567, but for the black female, only $6,747. Thus, the black female under consideration was saddled with an earning capacity only 79 percent that of the black male and 54 percent that of the white male.

Earlier it was pointed out that the median educational levels of black females were higher than those of black males over at least the past 50 years, but that, when translated into utilitarian terms, the differences between the sexes in median educational attainments were highly insignificant. A juxtaposition of income data by educational level is at least one way of dramatizing that insignificance. For income recipients 25+ years of age in 1969, the median income for black females with less than an eighth-grade education was approximately 40 percent that of their counterpart black males, falling to about 31·percent for those who had completed an eighth-grade education only.

Black females with one to three years of high-school training had incomes equaling about 43 percent of that of corresponding black males. For those completing high school only, the median black female income of $3,257 was 53 percent that of the black male median income of $6,144, while, for persons completing one to three years of college, the black female median of $4,247 was about 60 percent of the black male income of $7,051. Even when black females and males who had completed or gone beyond college were compared, the former earned only 78.8 percent as much as the latter in 1969, and only 54.2 percent as much as equivalent white males.

Such data as the above aids in highlighting the fabled myths surrounding black women. I am especially concerned about those fabled myths extant in education, occupation, employment and income, and about their relationships to family patterns. My most important concern in this connection is that such myths tend to reinforce unduly erroneous beliefs directly affecting social policies, which, in turn, adversely affect many black females. Despite the fact that black females have been severely disadvantaged in the labor market, there has yet to be sufficient emphasis placed upon the need for significant improvements in receipt of higher education and higher-level professional occupations accompanied by significantly higher incomes, particularly so for those very likely to remain or to become household heads.

The Myth of the Black Matriarchy

One important factor probably influencing that very lack of emphasis is the unnecessary persistence of the myths of black matriarchy and of black female emasculation of black males.[2] Too many social programs act as if black females appropriately submissive to male dominance would be blessed with "present" rather than "absent" black males. That assumption is sheer nonsense, for in line with the major purpose of this article, one must ask "But where are the males?"

The overall conclusion which must be reached and explicated in some detail is simply that there are not enough black males for black females, and since non-black males rarely marry black females, a sufficient supply of males for black females is not available at this point in time. Hence, in line with one prominent social policy, even if all available black males were to amass highly significant gains in their educational, occupational, employment and income levels tomorrow, some black female-headed households would remain, some black females would yet be without mates. Thus, there is a critical need to concentrate not only on improving socio-economic levels of black males so that they may be in better position to support their families (which, incidentally, form the vast bulk of black families); but there also must be simultaneous concentration on improving the socio-economic positions of black females who are very likely to be bereft of mates, so that they too may improve significantly the opportunities to be derived for themselves and their families.

Additionally, it is quite significant, as pointed out below, that blacks have had a "headstart" on whites in developing alternative forms of marital and familial life in the absence of a sufficient number of males. Recent trends in white society, such as the increase in the illegitimacy rate and in the divorce rate, suggest that whites are patterning themselves after blacks, not the other way around.

2. For works especially valuable in their critiques of these theories, see Robert Hill, "Black Families: Their Strengths and Stability" (forthcoming publication, Research Department, National Urban League, Washington, D.C.); H. H. Hyman and J. S. Reed, "'Black Matriarchy' Reconsidered: Evidence from Secondary Analysis of Sample Surveys" (Public Opinion Quarterly, 33:346-354, 1969); Jacquelyne J. Jackson, "Family Organization and Ideology" (forthcoming in R. M. Dreger and K. S. Miller, eds., Comparative Studies of Negroes and Whites in the United States, 1966-1970); Karl King, "A Comparison of the Negro and White Family Power Structure in Low-Income Families" (Child and Family, 6:65-74, 1967); Delores E. Mack, "Where the Matriarchal Theorists Went Wrong" (Psychology Today, 4:24+, 1971); Russell Middleton and Snell Putney, "Dominance in Decisions in the Family, Race, and Class Differences" (American Journal of Sociology, 65:605-609, 1960); Robert Staples, "The Black Woman's Burden: Racism and Sexism" (forthcoming, Zena, 1972), "The Myth of the Black Matriarchy" (The Black Scholar, January-February, 1970, pp. 9-16); and Warren Tenhoutten, "The Black Family: Myth and Reality" (Psychiatry, 33:145-173, 1970).

Also affecting the available supply of black males, it should be noted that intermarriage between blacks and whites has increased over the past several decades, with the modal white partner being female. That represents a further encroachment upon the limited supply of black males available to black females.

Black Sex Ratios

The question "But where are the males?" refers inevitably to that of the sex ratio (i.e., the number of males per one hundred females). One highly significant gap in almost all contemporary scientific, pseudo-scientific, and ideological concerns about black women—and especially about black female household heads—is that of the failure to consider the implications of the sex ratio itself. This gap can be attributed directly to the general tendency of social scientists and social policymakers to ignore the realities of the prevailing black sex ratios and concomitant factors, such as the aforenoted tendency of white females to seek black mates.

Such a gap is particularly deplorable in the social sciences, inasmuch as Oliver C. Cox [3] focused specific attention upon sex ratios and their implications at least as early as 1940. For present purposes, it is imperative to note that Cox indicated quite clearly the following:

1—Differences in the marital status of persons in different areas and communities may be due to differences in the ratio of marriageable men to women; [4]

2—The racial sex ratio varies considerably in the different regional divisions of the United States; [5]

3. Oliver C. Cox, "Sex Ratio and Marital Status Among Negroes," *American Sociological Review*, 5:937-947, 1940. Incidentally, no opportunity should be lost in pointing out anew that the significant contributions of Dr. Cox to American sociology, and particularly those valuable in knowing and understanding blacks, have been largely ignored by the white male-dominated American sociological establishment. At the 1971 annual meeting of the American Sociological Association, however, largely through the efforts of the Caucus of Black Sociologists, and Dr. James E. Conyers especially, the first DuBois-Johnson-Frazier Award was conferred upon Dr. Cox in recognition of such contributions. Earlier, the first annual DuBois Award established by the Association of Social and Behavioral Scientists (founded in 1935) was given to Dr. Cox in recognition of his distinguished achievements.

4. *Ibid.*, p. 937.
5. *Ibid.*

3–The percentage of Negro females married in cities is particularly sensitive to changes in the sex ratio, while the percentage of males married seems to respond almost not at all.[6]

Thus, as the black sex ratio rose, the percentage of black females who were married rose. As that sex ratio declined, so did the percentage of married black females.

Since 1940, the black sex ratio has actually worsened, if judged from the perspective of black females. Yet most contemporary literature is written as if there were one black male for each black female. That literature almost always fails to inquire about male availability levels for black females. Probably the most glaring example is *The Moynihan Report.*[7] Moynihan tended to assume that male unemployment was the critical factor affecting the proportion of female-headed households among blacks, but he failed miserably in dealing with the actual supply of black males for black females.

Census data clearly reveal that females have been excessive in the black population of the United States since at least 1850, or a period of more than 120 years. In 1850, the black sex ratio was 99.1, rising slightly to 99.6 in 1860, but declining to 96.2 in 1870. In 1880, it was 97.8; in 1890, 99.5; in 1900, 98.6; in 1910, 98.9; and in 1920, 99.2. Since 1920, the black sex ratio has decreased consistently, from 97.0 in 1930, to 95.0 in 1940, to 94.3 in 1950, to 93.3 in 1960, and, in 1970, to 90.8, or approximately 91 black males for every 100 black females. Thus, for the past 50 years, black men have been becoming scarcer and scarcer. It is not the case that they are more likely to be missed in the census counts, but that they are just not there![8]

If no adjustment is made for age, at least 1,069,694 of the 11,885,595 black females in the population of the United States in 1970 would have been without available monogamous mates. When age-adjusted and regional-adjusted data are presented, as shown in Table 1, the unadjusted pattern does not undergo any significant change. As can be seen in Table 1, in the United States as a whole, black females are not more numerous than black males only within one age group, that of 5 to 14 years. They are more numerous in all

6. *Ibid.*, p. 938.
7. Daniel P. Moynihan, *The Negro Family: A Case for National Action.* Washington, D.C.: U.S. Government Printing Office, 1965.
8. It may be interesting to note that some discussions of this point have brought retorts that the males are there, but simply avoid being counted. The chief argument here is that even if all of the black males throughout the United States were counted, the females would still remain excessive, due to a variety of reasons certainly warranting systematic investigations. Some, of course, are not there due to the unnecessarily high infant and childhood mortality rates especially affecting black males, while some others are dead, victimized by war and wanton killings.

of the remaining age groupings, and especially so during female childbearing ages. The same is true of the geographical divisions, with one exception occurring in the West among the 15 to 24 year-old grouping.

TABLE 1

Black Sex Ratios by Age and Geographical Location, 1970 °

		GEOGRAPHICAL LOCATION			
AGE (YEARS)	U.S.	NORTHEAST°°	NORTH CENTRAL°°	SOUTH°°	WEST°°
Total, all ages	90.8	87.5	91.3	98.8	97.6
Under 5	99.3	100.7	100.0	90.8	97.6
5–14	100.4	100.7	99.8	100.5	100.3
15–24	93.0	87.1	90.1	94.5	105.6
25–34	84.3	78.6	83.4	85.4	95.7
35–44	82.9	81.1	84.5	81.0	95.3
45–54	86.4	83.4	90.4	84.9	94.0
55–64	85.3	78.3	89.7	85.6	90.3
65+	76.4	71.7	81.4	76.2	76.3

° Source of raw data: U.S. Department of Commerce/Bureau of the Census. *1970 Census of Population, Advance Report,* "General Population Characteristics, United States," PC(V2)–1. U.S. Department of Commerce, Washington, D.C., February, 1971.

°° Northeastern states include Maine, New Hampshire, Vermont, Massachusetts, Rhode Island, Connecticut, New York, New Jersey, and Pennsylvania; North Central includes Ohio, Indiana, Illinois, Michigan, Wisconsin, Minnesota, Iowa, Missouri, North Dakota, South Dakota, Nebraska, and Kansas; the South includes Delaware, Maryland, District of Columbia, Virginia, West Virginia, North Carolina, South Carolina, Georgia, Florida, Kentucky, Tennessee, Alabama, Mississippi, Arkansas, Louisiana, Oklahoma, and Texas; and the West encompasses Montana, Idaho, Wyoming, Colorado, New Mexico, Arizona, Utah, Nevada, Washington, Oregon, California, Alaska, and Hawaii.

It is relevant now to inquire about alternative familial forms developed in the absence of a sufficient supply of males. Two of those forms, unnecessarily and irrationally viewed as "deviant" by the American white culture, are those of female-headed households and of illegitimacy. The nomenclature of "illegitimacy" is inappropriately applied to blacks for any number of reasons, but the common usage of such a concept does reflect a tendency of many whites to attempt to "desexify" blacks. It is quite important to add that the development of that term occurred at a time when white males exceeded white females in the United States. The application of the term was also grossly unfair to blacks who were already in the process of developing alternative familial forms in the absence of a sufficient supply of males, a condition not confronting whites until 1950.

The "problem" of female-headed households can only be perceived as a "problem" by those who act, again, as if there were identical supplies of males and females. When such is not the case, as it is clearly not in the case of blacks, then the phenomenon should be perceived as a rational alternative to an ineffective traditional system. It should be quite obvious that slavery is an insufficient factor to be used in explicating both illegitimacy and female-headed households, for, by the usual measures of family stability, as Frazier has noted, black family stability continued progressively throughout the latter half of the nineteenth century and up until about 1910.[9]

In fact, census data show that in 1900, for persons 15+ years of age, there were no significant differences in marital status by race or by sex between black and white females and males. But since then, as the black sex ratio has decreased, the marital status of black females in particular has also been affected, as Cox demonstrated.[10] The marital status of black females has been far more sensitive to that reducing sex ratio than have those of black males, which leads us into an exploration of one of the relationships which may exist between black sex ratios and familial patterns, specifically that of female-headed households.

As that sex ratio has decreased, the proportion of female-headed households among blacks has increased, suggesting thereby that a possible causative factor for the latter may be the former. If we examine available 1970 data on the black sex ratio and the proportion of female-headed households among blacks in each state and the District of Columbia, what will emerge will be a significant inverse relationship between those two variables ($r = -.68$, $df = 49$, and $p > .001$). In other words, as shown in Table 2, there is a tendency for the proportion of female-headed households to increase as the supply of males decreases. Conversely, when the supply of males increases, the proportion of female-headed households decreases. For example, the excess of black males over black females is greatest in Hawaii, where the proportion of black female-headed households ranks quite low. In fact, only two states (North Dakota and South Dakota) rank lower than Hawaii in the proportion of female-headed households among blacks. On the other hand, the sex ratio is lowest in New York (85.9, or approximately 86 males per every 100 females), and 32.1 percent of black families within the state were headed by females in 1970, exceeded only by Massachusetts, where 34.3 percent of black families were female-headed.

9. E. Franklin Frazier, *The Negro Family in the United States.* Chicago: University of Chicago Press, 1939. Here, perhaps, it should be noted that, contrary to a number of interpretations of Frazier, he did *not* characterize matriarchy as the *dominant* family type among blacks.

10. Cox, *op. cit.*

TABLE 2

Black Sex Ratios and the Percentage of Female-Headed Families and
Their Rank Orders in the United States, 1970 °

STATE	SEX RATIO	% FEMALE-HEADED FAMILIES	SEX RATIO RANK°°	% FEMALE-HEADED FAMILIES RANK°°
Hawaii	192.6	7.1	1.0	3.0
Montana	169.2	24.2	2.0	16.0
North Dakota	160.3	2.9	3.0	1.0
Idaho	158.5	9.0	4.0	5.5
South Dakota	157.0	6.2	5.0	2.0
Utah	151.6	21.6	6.0	10.0
Alaska	147.3	7.8	7.0	4.0
Vermont	139.3	13.0	8.0	8.0
Maine	136.9	9.0	9.0	5.5
New Hampshire	130.4	9.9	10.0	7.0
Wyoming	114.2	13.2	11.0	9.0
Washington	113.0	23.1	12.0	12.0
Colorado	105.2	22.1	13.0	11.0
Rhode Island	102.5	31.7	14.0	49.0
Minnesota	102.4	28.5	15.0	36.5
Arizona	102.2	25.5	16.0	21.0
New Mexico	101.1	24.3	17.0	17.5
Nevada	100.8	23.6	18.0	13.0
Oregon	100.5	26.1	19.0	26.0
Kansas	97.9	27.2	20.0	29.0
Iowa	95.9	28.9	21.0	42.0
California	95.2	28.1	22.0	34.5
Virginia	94.7	23.7	23.0	14.0
Wisconsin	94.0	30.8	24.0	46.0
Michigan	93.6	25.7	25.5	22.5
Nebraska	93.6	30.5	25.5	45.0
Kentucky	93.0	27.9	27.0	33.0
Maryland	92.8	27.0	28.0	27.0
Indiana	92.7	24.7	29.5	19.0
Delaware	92.7	28.1	29.5	34.5
Texas	92.4	24.0	31.0	15.0
North Carolina	92.1	25.8	32.0	24.0
Florida	91.7	28.5	33.0	36.5
South Carolina	91.4	26.0	34.0	25.0
Ohio	90.6	27.1	35.0	28.0
Mississippi	90.1	25.7	36.0	22.5
Louisiana	90.0	27.6	37.0	32.0
Arkansas	89.8	24.3	38.0	17.5
Connecticut	89.7	30.4	39.0	43.5
New Jersey	89.5	30.4	40.0	43.5
Illinois	89.4	28.8	41.0	40.5
Oklahoma	89.3	31.1	42.0	47.0
Missouri	89.1	28.8	43.0	40.5
Massachusetts	88.6	34.3	45.0	51.0

TABLE 2 (continued)

Black Sex Ratios and the Percentage of Female-Headed Families and
Their Rank Orders in the United States, 1970 *

STATE	SEX RATIO	% FEMALE-HEADED FAMILIES	SEX RATIO RANK**	% FEMALE-HEADED FAMILIES RANK**
Georgia	88.6	28.6	45.0	38.0
District of Columbia	88.6	28.7	45.0	39.0
Tennessee	88.3	27.9	47.5	30.0
Pennsylvania	88.3	31.3	47.0	48.0
Alabama	88.0	27.4	49.0	31.0
West Virginia	87.6	24.8	50.0	20.0
New York	85.9	32.1	51.0	50.0

* Source of raw data: U.S. Department of Commerce/Bureau of the Census. *1970 Census of Population, Advance Report,* "General Population Characteristics, United States," PC(V2)–1. U.S. Department of Commerce, Washington, D.C., February, 1971.

** Rank ordering for the sex ratio is from high to low. That is, the state with the highest sex ratio (Hawaii) is ranked 1.0, while that with the lowest (New York) is ranked 51.0. Rank ordering for the percentage of female-headed households is from low to high. That is, the state with the lowest proportion (North Dakota) is ranked 1.0, while Massachusetts, with the highest, is ranked 51.0.

Despite the fact that black females are excessive in the black population, that excess is not equitably distributed throughout the United States. In 19 states, black males outnumber females. Those states are Hawaii, Montana, North Dakota, Idaho, South Dakota, Utah, Alaska, Vermont, Maine, New Hampshire, Wyoming, Washington, Colorado, Rhode Island, Minnesota, Arizona, New Mexico, Nevada and Oregon—none are southern states. They are also states containing extremely minute proportions of aged (i.e., 65+ years) blacks, which suggests that they are probably less affected by the considerably shortened life expectancy rates of black males than is true of the remaining states. Thus, the proportion of widowed black females who may find it necessary to assume a status as household head is reduced.[11]

11. In this connection, it may be useful to remind the reader that while there is no significant proportional difference between widowed black and white females, there is a crucial difference in that black females are considerably more likely to become widowed at a much earlier age than are white females, which, among other factors, can be attributed directly to the fact that, as compared with whites and black females, black males are most disadvantaged by having the shortest rates of life expectancy. That is, on the average, black males die earlier than black females and whites. A number of consequences follow from that earlier death phenomenon, but one with which I am especially intrigued and in which I would personally like to interest a number of individuals and groups, especially in light of the 1971 White House Conference on Aging is a proposal I first made in 1968. Briefly, that proposal is that the minimum age-eligibility requirements for receipt of Old-Age, Survivors, Dependents, and

This geographical disproportionment in the distribution of black females and males also has consequences for familial patterns in that, as indicated above and as evident in Table 2, black females are generally least likely to be heads of households where the sex ratio is the highest. Thus, it may be that black male geographical mobility has been significantly different from that of black females, suggesting two different types of policy alternatives for those concerned about the proportion of black female-headed households. One implication may well be that greater geographical mobility could be encouraged among black females, especially those in such states as New York, Massachusetts, Pennsylvania, Oklahoma, New Jersey, and Connecticut, where such encouragement would include the lure of significant opportunities for receipt of higher education, professional occupation, and incomes approximating at least the median income of all individuals in the United States. That might help move the "girls" to "where the boys are."

A second but different type of implication might well be the continuing development of alternative familial forms, including that of polygyny, a system appropriate in the absence of a sufficient supply of males. Polygyny, of course, requires male participants with sufficient resources to maintain adequately one or more families. At the present time, almost no black males in the United States are economically equipped to participate in such a system, which forestalls any present concerns about the acceptability of such a system to black females. Nevertheless, as some keen observers have indicated in various private conversations, the legitimacy of polygyny could well benefit some females who are involved in "playing at polygyny," but who are legally denied any of the benefits to which they might otherwise be entitled.

For example, on a recent visit to Kampala, Uganda, the Vice-Chancellor of Makerere University noted that, in defense of polygyny, the women participating as spouses had a legal status of wife, not that of whore, slut, mistress, etcetera. Thus, not only did such wives not have illegitimate children, but both they and their children had legal protection under the law, which he regarded as a more "civilized" system than that existing in the "civilized" United States.

Health Insurance (OASDHI, Social Security) should be reduced for black males especially, so as to reflect their lower life expectancies and allow them, thereby, should they so desire, an equitable amount of time to receive those Social Security benefits for which they have paid during their working years. As it now stands, black males are especially disadvantaged in that they do not draw, on the average, such benefits for as many years as do white males, who tend to live longer than black males. Incidentally, for fuller discussion of this, see Jacquelyne J. Jackson, "Aged Blacks: A Potpourri Towards the Reduction of Social Inequities," *Phylon*, September, 1971.

He may have a point worth further investigation. In any case, it is quite clear that there is not one absolute system of marriage and family which must be adhered to at any cost and under any circumstance. Such is the case even among white Americans.

White Sex Ratios

It has already been established that females have been excessive in the black population since 1850. Table 3, which provides a com-

TABLE 3

Black and White Sex Ratios,
*1850–1970 ***

| | SEX RATIOS | |
YEAR	BLACK	WHITE
1850	99.1	105.2
1860	99.6	105.3
1870	96.2	102.8
1880	97.8	104.0
1890	99.5	105.4
1900	98.6	104.9
1910	98.9	106.6
1920	99.2	104.4
1930	97.0	102.9
1940	95.0	101.2
1950	94.3	99.1
1960	90.8	95.3
1970	93.3	97.3

* For whites in 1970, the data includes non-blacks. Sex ratios were obtained from census reports for the specified years.

parison of the black and white sex ratios, 1850–1970, clearly shows the evidence permitting the statement already made that blacks have had a "headstart" on whites in developing alternative familial patterns in the absence of a sufficient number of males. Blacks are at least 100 years ahead of whites in this respect. A cursory examination of such variables as those of marital status, illegitimacy rates, and intermarriage rates is invaluable in noting certain trends depicting whites as becoming more like blacks.

Table 4 provides some limited information on two of the three

TABLE 4
Selected Statistical Comparisons
Between Blacks and Whites

CHARACTERISTIC	BLACK	WHITE
Female marital status		
1900, 15+ years of age		
% single	39.8	40.1
% married	55.5	55.4
% divorced	0.2	0.3
% widowed	4.3	4.0
1940, 15+ years of age		
% single	23.9	26.0
% married, spouse present	44.2	56.9
% divorced	1.7	1.7
% widowed	15.8	11.1
1960, 14+ years of age		
% single	22.3	18.7
% married, spouse present	51.8	65.2
% divorced	3.6	2.7
% widowed	14.0	12.0
1970, 14+ years of age		
% single	28.0	21.3
% married, spouse present	42.0	60.3
% divorced	4.3	3.4
% widowed	13.5	12.4
Percent of female-headed families		
1950	17.6	8.5
1955	20.7	9.0
1960	22.4	8.7
1966	23.7	8.9
1970	26.4	9.1
1971	28.9	9.4
Percent of own children living		
with both parents as percent		
of all own children		
1960	75	92
1970	67	91
Percent change in estimated		
illegitimacy rates		
1940–1944 to 1955–1959	+166	+139
1955–1959 to 1968	−8	+53

Sources of data: U.S. Census Office, *Census Reports,* Vol. 2, Part 2, "Population," U.S. Govt. Printing Office, Washington, D.C., 1902; U.S. Bureau of the Census, *Sixteenth Census of the United States: 1940,* Vol. 2, "Population, Characteristics of the Population," U.S. Govt. Printing Office, Washington, D.C., 1943; U.S. Bureau of the Census, *U.S. Census of Population, 1960,* Vol. 1, "Characteristics of the Population," Part 1, "United States Summary," U.S. Govt. Printing Office, Washington, D.C., 1964;

The Social and Economic Status of Negroes in the United States, 1970, BLS Report No. 394, CPR, Series P-23, No. 38, Special Studies, U.S. Department of Commerce/ Bureau of the Census, Washington, D.C., July, 1971; and *Social and Economic Characteristics of the Population in Metropolitan and Nonmetropolitan Areas: 1970 and 1960*, Current Population Reports, Series P-23, No. 37, U.S. Govt. Printing Office, Washington, D.C., 1971.

variables referred to above, namely marital status and illegitimacy. If we examine female marital status by race from 1900 through 1970, we see that in 1900, when the black sex ratio was 98.6 and the white 104.9, there was no significant difference by race in marital status. In fact, a slightly higher proportion of the black females were returned as *married*, while a slightly larger proportion of the whites were returned as *divorced*, but slightly fewer as *widowed*. By 1940, when the black sex ratio had declined to 95.0 while that of the whites remained above 100, it is evident that the divorce rates by race were identical, while the widowhood rate was higher among blacks than whites. In addition, data available for persons married with spouses present (not available in the 1900 Census) showed that the decreasing sex ratio had affected the proportion of black females likely to fall within that category, while the whites remained relatively unaffected.

In 1960, when the sex ratios among both blacks and whites had declined to 93.3 and 97.3 respectively, we actually find that a larger proportion of females in both racial groups were returned as *married, with spouse present*. By that year, their divorce rates were no longer identical, but both were rising: 3.6 among the blacks, and 2.7 among the whites, as compared with the 1940 rate of 1.7.

By 1970, with the sex ratios continuing to decline (90.8 among blacks, 95.3 among whites), it is clear that the proportion of females *married, with spouse present* had declined *both* among black and white females from the percentage given in 1960. In 1970, 9.8 percent fewer black females and 4.9 percent fewer white females were so classified. The major factor contributing to that change may, perhaps, be found in the increased proportion of those single, which is over twice as high among the black females, 1960–1970, than among the white females. In 1970, as it may be recalled, over nine black females out of every 100 would have been theoretically classified as being without monogamous mates, true of only about five out of every 100 white females.

Thus, a partial explication of the differences in the marital status by race should not be sought, as is quite commonly done, within black family disorganization, but within the effects of sex ratios upon marital status. While the divorce rate in 1970 con-

tinued to be higher among black than among white females, the
rate among the latter also continued to increase from 1960 to 1970.

Data in Table 4 depicting the percent of female-headed families
does reveal, as expected, that the proportion of such families is
considerably higher among blacks than among whites. However, the
proportionate increase among blacks was less from 1960 to 1970
(119.6%) than it was from 1950 to 1960 (127.3%), whereas the
proportionate increase among whites was greater in 1960–1970
(104.6%) than between 1950–1960, when it was 102.4 percent. Consequently, although the sex ratios were continuing to decline among
both groups, the rate of increase in female-headed families among
whites continued to rise between 1950–1970, while it had begun to
decrease somewhat among blacks over the same time period.

A similar pattern emerges upon examination of the percentage
changes occuring over time in two other variables—the percentage
of own children living with both parents as the percentage of all
own children, and the percent change in estimated illegitimacy
rates. In the case of the former variable, from 1960–1970, the percentage of such children among both races declined, from 75 to 67
percent among blacks, and from 92 to 91 percent among whites, a
decrease which may also be related to their decreasing sex ratios and
increasing proportions of female-headed families.

While illegitimacy as usually defined remains higher among
blacks than among whites, it is very interesting to note that illegitimacy rates have been declining among blacks, while increasing
among whites, as also shown in Table 4. In other words, the rate
of illegitimate births is rising among whites while their sex ratio is
declining, which is a pattern not at all unlike that which transpired
much earlier among blacks. Thus, it appears that as females become
more excessive in the white population, the proportion seeking
family forms deviating from the traditional is on the increase. In this
sense—and a very important sense, to be sure—whites are following
trends mapped out earlier by blacks.

Whites, of course, have not yet "caught up" with blacks in developing various alternative patterns for several different reasons,
with the most important one probably being that black females are
yet more excessive in the black population than are white females in
the white population, particularly so during the childbearing years
of 15–44, as can be seen by inspecting the data provided in Table 5.
For the years 15–44 inclusive, the sex ratios are much lower among
blacks than whites, and especially so for the years 25–44, as of 1970.
Interestingly, however, for those 65+ years of age, the black sex
ratio is actually higher than that of the whites, a finding readily ex-
plicable by the greater longevity of white females as compared

TABLE 5

Differences in the Black and White
Sex Ratios, 15+ Years of Age, 1970 °

AGE GROUP	BLACK	WHITE	DIFFERENCE
15–24 years	93.0	98.8	5.8
25–34 years	84.2	97.8	13.6
35–44 years	82.8	96.2	13.4
45–54 years	86.3	93.8	7.5
55–64 years	85.1	90.2	5.1
65+ years	76.4	71.9	−4.5

° Source of raw data: U.S. Department of Commerce/ Bureau of the Census. *1970 Census of Population, Advance Report,* "General Population Characteristics, United States," PC(V2)–1. U.S. Department of Commerce, Washington, D.C., February, 1971.

with blacks and with white males. In passing, what may also be quite impressive about Table 5 is an inference that the significant differences in the sex ratios between blacks and whites are not reflected to the same extent in the differences between their illegitimacy rates. That is, given the fact again that white females are not so excessive in the white population as are black females within the black population, and considering also that white females have far greater access to black males as marital partners than do black females to white males, one must wonder why the white illegitimacy rate is as high as it is among whites and as low as it is among blacks!

Summary and Conclusions

By now it may be quite evident that there are at least three major and interrelated concerns running through this discourse about "But where are the men?" with the most important one being that there simply are not enough men available for black women to assure their conformity to traditional patterns of sex, marriage, and family living, as defined for them by the white American culture. More important, as the white sex ratio becomes more like that of blacks (as measured by excessive females within the population and particularly within the age ranges of 15–44 years), it is quite clear that whites are increasingly utilizing patterns or models already developed by blacks, who have had a "headstart" of at least 100 years.

Ultimately, black women must be concerned with resolution of the issue of an insufficient supply of males, and aid in developing means of increasing that supply (which can take a variety of tactics, not the least of which is improving the life expectancies of black men) or, should that fail, providing viable alternatives to this "supply-and-demand" problem, one of which may be aiding in reducing the supply of black males available to white females, a practice, incidentally, which seems to affect an unduly high number of black coeds on major campuses throughout at least most of the northern and western parts of the United States.

In closing, then, the critical issues confronting many black women are not those of black matriarchy or black female emasculation of the male, but merely that of, *"But where are the men?"*

III

POLITICS

1

A Portrait of Marcus Garvey

PHAON SUNDIATA

Marcus Manasseh Garvey was born August 17, 1887 in the town of St. Ann's Bay, Jamaica, one of the chain of Caribbean islands known as the West Indies. He was named after his father, Marcus Garvey Sr., whom he respected as a man of intellect and great courage. Marcus, Jr. said of his father in the September 1923 issue of the magazine *Current History*,[1] "He was afraid of consequences. He took human chances in the course of life, as most bold men do . . ." He wrote tenderly but lightly of his mother in this article, describing her as a "sober and conscientious Christian, too soft and good for the time in which she lived." To contrast his father's firm, determined and willful handling of situations and people, he noted that Mrs. Sarah Garvey was always ready to return a smile for a blow and to bestow charity on an enemy. Mr. Garvey Sr. was not much of a church-goer, but it is recorded that Mrs. Garvey attended services regularly. Cronon lists the younger Garvey's religious affiliation as Roman Catholic.[2]

Marcus and Sarah Garvey considered themselves to be of unmixed African stock, and the father is said to have been descended from the Maroons, those escaped African slaves whose heroic expoits in defense of their freedom form an important part of Jamai-

Long active in the Movement and widely published as a writer, PHAON SUNDIATA has written for a number of journals and periodicals such as *Muhammad Speaks, The Washington Afro-American, The Crusader Newsletter* and the *Negro History Bulletin*. He was employed for two years as an editorial assistant to Dr. William Leo Hansberry, first recipient of the Haile Selassie I Prize Trust Award for research in African history. Sundiata was Key Coordinator of the National Conference on Black Power in 1967. Sundiata received a BA in psychology from Howard University, and an MA in government from American University.

1. Marcus Garvey, "The Negro's Greatest Enemy," *Current History*, XVII, September, 1923, pp. 953-54.
2. Edmund David Cronon, *Black Moses*. Madison: University of Wisconsin Press, 1955, p. 5.

can history and folklore. The Maroons have always had a greater prestige than ordinary Jamaican blacks as a result of their success-ful struggle against slavery, a fight that was rewarded with a treaty of independence from the British in 1793.[3] Garvey was later to glory in the fact that he was a "full-blooded" black man without any taint of "white blood" in his veins, a feeling of superiority that may have stemmed in part from his Maroon ancestry.

Garvey claimed his education was secured through private tutors, Anglican elementary or grammar schools, the town high school and two colleges. The records of Birkbeck College, London, were par-tially destroyed during the blitz of 1940 and therefore cannot be reviewed. However, the registrar of the College verifies that Garvey may have attended classes there intermittently in 1912–13.[4] Young Marcus developed a fondness for books and reading patterned after his father's habits.

In his autobiography in *Current History,* Garvey made much of the fact that as a child he grew up in the midst of black and white playmates, not realizing the social distance that existed between the races until his early teens.[5] He took pains to draw attention to the fact that he refused to submit to whipping by teachers while in the public schools because humiliation and defeat always made him strive to conquer the person or situation dealing him an affront.

His youthful work experience centered around the printing trade, and he unabashedly pointed out that, due to his intelligence and "strong and manly" character, he was able to become manager of a print shop and director of other men at the early age of eighteen.

As he grew older his white companions of earlier years began to rebuff and ignore him more and more frequently, causing him to seek an active part in the political life of Jamaica. Undoubtedly this was an effort to come into control of the situation that daily dealt indignities to him and other blacks. He polished up his attempts at public speaking. He spent his Sundays visiting various churches to observe the techniques of delivery used by the most effective King-ston (Jamaica) preachers.[6] He practiced reading aloud passages

3. Martha W. Beckwith, *Black Roadways: A Study of Jamaican Folk Life.* Chapel Hill: University of North Carolina Press, 1929, pp. 183-97, cited by E. David Cronon, *op. cit.,* p. 5.

4. Cronon, *op. cit.,* p. 7.

5. This was an unusual state of affairs, contrasting greatly with the general trend of relations between the races in Jamaica at that time. One writer holds that the maintenance of "social distance" on racial grounds was a necessary adjunct to the sugar plantation economy. See, Eric Eustace Williams, *The His-torical Background of Race Relations in the Caribbean.* College Press: Port-of-Spain, Trinidad-Tobago, 1955.

6. *Ibid.,* p. 12.

from the school reader while trying out various gestures before the mirror in his room. More and more he spoke in public, especially at meetings of laborers, and thus gained sound training for his future years.

The touch of local politics piqued Garvey's interest in the conditions of black people in neighboring islands and in Central and South America, where he journeyed in 1910. He traveled to Costa Rica, Panama, Ecuador, Nicaragua, Honduras, Colombia and Venezuela—working on banana plantations. In Costa Rica and Panama Garvey tried to start newspapers but failed, principally because of indifference on the part of the workers.[7] Even when he visited Europe in 1912 he found color prejudice.[8]

Garvey credits his decision to be a race leader to a coupling of his visual observations during his travels and to the description of the hardships encountered by Negroes in the U.S.A., in the book *Up From Slavery* by Booker T. Washington.[9] The first full-length biography of Garvey, *Black Moses,* bears out this contention but also elaborates on the Africa-consciousness stirred up in Garvey by his association with the African author Duse Mohammad Ali. Garvey's contact with this scholar and editor of the *Africa Times and Orient Review* stimulated a keen interest in Africa, African cultures and the continent's administration under colonial rule. According to Cronon, it was through Ali plus other students from Africa and the West Indies, African nationalists, sailors and dock workers that Garvey compiled more information on the conditions of black people throughout the world and absorbed much of the African nationalism so characteristic of his later activities.

Returning to Jamaica, this ambitious young black man established on August 1, 1914 the organization that was henceforth to consume all his time and energy—The Universal Negro Improvement Association and African Communities (Imperial) League. Its manifesto stressed the need for racial unity and elaborated that its purposes were:

To establish a Universal Confraternity among the race; to promote the spirit of race pride and love; to reclaim the fallen of the race; to administer to and assist the needy; to assist in civilizing the backward tribes of Africa; to strengthen the imperialism of independent African states; to establish Commissionaries or Agencies in the principal countries of the world for the protection of all Negroes, irrespective of nationality; to promote a conscientious Christian worship among the native tribes of

7. *Ibid.,* p. 15.
8. Duse Mohammed, *In the Land of the Pharaohs.* London: Stanley Paul, 1911, cited by Cronon, *op. cit.,* p. 15.
9. M. Garvey, *op. cit.,* p. 953.

Africa; to establish universities, colleges and secondary schools for the further education and culture of the boys and girls of the race; to conduct a world-wide commercial and industrial intercourse.[10]

The founder was also appointed President and Traveling Commissioner; a Ladies' Division was formed, and his future wife, Amy Ashwood, was appointed Associate Secretary. Its motto was both stirring and succinct—"One God! One Aim! One Destiny!"

The UNIA, as it came to be known, started its work of "racial uplift" in Jamaica itself in an attempt to establish educational and industrial colleges for the island's black majority. These efforts, however, were actively opposed by the middle or mulatto class.[11]

One of the outstanding features of the Jamaican racial situation at that time was the separate status of this mulatto group. As in the case of many colonial areas where the white minority lives as a managerial or non-laboring class, the "mixed bloods" approximated a middle-class status. As a middle class, the mulatto group occupied a useful role in the eyes of the whites: it was useful for economic purposes, and it acted as a buffer between the two "unmixed" races. And since accommodation rather than protest is the dominant motive of the mixed blood, he assumes the role of a conformist anxious to defend his superior status.[12] There is a tendency for personal behavior to follow conformist patterns, since ambition is directed toward individual social and economic success. Many leaders are therefore drawn away from attempts to modify the system.

This "colored" population acted as a safety valve for any explosive racial discontent and tended eagerly to assimilate and to imitate English culture. This was aided by a general lack of pride in the African heritage and by the stigma attached to "Negro blood."

The blacks, despite their numerical superiority, were relegated to an inferior economic and social position. The blacks tended to be

10. *U. N. I. A. Manifesto*, Booker T. Washington MSS, Library of Congress, cited by Cronon *op. cit.*, p. 19.

11. Amy Jacques-Garvey, *Philosophy and Opinions of Marcus Garvey or Africa for the Africans*, II. New York: The Universal Publishing House, 1926, p. 127. For a comprehensive description of the characteristics of social classes, see, Reinhard Bendix and Seymour Lipset, *Class, Status and Power*, Glencoe, Illinois: The Free Press, 1957. For comments of the role of the hybrid in relation to the oppressed group, see, Robert L. Sutherland, *Introductory Sociology*, Chicago: J. B. Lippincott Company, 1956, p. 302.

12. Fernando Henriques, *Family and Colour in Jamaica*, London: Eyre and Spottiswoode, 1953, Ch. 2 and Ch. 3, especially pp. 33 and 42 passim. Also Melville J. Herskovits, *The American Negro*, New York: Columbia University, 1928, and J. Dollard, *Caste and Class in a Southern Town*, New York: Harbor, 1949, both cited by Henriques, *op. cit.* Everett Stonequist, *The Marginal Man: A Study in Personality and Culture Conflict*, New York: Scribners, 1937, p. 27, cited by Cronon, *op. cit.*, p. 9.

helpless for want of organization leadership. Black leaders were drawn into the colored class through marriage or through economic and social advancement. Neither whites nor mixed bloods were anxious for a change in the status quo, and they acted together to prevent any enlightenment of the black majority.

It was from this environment that Marcus Garvey drew much of his antipathy and distrust for any but the darkest-skinned blacks. Growing up as a black himself, Garvey understood the feelings of hopelessness and frustration among the more backward Jamaican Negroes and saw the need of expanding their outlook through greater educational and economic opportunities. Above all he desired to rebuild their racial self-respect through a new feeling of pride in the African heritage.

Dispirited by the prolonged rebuffs of the mulattoes and disillusioned by the inertia of the black masses, Garvey decided to visit America in order to meet Booker T. Washington, whose Tuskegee Institute, an agricultural and technical school, had done so much to inspire him in the first place. He planned to seek financial aid as well as inspirational advice. He gave some thought to starting a USA branch of the Universal Negro Improvement Association.[13]

As it turned out, Booker Washington died before Garvey reached New York City in the spring of 1916. Undeterred, the short, stocky West Indian came to Harlem anyway and soon became one of the many familiar sidewalk haranguers of the teeming black masses. In spite of a discouraging beginning here also, the Jamaican continued to speak on the streets and at various public gatherings in churches and elsewhere, and in 1917 he organized the New York Division of the UNIA.[14]

Garvey had hoped to get this branch started and then return to his headquarters in Kingston to direct affairs on an international basis. However, a few Negro politicians were attempting to turn the Association into a political vehicle. In the ensuing fight the organization disbanded.[15] After he made a new start and enrolled 1,500 members, a similar tug-of-war with the politicians began again, and Garvey resolved to stay in America and conduct organization affairs himself.[16]

During 1919 and 1920 the Universal Negro Improvement Associa-

13. Jacques Garvey, *op. cit.*, p. 128.
14. Cronon, *op. cit.*, p. 42.
15. Jacques Garvey, *op. cit.*, p. 128. Also Claude McKay, Harlem: *Negro Metropolis*, New York: Dutton, 1940; Burgit Aron; "The Garvey Movement," unpublished Master's thesis, Columbia University, 1947, both cited by Cronon, *op. cit.*, p. 43.
16. Jacques Garvey, *loc. cit.*

tion enjoyed a remarkable growth. Gravey traveled throughout the
United States, speaking and establishing branches. He also started
The Negro World, a weekly newspaper which soon became a leading Negro periodical and a most effective organ for the promulga-
tion of Garvey's program.[17] The UNIA bought an auditorium
seating 6,000 people, and capacity audiences nightly thronged "Liberty Hall," as it was named,[18] to hear this peppery, audacious new-
comer who was proud of his African heritage and his jet-black skin.

The Liberty Hall conclaves were exciting, colorful affairs frequently preceded by a parade which served to stimulate the interest
of outsiders in the UNIA. Many persons were captivated by the
lure of militarism and manhood suggested by the black and green,
gold-braided uniforms of the soldiers of the "Great Army of Africa."
The throb of scores of motorcycles in the African Motor Corps
called many a young black male to the UNIA standard. Women,
young and old, flocked to answer the call of the proud, inspiring
units of Black Cross Nurses. The parade was resplendent with Sam
Browne belts, dress swords, ceremonial costumes and plumed
knights.[19]

Marchers carried pictures of a black Madonna and child, an
Ethiopian Jesus, Antonio Maceo, Frederick Douglass and other
black heroes. Posters and placards read, "Africa, Mother of Civilization," "Princes Shall Come Out of Egypt," "Free Africa," "The Negro
Will Build Cruisers and Submarines," and "African Scientists Will
Win the War." [20] Doubtless, World War I with its shibboleths and
stirrings of subject minorities offered a volume of suggestions for
these sloganeers.

Inside the packed hall, massed bands accompanied the audience
in the singing of martial hymns and the Association's anthem "Ethiopia, Thou Land of Our Fathers." Black, green and crimson bunting

17. Claude McKay, "Garvey as a Negro Moses." *Liberator,* IV, April, 1922,
pp. 8-9. Also McKay, *Harlem, op. cit.,* pp. 147-48. Both cited by Cronon, *op.
cit.,* p. 45.

18. A name meant to symbolize the intent of the movement for the American blacks. It was considered particularly appropriate in view of the bloody
race riots that had taken place in Washington, D.C., around that time. Between
July 20 and July 28, 1919 the *New York Times* kept a running account of the
civil fracas in the nation's capital. Various headlines read "Sailors and Marines
Invade Negro Quarters," "Martial Law Called For," etc. *New York Times Index,*
July-Sept. 1919, New York: New York Times Corporation, 1919, p. 248. Origin
of name also mentioned in Case A. Garvey v. U.S. no. 8317, Ct. App., 2nd
Circ., Feb. 2, 1925. Case A refers to record on appeal.

19. A. F. Elmes, "Garvey and Garveyism—An Estimate." *Opportunity,* III,
May, 1925, p. 139.

20. Charles S. Johnson, "After Garvey—What?" *Opportunity,* I, No. 8,
August, 1923, p. 231.

abounded. Blackness was glorified in photographs, paintings symbols. On stage the "Court of Ethiopia" held sway with "Du "Duchesses" and "Ladies-in-Waiting" in ample attendance. Every gesture, every movement, every speaker had to conform to the official handbook on court etiquette.[21]

Preliminary to the entrance of their chief spokesman in person, "Knights" and "Sirs" of the UNIA offered the invocation, prayers and review of difficulties encountered by the organization. Frequently an average follower was called upon to attest to Garvey's greatness. Even the humblest supporter bore the title, "Fellowman of the Negro Race." [22] Here and there sat a visiting member of genuine African royalty or officialdom, adding a touch of authentic brilliance in his flowing robes and turban.

Upon signal that Garvey was about to enter the hall, the highest ranking officer present—usually a Knight Commander of the Distinguished Order of Ethiopia—took the floor and roused the crowd to new heights. He recalled their leader's humble beginnings; reiterated the loathsome tricks played on them by their enemies; he respectfully compared Marcus Garvey with the religious martyrs of history.

Six thousand people surged to their feet when the Chief Potentate of the Royal Order of the Nile, the Grand Sachem of the African Legion, the Provisional-President of Africa—Marcus Garvey himself—flanked by a security force, strode to the podium.

The "Redemption of Africa" was his battle cry. To his followers he trumpeted, "No one knows when the hour of Africa's redemption cometh. It is in the wind. It is coming one day like a storm. It will be here. When that day comes, all Africa will stand together—400 million strong." "Look for me in the whirlwind; look for me in the storm; look for me all around you, for with God's grace, I shall come and bring with me the countless millions of black slaves who have died in America and the West Indies and the millions in Africa to aid you in the fight for liberty, freedom and life. Up you mighty race, you can accomplish what you will!" [23] Garvey raised himself above mortals and made himself the "Saviour of the Black World." [24] The crowd was in a trance.

It was a black version of the same nationalism that then encompassed the globe. "India for the Indians!" "A Free Ireland!" "A

21. Roi Ottley, *Black Odyssey.* New York: Scribner's, 1948, p. 235.
22. E. Franklin Frazier, "Garvey, A Mass Leader." *The Nation,* CXXIII, No. 189, August 18, 1926, p. 147.
23. Cronon, *op. cit.*
24. "Marcus Garvey." *The Negro World,* February 14, 1925.

Nordic Blood Renaissance!" To these a black man was determined
to add "Free Africa!" [25]

Early in 1919 the Association projected the idea of an all-black
steamship company, the Black Star Line, which would link the
peoples of African descent throughout the world in commercial
and industrial intercourse.[26] By the early 1920's Garvey claimed
two million members and thirty branch offices of the UNIA.[27]

The August UNIA Convention of 1920 was a magnificent affair
judged by any standards. A history-making crowd of 25,000 black
people representing all sections of America and many parts of Africa
and the West Indies jammed Madison Square Garden.[28] The Association had launched a steamship line—an undertaking that staggered the imagination of a peasant folk and made them burst with
pride. The Negro Factories Corporation [29] had been chartered and
had developed a chain of cooperative grocery stores, a restaurant,
a steam laundry, a tailor and dressmaking shop, a millinery store
and a publishing house.[30] There was every reason to believe that the
organization would, in line with its stated purpose, "build and
operate factories in the big industrial centers of the United States,
Central America, the West Indies and Africa to manufacture every
marketable commodity." [31] Blacks were called upon, and were
demonstrably ready, to support this business enterprise in order to
ensure steady and profitable employment for their sons and daughters.[32] The Association's weekly periodical, the *Negro World*, proved
an immediate success and within a few months rivaled the circulation figures of other similar ventures that had been established for
years.[33]

The Universal Negro Improvement Association itself was organized on a business-like and characteristically American basis. Members were required to pay monthly dues, and paid-up participants,
as in most American fraternal lodges, were entitled to draw sickness
and death benefits from the organization. This fraternal aspect of
movement stemmed from Garvey's belief that the best approach to

25. "Garvey." *Opportunity*, II, October, 1924, p. 284.
26. W. E. B. DuBois, "Marcus Garvey." *Crisis*, XXI, pp. 58-60, December,
1920 and pp. 112-15, January, 1921.
27. A. Garvey, *op. cit.*, II, p. 129.
28. Cronon, *op. cit.*, p. 62.
29. *Negro World*, August 21 and September 11, 1920, cited by Cronon, *op.
cit.*, p. 60.
30. W. E. B. DuBois, "Back to Africa." *Century*, CV, February, 1923, p.
544. Also, Aron, *op. cit.*, p. 31. Both cited in Cronon, *op. cit.*, p. 60.
31. *Negro World*, September 11, 1920, cited by Cronon, *op. cit.*, p. 60.
32. *Ibid.*
33. McKay, *Liberator, op. cit.*, Aron, *op. cit.*, p. 29 cited by Cronon, *op. cit.*,
p. 45.

the black masses was through their universal search for security.[34]

The magic of Garvey's spell gave all the splendor and pageantry of a medieval coronation to the convention parade that spellbound Harlem. The militaristic Africa Legion, the immaculate Black Cross nurses, the lines of UNIA choristers, and the spirited juvenile auxiliary combined to give outsiders the impression that the UNIA was "going places."

But how did this untutored black immigrant to America accomplish this unparalleled feat? One of the oldest paradoxes presented to students of history is, "Do the times make the man or does the man make the times?" Without becoming immersed in a lengthy historical rundown on both sides of this proposition, it might be well, nevertheless, for us to first review the social conditions that made it possible for this black folk hero to act as a catalyst for popular currents already beginning to coalesce. Following this appraisal, we will isolate the techniques and the appeals he used to heighten and rally the emotions of his people and thus build the largest mass organization in the history of the black man in the West.

The Afro-American world during the period 1917–1923 was undergoing a series of profound social changes that would play no small part in the acceptance of Garvey's leadership by large numbers of American blacks.[35] There were many reasons why Afro-Americans would be receptive to Garveyism at this time, some stemming directly from the effect of World War I on life in the black community and others having their origin in factors that had been shaping the thoughts of many blacks for years prior to the war. The profound disillusionment felt by blacks at the end of the war had much to do with their widespread acceptance of a new and alien leader with an extreme program of racial nationalism. American blacks, expecting much and obtaining little in the way of improved status from the war to "make the world safe for democracy," were deeply discouraged over the results of the war here at home. This growing mood of frustration and despair on the part of many Afro-Americans was a favorable climate in which Garvey could promote his ideas of race redemption.

The magnitude of black migration from the South to war-industry centers of the North and West was tremendous. The exodus of 1916–18 was caused partly by economic conditions—the lure of Northern wages and the decline of Southern agriculture—and partly

34. Amy Jacques-Garvey, Kingston, Jamaica to K. David Cronon, cited by Cronon, *op. cit.*, p. 61.

35. Edmund David Cronon, *Black Moses*. Madison, Wisconsin: University of Wisconsin Press, 1955. This account is based in part on Cronon's work.

by the discriminatory treatment accorded blacks in the South.[36] Northern industrialists engaged in a studied campaign to lure black labor North to replace the immigrant labor now dwindled to insignificance by the war.[37] The Negro press was utilized to spread the word of the golden economic opportunities to be found in the North. In addition, the Negro press' militant campaign for racial justice, its violent criticism of the South and its strident advocacy of retaliation in kind for the barbarities of Southern whites found wide audience among Southern blacks.[38]

Another aspect of mounting dissatisfaction with conditions in the United States came from veterans, especially those who had been stationed in France where they enjoyed friendly and free movement throughout the entire community—an experience heretofore unknown to them.[39] The returning black soldier, emboldened and embittered, was in no mood to slip quietly back into the old pre-war caste system.

Race friction was on the rise both in the services and in civilian life. The gross and obvious differential in sentences passed on black servicemen involved in racial disputes did much to shake the confidence of the Afro-American world in the integrity of federal justice.[40]

The heavy and abrupt influx of Southern peasant black folk into Northern urban areas brought serious problems of accommodation and employment during a period when officials of Northern cities had little time to cope with them adequately. The bloody months from June to December 1919 were marked by 26 race riots in American cities, causing this period to be known as "the Red Summer." [41] The conflicts were not localized in any one section of the country but developed wherever the two races were living in close proximity and were competing for scarce housing and jobs. Blacks now showed a new willingness to defend themselves and their rights, a fact that added to the ferocity of some of the struggles.

The pattern of violence evidenced in the great increase of lynching and race riots demonstrated that Afro-Americans were now determined to adopt more militant measures in defense of their rights.

36. Emmett J. Scott, *Negro Migration During the War*. New York: Oxford Press, 1920, p. 3, cited by Cronon, *op. cit.*, p. 23.

37. *Ibid.*, pp. 36-37, cited by Cronon, *op. cit.*, p. 25.

38. Cronon, *op. cit.*, p. 25.

39. See for example, Robert L. Wolf, "Les Noires," *Messenger*, V, January, 1923, p. 578, cited by Cronon, *op. cit.*, p. 29.

40. For example, the summary trial and speedy execution of thirteen Negro soldiers involved in the September 1917 race riot in Houston, Texas particularly galled the Negro press and public. See John Hope Franklin, *From Slavery to Freedom: A History of American Negroes*. New York: Knopf, 1947, p. 452.

41. *Ibid.*, p. 472.

This new element of forceful protest indicated not only a deep dissatisfaction with the workings of American democracy but implied as well a fierce determination to improve the status of the colored citizen.[42]

Additionally, the fiery cross began to blemish the countryside again as the Ku Klux Klan experienced a dramatic resurgence due not only to the increased mixing of the races but also to a burgeoning reaction against wartime internationalism.[43] The Klan acted in such a way as to leave no doubts in minds of blacks as to its determination to make the United States a white man's country. The Knights of the Ku Klux Klan proposed that agents be sent among the colored population to emphasize the desirability of returning to their ancestral homeland.[44]

Just as the race riots after the war helped to shake the faith of blacks in their future as American citizens, so also the nocturnal activities of the KKK and its associated organizations caused many colored citizens to doubt whether they could ever hope to achieve equality of opportunity and treatment in the U.S.A. The great hopes of the war years dissolved into bitter cynicism in the face of the brutal realities of the post-war situation. It is not surprising that many blacks sought escape in radicalism or looked for a new leader to point the way to relief from the injustices of American life.

By 1919 the Afro-American was ready for any program that would tend to restore even a measure of his lost dignity and self-respect. Discontent with existing conditions was widespread, and the old "Uncle Tom" race leader was being replaced by more vigorous spokesmen, who spoke of equality in general rather than limited terms.

The black population of the North had greatly increased during the war and was concentrated in urban centers where mass organization could be more easily accomplished than in the predominantly rural South. Bad living conditions and poor job opportunities tended to discourage even the most optimistic Negro, while the outbreak of mass intolerance as evidenced in the violence of the race riots and the resurgence of the KKK seemed to prove the need of a new approach to the race problem. More and more blacks were beginning to agree with Cassy of *Uncle Tom's Cabin*, "There's no use calling on the Lord—He never hears." Rather they were coming to believe that more drastic steps would have to be taken before blacks could achieve their full rights.

Up to this time no Negro organization had either seriously at-

42. Cronon, *op. cit.*, pp. 32-33.
43. Franklin, *op. cit.*, p. 471.
44. *Chicago Defender*, May 5, 1923, cited by Cronon, *op. cit.*, p. 34.

tempted or succeeded in the marshaling of the black masses. None of the racial improvement groups such as the National Urban League or the NAACP had directed much attention to lower-class blacks, but had instead depended upon the upper-class whites and the Negro middle class for intellectual and financial support. This was a basic weakness that tended to separate the bulk of the Afro-American population from its leadership, and the unfortunate result was that blacks were denied any very effective racial group.[45] A really comprehensive alignment within the black world would gear its program to the suspicions, prejudices, aspiration and limited intellectual attainments of the black masses.

Black people were ready for a black Moses, and equally ready to lead them into the promised land was Marcus Garvey.

Garvey's philosophy has been characterized as more "pro-black" than "anti-white." [46] He consistently pictured for his black legions the historically verifiable days of grandeur of Ethiopia and Egypt and the renowned civilizations of Ghana and Timbuctoo.[47] He felt that white people would never of their own free will and without reservation look upon blacks as their equal. He deprecated the idea that the black man's highest goal in life should be to become "acceptable" to whites through acculturation and amalgamation.

As a uniting tactic Garvey frequently commiserated with his people over the past and present suffering of the blacks and set forth the beginnings of a racially angled program of rebuilding the confidence and self-respect of a people who doubted their self-worth after nearly three centuries of slavery and generations of physical and mental brutality.

He recommended economic and territorial independence of the white man. The religion he counseled, though it was one learned from Caucasians, made the strategically wise move of giving God and his heavenly consorts the physical appearance common to black men.[48] Though he was not a self-appointed messiah, the followers of Marcus Garvey made of him a "leader-hero" whose position of pre-eminence and admiration has yet to be equaled in the world of "Afro-affairs."

45. This division continues to the present day and has frequently been a point of attack for author Louis Lomax, among others. Cf., Lomax's *The Negro Revolt.* New York: Harper & Brothers, 1962.

46. Robert Lucas, "How Negroes Look at Whites," *Tomorrow*, IX, May, 1950, pp. 5-9.

47. See both W. E. F. Ward, *A History of Ghana.* London: George Allen Unwin Ltd., 1948, and E. W. Bovill, *The Golden Trade of the Moors.* London: Oxford University Press, 1958. Note here that Garvey classifies all persons indigenous to the continent of Africa as Africans.

48. "Garvey." *Opportunity*, II, October, 1924, p. 284.

The two-volume work, *The Philosophy and Opinions of Marcus Garvey*, contains reprints of speeches and copies of letters and various articles by Marcus Garvey. Although he is more widely known for his oral appeal to the masses, a review of his works in both forms of communication reveal a pattern of emphasis and repetition that is basically analogous. True to our previous findings, some of these ideas are the very themes which are widespread in social movements in general and seem almost universal among American Negro social movements. Foremost among these as stressed by Garvey are: discontent in the area of race relations, concern over the condition of the common black man, glorification of the past, the establishment of a religious context for his people's plight, the solution to their problems—in the areas of their acquisition of land, their self-image and their economic well-being—and his relationship to them and the times. Garvey, in contradistinction to other leaders of American mass movements described here, did not underline the necessity of his followers living by a rigid moral code.

Among the multiple solutions to the black man's problems proposed by the Universal Negro Improvement Association, the desire for a separate geographic area on another continent stood high. Following closely was a drive to build a new frame of reference for the black man—self-respect, racial unity and economic self-sufficiency. Marcus Garvey's task was to convince his people that it was no longer a bad thing to be black. He approached the subject from the standpoint of both his audience's belief in their dignity as human beings and their religious predilection.

Garvey's utterances were filled with references to strength, unity, self-defense and manhood. The lack of knowledge of their racial heritage and the consequent need for confidence in themselves as a people and as individuals were apparent to this youthful race leader. He plugged away at the concept of self-respect achieved through unity and strength.

The best we can do is to work and pray for the hastening of the time when we, too, will have become a united and strong people, able, by our force of character and achievement, to demand not sympathy but justice from all men, races and nations. Let us not waste time in breathless appeals to the strong while we are weak, but lend our time, energy and effort to the accumulation of strength among ourselves by which we will voluntarily attract the attention of others.[49]

In April 1923 he wrote, under the caption "Africa's Wealth,"

. . . We have allowed cowardice and fear to take possession of us for a long time, but that will never take us anywhere. It is no use being afraid

49. *Ibid.*, II, p. 12 f.

of these nations and peoples. They are human beings like ourselves. We have blood, feelings, passions and ambitions just as they have. Why, therefore, should we allow them to trample down our rights and deprive us of our liberty? Negroes everywhere must get that courage of manhood that will enable them to strike out, irrespective of who the enemy is, and demand those things that are ours by rights—moral, legal and divine.[50]

Innumerable times Garvey gave power to his appeals by stressing the numerical strength of the black people of the world, ". . . we are determined that four hundred million of us shall unite to free our Fatherland from the grasp of the invader." "We should say to the millions who are in Africa to hold the fort, for we are coming four hundred million strong."

Garvey gave high priority to black people becoming economically self-sufficient as well. This insistence was based not only on the desire to see Negroes become producers as well as consumers but also out of the fear that the white man would use his economic power to force the Negro into conformity or starve him out of existence. In 1922 the essay, "The Negro as an Industrial Makeshift," was published. It said:

A race that is solely dependent upon another for its economic existence sooner or later dies. As we have been in the past living upon the mercies shown us by others, and by the chances obtainable, and have suffered therefrom, so will we in the future suffer if an effort is not made now to adjust our own affairs.[51]

The President of the UNIA repeatedly attempted to interest Negroes in aiding the development of enterprises in Africa and into becoming black capitalists. The author's opinion on this subject appeared under the caption "Africa's Wealth" which warned:

An open appeal is now being made to the white capitalists of different countries to invest in the exploitation of the oil fields, diamond, gold and iron mines of the "Old Homeland." This means that in a short time Africa will become the center of the world's commercial activities, at which time the black man will naturally be relegated to his accustomed place of being the "under-dog" of the new African civilization. This is about to happen in the face of a highly developed Negro civilization in the Western world, wherein men of the Negro race seek the same opportunities in things economic as the other races of the world.[52]

and advised: "Why should we not go there and take an interest in its development, not for white men but for Negroes? The white man is now doing it, not with the intention of building for other

50. *Ibid.*, II, p. 63.
51. *Ibid.*, I, p. 48.
52. *Ibid.*, II, p. 63.

races, but with the intention of building for himself—for the white race."

". . . . Why should not Africa give to the world its black Rockefeller, Rothschild and Henry Ford? Now is the opportunity. Now is the chance for every Negro to make every effort toward a commercial industrial standard that will make us comparable with the successful businessmen of other races."

The overall militancy and aggressiveness of this molder of the "New Negro" aroused apprehension internationally—from colonial powers and opposition domestically—from both Negro and white spokesmen. Within the United States his statements did not go unchallenged. Opponents of the organization accused Garvey of preaching hatred and encouraging violence and violation of the laws. But Garvey's defense was couched in terms that appealed to Christian sentiment and materialistic logic:

We are organized for the absolute purpose of bettering our condition industrially, commercially, socially, religiously and politically. We are organized not to hate other men, but to lift ourselves, and to demand respect of all humanity. We have a program that we believe to be righteous; we believe it to be just, and we have made up our minds to lay down ourselves on the altar of sacrifice for the realization of this great hope of ours based upon the foundation of righteousness. We declare to the world that Africa must be free, that the entire Negro race must be emancipated from industrial bondage, peonage and serfdom; we made no compromise, we made no apology in this our declaration. We do not desire to create offense on the part of other races, but we are determined that we shall be heard, that we shall be given the rights to which we are entitled.[53]

Nevertheless the charge of "preaching hate" and inciting to violence stuck. And Garvey's injudicious identification of his group with the Ku Klux Klan, the Anglo-Saxon Clubs of America and other white supremacy groups didn't help matters.

It might be noted in passing that he made a few favorable references to white persons or white majorities. These expressions, however, were obviously dictated by a desire to win favor with the existing power structure.

In general, Garvey's philosophy concerning races was basically egalitarian with an understandable "pro-black" emphasis to aid his people to overcome three hundred years of inferiority-complex—producing propaganda aimed at them. For a people who had been made to feel inferior in so many ways—even to the extent that there was a negative connotation to the word "black" in the everyday usage of the English language—one of Mr. Garvey's biggest jobs

53. *Ibid.,* I, p. 73 f.

was to inculcate a sense of self-respect in the Negro people. With a genius sense of recognizing the causes of the malaise that afflicted his race, Garvey's approach to curing black self-doubt and self-hatred was both practical and pragmatic. He built upon his people's religious precepts to emphasize their oneness with the rest of mankind. He inspired them with visions of what four hundred million united people could accomplish. He enthralled them with a type of verbal brinkmanship that replaced the so-called Negro qualities of humility and eternal patience with combative spirit, unqualified courage and undaunted manhood.

As in so many other instances, Garvey was thoroughly realistic in seeking a new land in which to build a new way of life. He recognized the immense difficulty in building and maintaining a separate identity in the midst of a society where one was bombarded with what were frequently diametrically opposed values and standards.[54] He underlined the need for marshaling material and manpower resources for racial respect and defense. As could be expected with a nationalistic movement, a major effort was made to establish a tangible, territorially distinct state.

How was it then that in less than five years, that which had seemed so certain to succeed was crumbling into an inglorious retreat on every side?

Misuse of funds was the prime cause of the dissolution of the dreams of Marcus Garvey. After performing the near-miracle of collecting over $750,000, more than three-quarters of a million dollars [55] from the sweat-stained salaries of Negro maids, janitors and sanitation workers, in two years of operation the Black Star Line squandered $600,000 of this amount.[56] The chief cause of the collapse of the steamship corporation was the deliberate bilking of the line by white agents who advised purchase and maintenance of a series of decrepit and unseaworthy hulks on a group of people who could in no way be expected to understand the intricacies of higher finance and the mechanics of operating ocean-going vessels.[57] Further, Garvey himself pointed out many cases of theft and misappropriation of funds by trusted "fellowmen of the Negro Race" employed by the B.S.L.[58]

Secondly, general lack of business acumen and competent advisors frequently caused both the Universal Negro Improvement

54. "Can We Integrate Without Losing Identity?" *The National Jewish Monthly*, Vol. 77, No. 11, July-August, 1963, p. 5.

55. Cronon, *op. cit.*, p. 114.

56. *Ibid.*, p. 104.

57. *Ibid.*, p. 115.

58. *Ibid.*, pp. 79, 83, 90, 101.

Association and the Black Star Line operations to suffer. Garvey tended to place higher regard on personal loyalty than on professional competence in appointing corporation officers.[59] The resultant disorder in office and shipboard procedure and the improper keeping of financial records proved catastrophic.[60] Lack of adequate legal counsel, on more occasions than one, led this energetic organizer into prolonged and costly lawsuits mainly over verbal or printed indiscretions on his part.[61]

The opposition of the Negro intelligentsia, particularly those who had easy access to the Negro press, dealt another major blow to "The Tiger's" [62] hopes to found a lasting network of financially sound enterprises out of the nationalistic fervor and emotions of the masses. The publisher of the powerful race weekly the *Chicago Defender* [63] and the editor of the vitriolic Marxist monthly *Crusader* [64] led the pack in their attack on this black champion of the common people, and their ferocity increased as their editorial and legal blows began to tell. Some of the opposition was prompted by a genuine fear that this organizer of the black masses was willfully misusing the people's confidence and their money.[65] Some of it grew out of the bitter jealousy that permeates the would-be leaders of the lower-class urban Negro, with its corollary fears of too much money and too much prestige accruing to the "other fellow." [66] Undoubtedly some of Garvey's bourgeois Negro critics were prompted by a desire to prove to the national power structure that they were just as concerned about the growing power of this immigrant upstart as certain white authorities were. Consider, for an instance, the scurrilous letter sent to the U.S. Attorney General by eight prominent middle-class Negroes that was rife with libelous half-truths and slanderous innuendo.[67] However, Garvey was under so much

59. *Ibid.*, pp. 76, 79.

60. Marcus Garvey, Kingston, Jamaica to the American Consul at Kingston, June 7, 1921: Case B, U.S. v. Garvey, no. C33-688, S.D. N.Y., June 19, 1923, cited by Cronon, *op. cit.*, pp. 78-79, 114.

61. Cronon, *op. cit.*, p. 77.

62. *Ibid.*, p. 134. This was the nickname given Garvey by a U.S. lawyer during the lengthy B.S.L. mail-fraud trial.

63. Arna Bontemps and Jack Conroy, *They Seek a City.* Garden City, N.Y.: Doubleday, Doran, 1945, pp. 171-72; *Chicago Defender*, August 6, 1921, cited by Cronon, *op. cit.*, p. 75.

64. *Crusader Bulletin*, February 18, 1922, cited by Cronon, *op. cit.*, p. 75.

65. DuBois, "Marcus Garvey," *op. cit.*, pp. 58-60 and 112-115.

66. E. U. Essien-Udom, *Black Nationalism.* Chicago: University of Chicago Press, 1962, p. 332. See also, Chancellor Williams "The Socio-Economic Significance of the Store-Front Church Movement . . ." (unpublished Doctoral dissertation, American University, Washington, D.C., 1949), p. 181 f.

67. A. Garvey, *op. cit.*, II, p. 294.

pressure at the time and in such dire financial straits that they had little desire to be accurate in their charges and had no fear of retaliation.

Finally, and the letter to the U.S. Attorney General made much of this, the UNIA's increasing acts of comradeship with the Ku Klux Klan, the Anglo-Saxon Clubs and other quasi-legal white supremacist groups bewildered and infuriated the established Negro leadership and its press.[68] Garvey's invitations to representatives of such groups to speak before his followers was based on their common platform of "racial purity," plus his thesis that the black would never receive justice in America or elsewhere from any white race.[69] Unfortunately for him the more prevalent image of such groups was one of their hatred of all blacks and violence condoned in its use against blacks. This strategic error, coupled with some isolated instances of overenthusiasm on the part of some UNIA members which resulted in real or imputed acts of violence, combined to cause the eight Negro professionals mentioned earlier to openly push a federal case against Garvey and his associates for allegedly "using the mails to defraud."[70] This trial ended in Garvey's being sentenced to five years in a federal penitentiary and marked the point of no return for his program and desires "to promote the spirit of race pride and love . . . (and) to conduct a world-wide commercial and industrial intercourse"[71] for his people.

After going to jail in June 1923 in connection with the Association's activities involving its subsidiary corporation "The Black Star Line," Garvey issued his, "Statement to Press on Release on Bail Pending Appeal" (September, 1923). It said,

My personal suffering for the program of the UNIA is but a drop in the bucket of sacrifice. Service to my race is an undying passion with me, so the greater the persecution, the greater my determination to serve. To correct the evils surrounding our racial existence is to undertake a task as pretentious and difficult as dividing the sea or uprooting the Rock of Gibraltar; but, with the grace of God, all things are possible, for in truth there is prophecy that Ethiopia shall stretch forth her hand, and Princes shall come out of Egypt.[72]

Garvey viewed himself as one thoroughly committed to live and die for his race. No biographer has accused him of cupidity or venal motives in his lifelong dedication to uniting the scattered African

68. Marcus Garvey to William Pickens, July 10, 1922, and Pickens to Garvey, July 24, 1922 quoted in *Chicago Defender,* July 29, 1922, cited by Cronon, *op. cit.,* p. 106.

69. A. Garvey, *op. cit.,* II, pp. 97-98.

70. Cronon, *op. cit.,* p. 110 ff.

71. UNIA Manifesto, *op. cit.*

72. *Ibid.,* II, p. 229.

peoples of the world. The record of his activities with both the United Negro Improvement Association and the Black Star Line mark him as a man of vision and worthwhile ideals hemmed in by lack of experience and lack of understanding cooperation from potentially helpful members of his own race.

His tirades against mulatto leaders for opposing him as much for reason of color as for reasons of fact had much truth in it. He could not comprehend how black politicians and Negro men of the cloth could oppose his aim of unity or his portraying Jesus and other central figures of Christianity as black men. His conclusion that they were protecting the source of their money income was certainly a valid one in some cases, to which might be added the universal human disinclination to change established beliefs and modes of behavior.

Garvey's statement that "service to my race is an undying passion with me" was the swan song of a dedicated but tragic figure, an apt capsule of his *raison d'être* and a fitting finale for a martyr.

2

Black Guerrilla Warfare: Strategy and Tactics

MAX STANFORD (*Muhammad Ahmad*)

The most significant recent development in the African-American struggle for national liberation has been the internationalization of its intelligentsia and broad masses. The three main personalities who have contributed to this have been the leader of the Nation of Islam, Honorable Elijah Muhammad, Robert F. Williams, and the late Malcolm X.

But in order for the Afro-American to have a correct perspective, he must first destroy the philosophy of defeatism in the black community. We must understand our historical destiny and development in the world in order to have a clear view of our position in the black revolution. First of all, we must forget about whether or not we now have all the arms and must stop thinking that because we don't have any or all of the arms, we can't win. In order to free ourselves mentally, we must *know* the power black people have in this country.

These powers are: one, the power to stop the machinery of government—that is, the power to cause chaos and make the situation such that nothing runs. Two: the power to hurt the economy. With black people creating mass chaos—especially in the major urban areas in the North—and disrupting the agricultural setup in

MUHAMMAD AHMAD (s.n. MAX STANFORD), national field chairman of RAM (Revolutionary Action Movement) during the mid-sixties, has long been instrumental in laying the foundation for a black ideology. A former student at Central State University (Ohio), Ahmad has worked closely with Malcolm X, Jesse Gray, LeRoi Jones, Stokely Carmichael, Rap Brown, James Forman and Robert Williams in founding black liberation projects. In 1968 he helped organize the Third National Black Power Conference and was its political workshop co-chairman. Now 31 years old, Ahmad has consistently worked over the years for a black unified front. He is national chairman of the African People's Party and a frequent contributor to *The Black Scholar*.

the South, the economy of the oppressor would come almost to a standstill. Three: the power of unleashing violence. This is the power that black people have to tear up "Charlie's" house. This is something that every Asian, African, and Latin American revolutionary probably wishes he could do. But this goody is left to the Afro-American.

All Afro-Americans must begin to think like guerrilla fighters, since we are all "blood brothers" in the struggle. Let us learn from our mistakes in the past. Appealing to a power structure does no good. The only thing that power reacts to is more power. If we don't think we can win, then there is no use in trying. Cowards give up when the odds look bad. A guerrilla fighter knows he or she is right and attempts to win no matter what the odds are. Many of us think we can create chaos but can't take state power. This is not true. Others say we cannot be successful without the physical help of our Asian, African, and Latin American revolutionary brothers. This is also a degree of defeatism.

It is true that our struggle is part of a world black revolution, and that we must unite with the "Bandung" forces, but it is incorrect and defeatist to say that we cannot win under any circumstances. We must, under all conditions, be united with our Asian, African, and Latin American brothers and sisters, but as Fidel Castro says, "revolutionaries must make the revolution." This means that we (Afro-Americans) must make our own revolution. Also, we must be willing to accept the responsibility of revolution and be willing to go all the way, no matter what happens.

Robert F. Williams in February of 1964 advanced the theory of "urban guerrilla warfare." Since that time, mass eruptions have occurred in over 100 U.S. cities where Afro-Americans have fought gallantly against superior military forces. The most noticeable rebellion has been the Watts, Los Angeles, California, rebellion of 1965. These uprisings take on a different character in the present world scene, for they become an integral part of the World Black Revolution. The Afro-American is the vanguard of the World Black Revolution, being America's Achilles heel. RAM states that *the Afro-American will be "the single spark that starts the prairie fire" in the World Black Revolution.* Malcolm X in 1964 stated, ". . . any kind of racial explosion that can be confined to the shores of America. It is a racial explosion that can ignite the powder keg that exists all over the planet we call earth."

Each year more rebellions occur in American cities, and each year they obtain more support among the black masses, are linked more with organized resistance and are tied more to revolutionary slogans and programs. In 1966 many of the eruptions came under the psychological influence of the Black Power slogan raised by Stokely Carmichael, chairman of SNCC (Student Non-Violent Coordinating Committee). There is a dialectical progression arising and developing as a result of these rebellions. It is a revolutionary national consciousness (Black Nationalism) which sees itself linked to the World Black Revolution. The rebellions are "curtain raisers" to a developing Afro-American people's war. "A people's war inevitably meets with many difficulties, with ups and downs and setbacks in the course of its developments, but no force can alter its general trend towards inevitable triumph . . . To despise the enemy strategically is an elementary requirement for a revolutionary.

Without the courage to despise the enemy and without daring to win, it will be simply impossible to make revolution and wage a people's war, let alone to achieve victory. . . ." "It is also very important for revolutionaries to take full account of the enemy tactically. It is likewise impossible to win victory in a people's war without taking full account of the enemy tactically, and without examining the concrete conditions, without being prudent and giving great attention to the study of the art. of struggle and without adopting appropriate forms of struggle in the concrete practice of the revolution in each country and with regard to each concrete problem of the struggle." [1]

RAM is the only known national Afro-American organization that does not attempt to project itself publicly (using the oppressor's mass media). Williams states that the concept of urban guerrilla warfare that is taking place inside the U.S. is a new concept of revolution. . . . "The concept is lightning campaigns conducted in highly sensitive urban communities and spreading to the farm areas. The old method of guerrilla warfare, as carried out from the hills and countryside, would be ineffective in a powerful country like the U.S.A. Any such force would be wiped out in an hour. The new concept is to huddle as close to the enemy as possible so as to neutralize his modern and fierce weapons. The new concept creates conditions that involve or not. It sustains confusion and destruction of property. It dislocates the helpless, sprawling octopus. During the hours of day sporadic rioting and massive sniping take place. Night brings all-out warfare, organized fighting and unlimited terror against the oppressor and his forces.

Urban guerrilla warfare is an ever-growing concept as a solution to the end of oppression among the black masses in America. As racists continue to attack Afro-Americans, blacks will resort more and more to guerrilla warfare. This will bring a confrontation be-

1. Robert Williams, "Revolution Without Violence." *The Crusader*, V, No. 2, February, 1964.

tween the black and white races in America . . . "When massive violence comes, the U.S.A. will become a bedlam of confusion and chaos. The factory workers will be afraid to venture out on the streets to report to their jobs. The telephone and radio workers will be afraid to report. All transportation will come to a complete standstill. Stores will be destroyed and looted. Property will be damaged and expensive buildings will be reduced to ashes. Essential pipelines will be severed and blown up, and all manner of sabotage will occur. Violence and terror will spread like a firestorm.

"A clash will occur inside the armed forces. At U.S. military bases around the world, local revolutionaries will side with Afro-G.I.'s. Because of the vast area covered by the holocaust, U.S. forces will be spread too thin for effective action. U.S. workers who are caught on their jobs will try to return home to protect their families. Trucks and trains will not move the necessary supplies to the big urban centers. The economy will fall into a state of chaos." [2]

"The weapons of defense employed by Afro-American freedom fighters must consist of a poor man's arsenal. Gasoline fire bombs (Molotov cocktails), lye or acid bombs (made by injecting lye or acid into the metal ends of light bulbs) can be used extensively. During the night hours such weapons, thrown from rooftops, will make the streets impossible for racist cops to patrol. Hand grenades, bazookas, light mortars, rocket launchers, machine guns and ammunition can be bought clandestinely from servicemen anxious to make a fast dollar. Freedom fighters in military camps can be contacted to give instruction on usage . . . Extensive sabotage is possible. Gas tanks on public vehicles can be choked up with sand. Sugar is also highly effective in gasoline tanks. Long nails driven through boards and tacks with large heads are effective to slow the movement of traffic on congested roads at night. This can cause havoc on turnpikes. Derailing of trains causes panic. Explosive booby traps on police telephone boxes can be employed. High-powered sniper rifles are readily available. Armor-piercing bullets will penetrate oil storage tanks from a distance. Phosphorus matches (kitchen matches) placed in air conditioning systems will cause delayed explosions which will destroy expensive buildings. Flame throwers can be manufactured at home. Combat-experienced ex-servicemen can easily solve that problem . . ." [3]

In the process of revolution, the mass communications system would be the first to go. Why? Because the enemy's populace and supporters rely on the mass communications system to know how to

2. *Ibid.*
3. Robert Williams, The Potential of a Minority Revolution, Part I. *The Crusader,* V. June, 1964.

relate to events. By destroying the oppressor's communication system the revolutionary nationalist creates a vacuum in the oppressor's apparatus and isolates him from his machinery. Also, it sets the oppressor at a disadvantage because he will have to attempt to rebuild his system in the middle of a battlefield. The electrical plants should be the first target, then radio and T.V. stations, newspaper buildings, etc. In urban areas transportation lines would be the number-two target—sabotage of subway systems, derailing of trolleys or trains, etc. The destruction of airports, especially the tower, dents the beasts' transportation system; telephone lines should be out. In rural areas the roads leading in and out should be set up for ambush and traps for trucks, etc. In urban areas gasoline across highways and road blocks can hold up traffic for hours.

With Wall Street, Madison Avenue, and half of the complex in Washington blown to bits, the oppressor will have to function under wartime plans. The destruction of property (the concept of private property being the basis of the system) would be the chief concern of the revolutionary National Liberation fighters. The demolition of industry would come after communication and transportation. The destruction of steel plants, auto plants (the Detroit complex), chemical plants, oil fields and plants would divide the energies of the oppressor. The complex outside the cities like New York, Detroit, Chicago, Buffalo, N.Y., Lansing, Mich., Philadelphia, Cleveland, etc., are convenient for revolutionary Nationalists. The destruction of such complexes could be achieved by stationary mortars or mortars from an automobile. The mayors' areas should also be completely demolished. This keeps the lower elite section of the capitalist ruling class isolated in the suburbs for days without communication with the outside world. Bombs on trains would stop the commuter system entirely; occasional terror raids in the "super elite" sections, killing important executives, would create chaos in the oppressor's communities and would hold, maintain and sustain it.

If psychological warfare is used with the physical, then the oppressor's forces and supporters will be put at considerable disadvantages. We can see through phase one—destruction of communications systems, destruction of transportation systems, destruction of important property of the oppressor's (Wall Street, Madison Ave., etc.) industrial complexes, steel, iron, chemical, oil, gas industries etc. . . . Birmingham, Ala. is the main industrial complex in the South. Being that the social, economic and political structure is divided into two different categories, our partisan war of National Liberation must have a dual front. The South is a rural area, but because of communication, terrain (basically flat) and transportation (highways), it takes on a semi-urban character. The North is highly industrialized, being urban—almost super-urban—on the East Coast.

The dual front of our forces would be a semi-urban campaign in the South and an urban campaign in the North. The struggle in the North would be to wreck the oppressor's political and economic apparatus—government buildings, assassination of government officials, state and city, police machinery, army, etc., business executives and business buildings. Strategic raids in certain suburbs at night, blowing up executives' homes, would result in total dislocation of major cities. These raids will be the type of activity of the Northern campaign. While in the South, there would be semi-urban guerrilla warfare with more emphasis on occupying (liberating) certain areas to establish the people's governments and wage campaigns against the enemy. This type of warfare would take place within the Black Belt area—Louisiana, Mississippi, Georgia and South Carolina. In this area black people constitute nearly the majority, and they live in an area that extends from the Atlantic coast to the Gulf of Mexico. Partisan warfare and the establishment of people's liberation bases could cut the oppressors in half. Blacks constitute at least 45 per cent in Alabama, 50 per cent in Georgia, and 55 per cent in South Carolina. The revolution would probably spread from the northern cities to southern cities, then to southern rural areas; then the initiative would fall on the rural areas to defeat the enemy in small campaigns while liberating the community.

The southern front would quickly shift from guerrilla to mobile warfare. At this time the oppressor would be forced to call in the National Guard, and the army battle forces would be divided because of internal dissension due to the racial issue. The National Guard and the Army would be called in to crush mobile warfare in the rural areas because it would be the most advanced form of guerrilla warfare. At this time guerrilla units in urban areas could engage the enemy in "mass ambush" while the enemy is preparing to mobilize against the southern front. The elite of the mobile guerrilla southern forces would wage an encirclement offensive on one of the major southern work centers.

At the same time the northern guerrilla could wage a suburban offensive, throwing the northern military apparatus far into white America; then the southern mobile guerrilla could close the encirclement which would extend the war in a protracted manner, splitting the enemy forces in two. The occupying of cities—black communities—would be basically in the South where there are a great number of black people both within and outside of the city.

The play of movement would develop sabotage within a southern city with mass riot in far areas, taking over plantations, etc. . . .

Organization would require many facets. Groups dedicated to militant demonstrations would have to apply constant pressure to the power structure, create chaos and confusion and force the oppressor to unmask his ugly face before the world by his reacting even more brutally and indiscriminately against constitutional forces. This would expose the true nature of the power structure and inspire greater resistance to it.

Armed defense guards would have to be formed throughout the land. These groups would be organized within the confines of the law and possibly become sporting rifle clubs affiliated with the National Rifle Association. They would function only as defense units to safeguard life, limb, and property in ghetto communities. Some form of central direction would be necessary. A tightly organized and well-disciplined underground guerrilla force would also have to be formed to perform a more aggressive mission. It would have to be clandestinely organized and well-versed in explosives. Its mission would be retaliation, but it could be used as a force to pin down and disperse concentrated facist power. It would prevent the power structure from rushing reinforcements to encircle and crush other defense groups engaged in battle against terrorist forces by ambushing, sniping, bombing bridges, booby trapping, and sabotaging highways. A welfare corps would have to be organized to build morale, raise funds, promote legal defense and take charge of the general welfare of the fighting forces and their families. Many of the members of the welfare organization front would not understand their total function. They would be recruited on a humanitarian basis.

The most aggressive and irrepressible arm of the overall organization would be the fire teams. They would work in complete secrecy and would be totally divorced, in the organizational sense, from the main bodies of defense and other forces. They would enjoy complete autonomy. The group's only tangible loyalty to them would be in times of stress. Their legal aid in court defense would be rendered by Afro-Americans giving legal aid to victims of kangaroo court systems, where as is commonly known, black people stand no chance of obtaining justice. This would be similar to, but more vigorous and militant than, the NAACP's role. The fire teams' mission would be sabotage. Thousands of these groups would be organized throughout racist America. These teams would consist of three or four persons. They would only know the members of their immediate team. They would not identify with the civil rights movement. They would appear to be apathetic and even Uncle

Toms. They would sometimes masquerade as super-patriots and be more than willing, in a deceptive way, to cooperate with the police. They would even infiltrate the police force and armed forces when possible and work in the homes of officials as domestics. There would be no official meetings and discussions, only emergency calls and sudden missions.

The mission of these thousands of active fire teams would be setting strategic fires. They could render America's cities and countryside impotent. They could travel from city to city placing lighted candles covered by large paper bags in America's forests, and have time to be far removed from the scene by the time the lighted candle burned to the dried leaves. While unsparingly setting the torch to everything that would burn in the cities and while concentrating on guerrilla warfare, they would not neglect the rural countryside. Aside from the devastating damage that it could visit upon the countryside, such a mission could serve a twofold purpose. It would also divert enemy forces from the urban centers. State forces would be forced to spread their ranks and would not be able to sustain massive troop concentrations in a single community.

The heat and smoke generated from the fires would render some of the highways impassable for repressive troop reinforcements. The rural countryside covers vast areas and would require exhaustive manpower, equipment, and security forces. America cannot afford to allow its rich timber resources and crops to go up in smoke. The fire teams roving in automobiles would find unguarded rural objectives even more accessible. A few teams could start miles and miles of fires from one city to another. The psychological impact would be tremendous. By day the billowing smoke would reflect reddish flames that would elicit pain and a feeling of impending doom. Operating in teams of twos and threes, one freedom fighter could toss a lighted candle into public waste baskets earlier prepared by others who could pour lighter fluid into them from small flasks. Near closing time, kitchen matches could be placed in the air conditioning systems of industrial and public buildings. The property of racists would be designated as priority objectives. Through this method, the racist oppressors could be reduced to poverty in a short span of time.[4]

In order to unite the black community, revolutionary Afro-American organizations would have to be united into a Black Liberation Front. This is revolutionary action. A black general strike to stop the oppressor's system would have to be called in order to throw

4. Robert Williams, "The Potential of a Minority Revolution, Part 2." *The Crusader*, VII, No. 1, August, 1965, pp. 5, 6.

into chaos the oppressor's economy and disturb his social system. When all the black servants are no longer there or cannot be trusted for fear they may poison, maim or murder, the enemy will be faced with a social crisis. The black general strike will cause complete social dislocation within the American racist system. Youth, especially those in gangs, would have to be organized into a political Black Liberation Army. This liberation army would become black America's regular guerrilla army that would become the "shock force" of liberation. All forms of revolutionary order would have to be established to keep superior community organization within the liberation forces ranks. A revolutionary Afro-American government would be established to govern the liberated areas. In non-liberated areas, it would exist in the form of instituting revolutionary justice. Organizations would have to be structured on the cadre level . . .

". . . A cadre organization cannot be made up of just enthusiastic and eager people. Its essential core must be cold, sober individuals who are ready to accept discipline and who recognize the absolute necessity of a strong leadership which can organize and project a strategy of action to mobilize the conscious and not-so-conscious masses around their grievances for a life-and-death struggle against those in power." Such a cadre must be able to continue the revolutionary struggle despite the setbacks that are inevitable in every serious struggle, because the members of the cadre feel that it is only through the revolution that their own future is assured.

At the same time that it recognizes the inevitability of setbacks, such an organization must build itself consciously upon a perspective of victory. This is particularly necessary in the United States, where the idea of perfect defeat of the black man has been so systematically rooted into the black people themselves that a tendency to self-destruction or martyrdom will lurk unconsciously within the organization unless it is systematically rooted out of every member, leader and supporter. The movement for Black Power cannot afford other Malcolms, other Emmett Tills, other Medgar Everses, but must build first and foremost the kind of organization which has the strength and discipline to assure that there will be no more of these.[5]

The failure to realize our power and position in this country has been the failure of Afro-Americans to see themselves as revolutionary nationalists. In doing this, they don't see our struggle as a national liberation struggle. Instead, our struggle has previously been defined along class lines only. This leads to confusion and failure to make a clear analysis, because there are more factors in-

5. James Boggs, *Racism and the Class Struggle*. Monthly Review Press, 1970.

volved than class. What most young black intellectuals must do is
stop seeing themselves, our people, and our struggle through
"Charlie's" eyes. We must become familiar with our revolutionary
history as an oppressed nation.

For a period of three hundred years, the United States was the
scene of constant revolt. During this period, white Americans—especially in the South—developed a fear of the "black hordes." The
South was an armed camp, with every white man delegated with
the authority of law and order in matters concerning the black man.
But then, as now, law and order meant the enslavement of a black
nation. What most young intellectuals fail to do is thoroughly study
the slave system, the development of slavery from the sixteenth
century on to the twentieth century, how our nation was taken into
bondage, and the psychology of white America during this period.

Contrary to the oppressor's statistics, the slave revolts were well
organized, involved thousands of slaves, and sometimes had international implications. These revolts occurred on an average of
every three weeks for a three-hundred-year period. The international perspective of the Denmark Vesey revolt with his attempted
coordination with Toussaint L'Ouverture (military leader of the
Haitian revolt which had defeated both the French and British
armies in liberating Haiti) shook white America to its roots . . .
With the population of African captives in the United States much
greater than "Charlie" has ever been willing to admit, white Americans were faced with a black take-over or black revolution. Black
revolution plagued them constantly. There was never any peace of
mind. The fear of having a Haitian revolution on United States soil
played a major role in the official abolishment of the slave system
when black revolution became an *entirely* feasible and practical concept.

Contrary to what most white historians would have us believe,
the Turner revolt was so well coordinated and planned that it involved hundreds of slaves. Turner struck fear into all of white
America by his tactic of "strike by night and spare none." Though
the revolt was short-lived, many persons in positions of power realized that they would have to cope with a black revolution if the
slave system wasn't destroyed. They knew that if they didn't do
something quick, the slaves would develop national organization
and they feared that the "blacks" would take over the country. The
horror of thinking what the "blacks" would do to the whites if they
were in power was the nightmare of America. The slave system
would have to go in order to "save the Union" (white America).
This was the situation that led to the Civil War. White power had
to fight white power in order to keep control over the "blacks."

The next step is to develop the tactics for national liberation as "black brothers and sisters" in the struggle. What we must understand is that "Charlie's" system runs like an IBM machine. But an IBM machine has a weakness, and that weakness is its complexity. Put something in the wrong place in an IBM machine, and it's finished for a long time. And so it is with this racist, imperialist system. Without mass communications and rapid transportation, this system is through. The millionaires who control this country would be isolated from their flunkies who do their dirty work. When war breaks out in this country, if the action is directed toward taking over institutions of power and "complete annihilation" of the racist capitalist oligarchy, then the black revolution will be successful. Guns, tanks, and police will mean nothing. The Armed Forces will be in chaos, for the struggle of black revolution will be directed against the racist government of white America. *It will be a war between two governments: the revolutionary Afro-American governments in exile against the racist, imperialist white American government. It will also be a war of the forces of the Black Liberation Front against the ultraright coalition.*

Black men and women in the Armed Forces will defect and come over to join the Black Liberation forces. Whites who claim they want to help the revolution will be sent into the white communities to divide them, fight the facists, and frustrate the efforts of the counter-revolutionary forces. Chaos will be everywhere, and with the breakdown of mass communications, mutinies will occur in great numbers at all levels of the oppressor's government. The stock market will fall; Wall Street will stop functioning; Washington, D.C., will be torn apart by riots. Officials everywhere will run for their lives. Thus the William Buckleys, Goldwaters, Duponts, Carnegies, Rockefellers, Kennedys, Vanderbilts, Hunts, Johnsons, Wallaces, Burnetts, etc. will be the first to go. The revolution will "strike by night and spare none." Mass riots will occur in the day with the Afro-Americans blocking traffic, burning buildings, etc. Thousands of Afro-Americans will be in the street fighting, for they will know that this is it. The cry will be "It's on!" This will be the Afro-American's battle for human survival. Thousands of our people will get shot down, but thousands more will be there to fight on. The black revolution will use sabotage in the cities—knocking out the electrical power first, then transportation—and guerrilla warfare in the countryside in the South. With the cities powerless, the oppressor will be helpless.

Nat Turner's philosophy of "strike by night and spare none" is very important because it shows us that Turner knew the psychology of white America, and that we had leadership with the guerrilla instinct. Turner knew what black terrorism meant to the whites, and he struck, even though the odds were against him. His sense of annihilation of the enemy is very important for our struggle even today, because, unlike Asians, Africans and Latin Americans, the Afro-American has a great bulk of the mass against him. White America can be neutralized only by fear of high stakes. That is, if they know that whole families, communities, etc. of their loved ones will be wiped off the face of the earth if they attack Afro-Americans, they won't be too eager to go to war against us. This will be especially true if the Afro-American revolutionary forces make it clear that they are fighting the capitalist ruling class oligarchy and if white Americans fight on the side of the white racist oppressor's government, they will be wiped out with no questions asked. For to support the oppressor's government is to be murderers, and they would be treated like murderers. With the terms of the revolution spelled out, this will divide white America; so we can see that just by observing Nat Turner we can gain something for our coming revolution.

The whites have had to use terrorism in order to control black America. By the proportion of the population—in the South especially—Afro-Americans constitute a nation within a nation. As in slavery times, the only thing that has kept us enslaved is the white man's superior political machinery. By political machinery, I mean the governmental machinery that controls the mass communications and transportation that have kept the white man in power. If we would look at our situation today, we would see that if the white man didn't deny us the right to vote or gerrymander our vote in the North, we would have significant political power—if not political control of this country.

We see that in the southern states—especially Mississippi—where the blacks outnumber whites by a very large proportion—the situation would be completely turned around. And with us controlling our communities in the North, we could have the ten major urban centers tied up. If white America wasn't a racist, capitalist state, half of Congress would be black. The whites in control know this, and this is why the federal government will never do anything about it to change its racist character. Yes, it's the United States government that perpetrates racism. The southern "cracker" (bigot) doesn't count, because the U.S. government is a "cracker" government. Knowing our position, our historical destiny, we should be willing to go all the way.

Neither the CIA, FBI, National Guard, Army or local police will be able to control our people, due to their internal conflicts. The oppressor's racist government will weaken and begin to fall more and more with every day of revolutionary struggle on its hands. Foreign imperialists' holdings will be seized by the various revolutionary movements in Asia, Africa and Latin America. U.S. lackey governments will topple everywhere once the racist white American government is no longer able to come to their aid. With the white American ruling class wiped off the face of this planet and the remaining reactionary forces suffering eventual defeat, *the revolutionary American government of the Afro-Americans will call on the help of other revolutionaries and revolutionary governments to help restore order and to fulfill the ultimate objectives of the World Black Revolution.*

Thus we will have the fulfillment of four hundred years' destiny, and with the Beast (western imperialism) destroyed—the birth of a New World! We must realize that we are the key to the World Black Revolution and that the rest of the world is waiting for us. We must remember that history is on our side. Not only can we win, we *will* win!

Politically, Africa as a continent, and the African people as a people, have the largest representation of any continent in the United Nations. Politically, the Africans are in a more strategic position and in a stronger position whenever a conference is taking place at the international level. Today, power is international, real power is international; today, real power is not local. The only kind of power that can help you and me is international power, not local power. . . .

MALCOLM X

3

African Socialism: Ujamaa in Practice

JULIUS K. NYERERE

In the individual, as in the society, it is an attitude of mind which distinguishes the socialist from the non-socialist. It has nothing to do with the possession or non-possession of wealth. Destitute people can be potential capitalists—exploiters of their fellow human beings. A millionaire can equally well be a socialist; he may value his wealth only because it can be used in the service of his fellow men. But the man who uses wealth for the purpose of dominating any of his fellows is a capitalist. So is the man who would if he could!

A millionaire can be a good socialist, but a socialist millionaire is a rare phenomenon. Indeed he is almost a contradiction in terms. The appearance of millionaires in any society is no proof of its affluence; they can be produced by very poor countries like Tanganyika just as well as by rich countries like the United States of America. For it is neither efficiency of production nor the amount of wealth in a country which makes millionaires; it is the uneven distribution of what is produced. The basic difference between a socialist society and a capitalist society does not lie in their methods of producing wealth, but in the way that wealth is distributed. Therefore, while a millionaire could be a good socialist, he could hardly be the product of a socialist society.

Since the appearance of millionaires in a society does not depend on its affluence, sociologists may someday find it interesting to try to find out why our societies in Africa did not produce any mil-

JULIUS K. NYERERE, President of Tanzania, was born in Tanganyika in 1922. An advocate of East African federation, Nyerere is the first president of the newly formed state of Tanzania. Architect of the doctrine of African Socialism, President Nyerere advocates communal cooperation, agricultural development, and *ujamaa*, self-sacrifice and obligation to the nation-family. President Nyerere lives a simple life with his wife and eight children in Dar es Salaam.

lionaires—for we certainly have enough wealth to create a few. I think they will discover that it was because the organization of traditional African society—its distribution of the wealth it produced—was such that there was hardly any room for parasitism. They may also say, of course, that as a result of this Africa could not produce a leisured class of landowners, and that therefore there was nobody to produce the works of art or science of which capitalist societies can boast. But the works of art and the achievements of science are products of the intellect—which, like life, is one of God's gifts to man. And I cannot believe that God is so careless as to have made use of one of his gifts depend on the *mis*use of another!

Defenders of capitalism claim that the millionaire's wealth is the just reward for his ability or enterprise. But this claim is not borne out by the facts. The wealth of the millionaire depends as little on the enterprise or abilities of the millionaire himself as the power of a feudal monarch depended on his own efforts, enterprise or brain. Both are users, exploiters of the abilities and enterprise of other people. Even when you have an exceptionally intelligent and hardworking millionaire, the difference between his intelligence, his enterprise, his hard work, and those of other members of society cannot possibly be proportionate to the difference between their "rewards." There must be something wrong in a society where one man, however hard-working or clever he may be, can acquire as great a "reward" as a thousand of his fellows can acquire among themselves.

Apart from the anti-social effects of the accumulation of personal wealth, the very desire to accumulate it must be interpreted as a vote of "no confidence" in the social system. For when a society is so organized that it cares about its individuals, then, provided he is willing to work, no individual within that society should worry about what will happen to him tomorrow if he does not hoard his wealth today. Society itself should look after him, or his widow, or his orphans.

This is exactly what traditional African society succeeded in doing. Both the "rich" and the "poor" individual were completely secure in African society. Natural catastrophe brought famine, but it brought famine to everybody—"poor" or "rich." Nobody starved, either for food or for human dignity, because he lacked personal wealth; he could depend on the wealth possessed by the community of which he was a member. That was socialism. That is socialism. There can be no such thing as acquisitive socialism, for that would be a contradiction in terms. Socialism is essentially distributive. Its concern is to see that those who sow reap a fair share of what they have sown.

The production of wealth, whether by primitive or modern methods, requires three things. First, land. God has given us the land, and it is from the land that we get the raw materials which we reshape to meet our needs. Secondly, tools. We have found by simple experience that tools do help. So we make the hoe, the axe, or the modern factory or tractor, to help us produce wealth—the goods we need. And thirdly, human exertion—or labor. We don't need to read Karl Marx or Adam Smith to find out that neither the land nor the hoe actually produces wealth. And we don't need to take degrees in economics to know that neither the worker nor the landlord produces land. Land is God's gift to man—it is always there. But we do know, still without degrees in economics, that the axe and the plough were produced by the laborer.

In traditional African society *everybody* was a worker. There was no other way of earning a living for the community. Even the elder, who appeared to be enjoying himself without doing any work and for whom everybody else appeared to be working, had, in fact, worked hard all his younger days. The wealth he now appeared to possess was not his personally; it was only "his" as the elder of the group which had produced it. He was its guardian. The wealth itself gave him neither power nor prestige. The respect paid to him by the young was his because he was older than they and had served his community longer; and the "poor" elder enjoyed as much respect in our society as the "rich" elder.

When I say that in traditional African society everybody was a worker, I do not use the word "worker" simply as opposed to "employer" but also as opposed to "loiterer" or "idler." One of the most socialistic achievements of our society was the sense of security it gave to its members, as well as the universal hospitality on which they could rely. But it is too often forgotten nowadays that the basis of this great socialistic achievement was this: that it was taken for granted that every member of society—barring only the children and the infirm—contributed his fair share of effort towards the production of its wealth. Not only was the capitalist, or landed exploiter, unknown to traditional African society, but we did not have that other form of modern parasite—the loiterer, or idler, who accepts the hospitality of society as his "right" but gives nothing in return.

Those of us who talk about the African way of life and, quite rightly, take a pride in maintaining the tradition of hospitality which is so great a part of it might do well to remember the Swahili saying: "Treat your guest as a guest for two days; on the third day give him a hoe!" In actual fact, the guest was likely to ask for the hoe even before his host had to give him one—for he knew what was expected of him and would have been ashamed to remain idle any longer.

There is no such thing as socialism without work. A society which fails to give its individuals the means to work or, having given them the means to work, prevents them from getting a fair share of the products of their own sweat and toil, needs putting right. Similarly, an individual who can work—and is provided by society with the means to work—but does not do so, is equally wrong. He has no right to expect anything from society because he contributes nothing *to* society.

The other use of the word "worker," in its specialized sense of "employee" as opposed to "employer," reflects a capitalist attitude of mind which was introduced into Africa with the coming of colonialism and is totally foreign to our own way of thinking. In the old days the African had never aspired to the possession of personal wealth for the puprose of dominatng any of his fellows. He had never had laborers or "factory hands" to do his work for him. But then came the foreign capitalists. They were wealthy. They were powerful. And the African naturally started wanting to be wealthy too. Unfortunately there are some of us who have already learned to covet wealth—and who would like to use the methods which the capitalist uses in acquiring it. That is to say, some of us would like to use, or exploit, our brothers for the purpose of building up our own personal power and prestige. This is completely foreign to us, and it is incompatible with the socialist society we want to build here.

Our first step, therefore, must be to re-educate ourselves; to regain our former attitude of mind. In our traditional African society we were individuals within a community. We took care of the community, and the community took care of us. We neither needed nor wished to exploit our fellow men. And in rejecting the capitalist attitude of mind which colonialism brought into Africa, we must reject also the capitalist methods which go with it. One of these is the individual ownership of land. To us in Africa, land was always recognized as belonging to the community. Each individual within our society had a right to the use of land, because otherwise he could not earn his living, and one cannot have the right to life without also having the right to some means of maintaining life. But the African's right to land was simply the right to *use* it; he had no other right to it, nor did it occur to him to try to claim one.

The foreigner introduced a completely different concept—the concept of land as a marketable commodity. According to this system, a person could claim a piece of land as his own private property *whether he intended to use it or not*. I could take a few square miles of land, call them "mine," and then go off to the moon. All I would have to do to gain a living from "my" land would be to charge a rent to the people who wanted to use it. If this piece of land was in an urban area I would have no need to develop it at all; I could leave it to the fools who were prepared to develop all the other pieces of land surrounding "my" piece, and in doing so automatically to raise the market value of mine. Then I could come down from the moon and demand that these fools pay me through their noses for the high value of "my" land—a value which they themselves had created for me while I was enjoying myself on the moon! Landlords, in a society which recognizes individual ownership of land, can be— and they usually are—in the same class as the loiterers I was talking about: the class of parasites.

The Tanganyikan African National Union government must go back to the traditional African custom of land holding. That is to say, a member of society will be entitled to a piece of land *on condition that he uses it*. Unconditional, or "freehold," ownership of land (which leads to speculation and parasitism) must be abolished. We must regain our former attitude of mind—our traditional African socialism—and apply it to the new societies we are building today. T.A.N.U. has pledged itself to make socialism the basis of its policy in every field. The people of Tanganyika have given us their mandate to carry out that policy, by electing a T.A.N.U. government to lead them. So the government can be relied upon to introduce only legislation which is in harmony with socialist principles.

Just as the elder in our former society was respected for his age and his service to the community, so in our modern society this respect for age and service will be preserved. And in the same way as the "rich" elder's apparent wealth was really only held by him in trust for his people, so today the apparent extra wealth which certain positions of leadership may bring to the individuals who fill them, can be theirs only insofar as it is a necessary aid to the carrying out of their duties. It is a "tool" entrusted to them for the benefit of the people they serve. It is not "theirs" personally, and they may not use any part of it as a means of accumulating more for their own benefit, nor as an "insurance" against the day when they no longer hold the same positions. That would be to betray the people who entrusted it to them. If they serve the community while they can, the community must look after them when they are no longer able to serve it.

In tribal society, the individuals or the families within a tribe were "rich" or "poor" according to whether the whole tribe was rich or poor. If the tribe prospered, all the members of the tribe shared in its prosperity. Tanganyika, today, is a poor country. The standard of living of the masses of our people is shamefully low. But if every man and woman in the country takes up the challenge and works to the limit of his or her ability for the good of the whole society, Tanganyika will prosper, and that prosperity will be shared by all her people. But it must be *shared*.

The true socialist may not exploit his fellows. If the members of any group within our society are going to argue that because they happen to be contributing more to the national income than some other groups, they must therefore take for themselves a greater share of the profits of their own industry than they actually need; and if they insist on this in spite of the fact that it would mean reducing their group's contribution to the general income and thus slowing down the rate at which the whole community can benefit, then that group is exploiting (or trying to exploit) its fellow human beings. It is displaying a capitalist attitude of mind.

There are bound to be certain groups which, by virtue of the "market value" of their particular industry's products, *will* contribute more to the nation's income than others. But the others may actually be producing goods or services which are of equal or greater *intrinsic* value though they do not happen to command such a high *artificial* value. For example, the food produced by the peasant farmer is of greater social value than the diamonds mined at Mwadui. But the mineworkers of Mwadui could claim, quite correctly, that their labor was yielding greater financial profits to the community than that of the farmers. If, however, they went on to demand that they should therefore be given most of that extra profit for themselves, and that no share of it should be spent on helping the farmers, they would be potential capitalists!

As with groups, so with individuals. There are certain skills, certain qualifications, which command a higher rate of salary for their possessors than others. But, here again, the true socialist will demand only that return for his skilled work which he knows to be a fair one in proportion to the wealth or poverty of the whole society to which he belongs. He will not, unless he is a would-be capitalist, attempt to blackmail the community by demanding a salary equal to that paid to his counterpart in some far wealthier society.

European socialism was born of the agrarian revolution and the industrial revolution which followed it. The former created the "landed" and the "landless" classes in society; the latter produced the modern capitalist and the industrial proletariat. These two revolutions planted the seeds of conflict within society, and not only was European socialism born of that conflict, but its apostles sanctified the conflict itself into a philosophy. Civil war was no longer looked upon as something evil or something unfortunate but as something good and necessary. As prayer is to Christianity or to Islam, so civil war ("class war") is to the European version of socialism—a means inseparable from the end. Each becomes the basis of a whole way of life. The European socialist cannot think of his socialism without its father—capitalism.

Brought up in tribal socialism, I must say I find this contradiction quite intolerable. It gives capitalism a philosophical status which it neither claims nor deserves. For it virtually says, "Without capitalism, and the conflict which capitalism creates within society, there can be no socialism." African socialism, on the other hand, did not have the "benefit" of the agrarian revolution or the industrial revolution. It did not start from the existence of conflicting "classes" in society. Indeed I doubt if the equivalent for the word "class" exists in any indigenous African language; for language describes the ideas of those who speak it, and the idea of "class" or "caste" was non-existent in African society.

The foundation, and the objective, of African socialism is the extended family. The true African socialist does not look on one class of men as his brethren and another as his natural enemies. He does not form an alliance with the "brethren" for the extermination of the "non-brethren." He rather regards *all* men as his brethren—as members of his ever-extending family. *Ujamaa,* then, or "family-hood," describes our socialism. It is opposed to capitalism, which seeks to build a happy society on the basis of the exploitation of man by man; and it is equally opposed to doctrinaire socialism, which seeks to build its happy society on a philosophy of inevitable conflict between man and man.

We in Africa have no more need of being "converted" to socialism than we have of being "taught" democracy. Both are rooted in our own past—in the traditional society which produced us. Modern African socialism can draw from its traditional heritage the recognition of "society" as an extension of the basic family unit. But it can no longer confine the idea of the social family within the limits of the tribe, nor, indeed, of the nation. For no true African socialist can look at a line drawn on a map and say, "The people on this side of that line are my brothers, but those who happen to live on the other side of it can have no claim on me." Every individual on this continent is his brother.

It was in the struggle to break the grip of colonialism that we learned the need for unity. We came to recognize that the same socialist attitude of mind which in the tribal days gave to every individual the security that comes of belonging to a widely extended family must be preserved within the still wider society of the nation.

But we should not stop there. Our recognition of the family to which we all belong must be extended yet further—beyond the tribe, the community, the nation, or even the continent—to embrace the whole society of mankind.

4

Prison or Slavery?

KAIDI KASIRIKA (*Kenneth Divans*)
and MAHARIBI MUNTU (*Larry M. West*)

Men and women come to jail primarily because of their economic status. Over 80% of prisoners enter prison with crimes concerned with obtaining money—whether it's murder-robbery, first degree robbery, second degree robbery, grand theft, petty theft, picking pockets, till-tapping, first or second degree burglary, passing checks, forgery, pimping and pandering, selling narcotics, etc. All these crimes are committed to obtain money, to secure food, clothing and shelter in some manner.

The crimes, most being petty in nature, are usually committed by the unemployed, under-employed or disabled. The people, the black and poor people who are in desperate need, seek to provide for themselves the essentials of life.

Many who read this article may disagree with the conclusions I have reached above because they fail to see that the systematic educational process in this country conditions us to accept competition and imbeds within each person the desire to exploit his fellow being —to try to obtain the maximum selfish benefit for the minimum output. So it is only natural that when forces beyond the individual's control ensnare him and impede his economic progress he utilizes those resources at his immediate command to break through those barriers erected to his detriment.

It would be interesting to see what percentage of black men and women would be sent to prison if they were not subjected to

LARRY WEST is serving a life sentence for kidnap and robbery. Generally acknowledged as one of the best legal minds in prison, Brother West and Ruchell Magee have collaborated on a number of legal writs. He was recently transferred from San Quentin to Folsom Prison because of his legal activity on behalf of inmates and for his particular assistance of Ruchell Magee. In his words, "When you talk about August 7, 1970, that's not an escape. It's a slave rebellion."

racism and discrimination, were granted a relevant education and an equal opportunity to prosper as other American citizens, and were spared the psychological sabotage that has been directed upon their minds.

However, black and poor people are also exploited as a class and forced to work for slave wages. They are subjected to a luxurious society that advocates the acquiring of wealth as the means to happiness and prosperity; a society that incessantly displays a multitude of riches, yet denies them the means to acquire same; a society that makes every action a crime and yet only black and poor people are subjected to prosecution.

If we are to understand the prison system it is necessary to take a critical and honest look at the system as a whole, as Chairman Mao states:

It is well known that when you do anything, unless you understand its actual circumstances, its nature and its relations to other things (the part correlated to the whole), you will not know the laws governing it or know how to do it or be able to do it well.

Or be able to deal with it effectively, you dig?

White racism and materialism (private ownership) are the two components of capitalism. One component without the other would severely cripple, if not destroy, the capitalistic system. The prison slavery system manifests itself as the primeval means of production for capitalism. The majority of the minority groups that overcrowd the prisons are the direct results of white racism. There is no divorce of the prison and capitalistic system, as some may think. The prisons are merely one part of the exorbitant afterbirths of a backwards government and politics. In attacking the prison system, we are merely assailing one of the tendrils of the octopus as a necessary prelude for the inevitable removal of its head, i.e., the American capitalistic system.

The prison system is a slave system. A slave is one who is held captive without freedom of choice and must labor until death or until his freedom is bought. The California prison system is a slave system, patterned after that of the original 13 colonies. The immense power wielded by this state slave system ascends to the president. From the womb to the tomb, juveniles are forced into crime and eventually become adult offenders.

It's more than a coincidence that 80% of today's prisoners started being rehabilitated at ages 11 or 12, and yet at ages 35 and 40 no rehabilitation has occurred for them. Doesn't this high percentage of state-raised prisoners attest to the fact that the system is designed to preserve a prison labor force? A prisoner (slave) is sentenced for an indeterminate term, and the only sanctioned way to freedom is to work and produce—in other words, make the captor a profit. Look into the California Department of Corrections industry books and see the millions of dollars profited each year. The prison industries maintain a cooperative relationship with society and produce for private enterprises. How many people realize that the profits of the San Quentin prison canteen pay the yearly salaries of 133 prison employees? No prisoner is issued money, only ducats. All monies are deposited in an interest-earning bank account, of which prisoners never receive any share.

The slave must be forced to realize that every day he works he is lengthening his prison term. The majority of the California prisoners are ignorant to the fact that they have the absolute power to destroy the slave prison system by not cooperating with it, by not working. The slaves en masse fail to perceive the reality of their situation i.e., *SLAVERY*. The prison system is a business that must profit to survive. A primary tenet of business is that each employee must produce so many units. Any business that has more employees than units produced is headed for bankruptcy. The same principle applies to the prison slave system, therefore its very existence depends on production. This is why the prison administration thwarts prison-worker strikes by inflating and agitating race riots. The strike is forgotten, and prisoners find themselves ensnared in a racial crisis. And the slavemasters' cheap slave labor force is no longer threatened by demands for higher wages, prison reforms, etc.

Finally, when one's labor has earned the system a sufficient amount of capital, he is rented out to the outside world (which is also slavery if he happens to be black and/or poor), for weeks, months or years, until he is eventually brought back to the plantation (prison). This is a never-ending cycle. Indeterminate sentences, strict paroles, lack of rehabilitation facilities, sexual and financial castration and restrictions on visiting and mail are the main forces that constitute this never-ending cycle of enslavement.

Indeterminate Sentence

The abrogation of the indeterminate sentence is the first and foremost proposal that must be submitted to the legislature. This is more paramount than any facet of reform in relation to the penal system in California.

Any sane convict would prefer less time and knowing when his release is scheduled than the various pacification and alteration programs presently being instituted in prisons.

The indeterminate sentence was initiated to give the adult authority complete power in granting and denying paroles, and as a safeguard from the possibility of a prisoner being released before he is thoroughly rehabilitated. This plan might have been plausible if it had really achieved rehabilitation. After this enactment of power to secure the "free" society, the policymakers failed to institute any meaningful facilities for the purpose of improvement. This has inevitably reduced the prison-slave system to human warehouses that do great harm and little or no good.

To the newly convicted, the indeterminate sentence is a psychological burden that blunts his motivational edge for improvement. If one is serving a five year to life term, he knows he has got to do at least three and one-half years, and who knows how much after that. This inspires him even less to participate in the quasi-programs available.

All prison terms should be set at a definite date. The prisoner—within 90 days after commencement of sentence—should be informed exactly of his possible release date.

For further incentive, a point system should be utilized based upon work, skill trades, educational and extracurricular prison activities. Once the time is set, the prisoner should then be informed that he can reduce his time by earning points and optimal evaluations. During the initial 90 days the prisoner's educational deficiencies must be exposed and his program of prison release tailored to overcome this deficiency.

Once a prisoner comes to the realization that he is actually setting his own time, the desire to be free will be the panacea for all prison conflict. These types of procedures will promote an optimistic attitude, while simultaneously requiring a complete education, trade, etc., for an early release.

However, before anything is implemented the general attitude of the policy maker must change toward prisoners. Prisoners must be provided with humane treatment and be discerned as culturally deprived people in need of support and understanding, not looked upon as animals and maniacs to be mutilated and twisted into formless objects.

Discipline

The amount and type of disciplinary actions received by a prisoner determines when he will be paroled. The "correctional officer" (prison guard) who charges the offense that greatly affects the amount of time a prisoner may serve has no training and in most cases doesn't fully know the prison rules. Thus, the prisoner's action at best is whimsical, but based upon this ill-trained prison guard's evaluation is the criterion used by the adult authority to determine whether a prisoner is fit for society.

When a prisoner is accused of violating a prison rule (for example, stabbing another prisoner), in nine out of ten cases this is not witnessed by a guard, as most guards could not identify most prisoners in any event. When the prisoner is brought before a hearing, he is not allowed confrontation with any of the witnesses against him or with his accuser. The only defense he has is to convince a hostile prison official that he is innocent. This is close to impossible to do, as other prison officials will state that they received some "anonymous" note or other communication identifying the accused prisoner as the culprit. Under this type of setting it matters not whether the prisoner is innocent or guilty of the offense charged since he is invariably found guilty.

However, even before the so-called hearing, the prisoner is allowed nothing—papers, toothbrush, toothpaste, soap, etc. Under such conditions he must wait sometimes up to 30 days for the committee to convene. If the prisoner is so-called "lucky," he is found guilty and sentenced to time served. If not, he is sentenced to the hole, for any duration from 5 days to the end of his sentence, which in many cases is life.

There are a number of prisoners, including the authors, who have been in the hole for two, three, four, even five or more years, where the food is cold and grossly insufficient to sustain life, where there is no sunlight, where most days you are confined to the cell for 24 hours, and on others you are allowed out for 30 minutes to an hour, twice a week.

The mode of disciplinary hearings does much to mentally scar a prisoner as far as fairness is concerned; it substantiates the fact that racism permeates American society in and out of prison, especially when prison officials' words or statements are involved. However, nothing is done to remove the programmed racism that is omnipresent, in and out of prison-slavery. To supplement the programmed racism and to further polarize prison-slaves, the oppressive captor has invoked and utilized to maximum benefit a class stratum where some slaves are "permitted" more privileges than others.

Rehabilitation

The historical focus of the prison system has transmuted from practical punishment to theoretical rehabilitation. At present, rehabilitation is a myth, and to make it a reality entails an amount of funds, staff members and a complete overhaul of the prison system, which the state refuses to provide.

More psychiatrists, psychologists, sociologists and relevant programs related to existing occupations in society are needed; not more prison guards, tear gas, night-sticks, strip-cells, guns, restricted diets and the like.

To effectuate rehabilitation the prison system must be operated on a basis relevant to the modes of existing cultures, based upon the theory that a man will be back unless properly trained. The idea of punishment must be completely liquidated. The main purpose of rehabilitation is to prepare one for return to society. Therefore we find it necessary for the prisoner to stay in contact with those with whom he will affiliate and to whom he will relate on his return to the community. It is impracticable (blinking reality) for prisoners to be completely alienated, for years in a microcosm of madness and sickness, from free people in society, then be returned to society and be expected to function as normal people.

This contradiction is manifested by the reality that the prisoners most likely to gain parole (in a minimum amount of time) are the ones who adapt to the autocratic rule of the prison—those who so-called adjust by becoming mindless objects, robots, and mechanical men—those who cease to think, because all decisions are made for them. They react to buzzers, bells, horns, whistles, etc. Those sounds relate—telegraph to the lobotomized cerebrum—when to eat, sleep, wake, go, stop, work, etc., etc. A constant reaction to these sounds generates a habitual mechanical functioning that requires little or no mental thought. It is a conditioned reflex: ring the bell—the animal reacts—the prison slave reacts. These types of prisoners, although the most likely to receive parole, are likewise most probably the ones who will fail outside the prison, because decisions are no longer made for them. They have been programmed to a false tempo, thereby putting them out of rhythm to the beat of society. Keeping a man locked up for many years, never allowing him to make independent decisions, and then flinging him unceremoniously into the free-world society is in contradiction to the rules and principles of rehabilitation.

Sexual and Financial Castration

The California correctional institutions (prison-slave camps) have broken up thousands of families because of their maximum restrictions. Among them is conjugal contact. At present, the prison system has mildly relented in this direction with the advent of conjugal visits restricted to married men only in certain privileged institutions. Actually a class system is used, for only a few prisoners have this privilege, and it is held as a shining example to married slaves, as to what the future holds (in slavery) for those obsequious slaves. In short, the conjugal visit is used as a lever by the oppressor to control.

The conjugal visit privilege should not be restricted to married men, but should extend to all men. For what is marriage but a piece of unfeeling paper that expresses nothing? Love needs no certification, nor does a sexual act between man and woman, for only they enjoy the fruits of their labor and reap the reward.

The system purports to frown upon homosexuality. Yet its very insular rules breed what it allegedly seeks to stamp out. Every man should have the right to unity with his so-called common-law wife or any consenting female. (The same applies to female prisoners.) Sexual intercourse between man and woman is as essential as life itself. The separation of man from woman is one of the greatest inhumanities to man and woman because it denies man the very creature who makes him whole and complete, and no man should be subjected to this emasculation, regardless of his crime. Not only has the ban on sex broken up families on the outside, but it has created more problems inside prisons. Young prisoners are constantly harassed, attacked, raped and forced into homosexuality for merely the sexual gratification. Prisoners also lie, cheat, steal and kill over homosexuals or potential bed partners.

Another home-wrecker is the financial castration of convicted men. Prisoners should have the opportunity to support their families while in prison. Hence the wages in the prison factories and other prison facilities should be tantamount to the federal minimum wage. This would enable prisoners to make allotments to their families, thus maintaining their status as the bread-winner.

Sexual and financial castration are the two components of home-wrecking. When a man is convicted and sent to prison, his woman or wife must and will continue her sex life and find a suitable bread-winner for the family. Prisoners should be allowed to maintain their responsibilities as providers and to continue their sex life. These are the two components essential for his manhood. Should a prisoner be denied his manhood because he is a prisoner?

Visiting and Mail Restrictions

Various programs must be established to keep prisoners active and in contact with the outside world. The restrictions on correspondence and visits should be completely abolished. At present, the strictness on mailing and visiting impedes the prisoner's right and desire for expression, foils the establishment of any new relationships and prohibits the receiving of services from outside agencies.

The present prison system is designed to keep and hold a prisoner incommunicado by placing restrictions upon his mailing and visiting. What type of prison system refuses to allow a prisoner to write a person he doesn't know simply because he is in prison? Surely not a system that purports to be preparing a prisoner for re-entry into society. Yet this system denies, obstructs and stymies the prisoner's contacts with free-world society. Prison officials redundantly state that the reason prisoners are prohibited from writing anyone is that society must be protected. However, such statements negate the fact that 98 per cent of all prisoners are eventually released back to society. Hence, if you can't trust a prisoner to write, how can you permit him back into society? A large portion of insecurity derives from having little or no meaningful communications or relations.

Also, there is the legal mail problem. The prison guards should not be allowed under any circumstances to censor or handle the mail (legal or personal) as is presently done. Usually the guards who censor and deliver the mail are the very guards against whom the prisoner is filing a complaint. Further, when court action is involved the attorney general and other legal adversaries obtain copies of prisoners' legal documents before the court does (without his permission). In a lot of cases the prisoner's legal mail never gets to court, especially when he has a winning case but has no outside help. Prison officials, acting on orders of the attorney general, etc., will shake down (search) prisoners' cells and take writs, lawbooks, and other legal documents. Many writs and cases are allegedly lost by the prison officials who are conspiring with the attorney general. Prison officials should not be allowed to tamper with prisoners' mail and legal property, because prison officials are the prisoners' adversaries. The only way to stop this is to take the mail completely out of the prison personnel's hands and authority. A federal postal employee should pick up and deliver all mail.

The restrictions on books, newspapers, and correspondence courses should also be abolished. Most prisoners like to read books of a relevant nature. But prison officials frustrate prisoners' efforts to obtain meaningful reading material and put at his disposal Christian Science newspapers, San Quentin newspapers, sex books and westerns. It is ironic that a prisoner has unimpeded access to such tools of destruction as dope, homosexuality, knives, guns, narcotics, etc., but that it is extremely difficult for him to obtain a good book.

Eradicate the Slave System

Today the rallying cry is, "free all political prisoners," although a more apt description is "free the slaves." A political prisoner is one whose ideology has brought him into combat with the oppressor, while a slave is one whose environmental factors cause him to be oppressed. We have previously defined a slave as one held captive without freedom of choice who must labor till death or his freedom is bought.

Our plight is exactly that of a slave. Our purpose is to awaken the people that their idleness indicates their approval of the enslavement of their friends, family, and loved ones. Not until the true situation of these enclosed microcosms is apparent will any meaningful moves be implemented to liberate the slaves. For none should deny that as long as he does not know that he, his family, friends or loved ones are slaves, there will be no will to resist. We must not overlook the fact that the only thing necessary for the triumph of evil, exploitation, and subjugation is that the conscientious people do nothing.

In all cases theory must precede action, and knowledge must precede both. The prison slave system must be opened, exposed, and eradicated. The first step to attainment is to elevate the consciousness of the people. Who among you dares to quarrel with the maxim, "He who controls minds has very little to fear from bodies"? The speediest and surest way to annihilate this prison system is to quit cooperating with it. Too many poor, oppressed, and innocent people are falling victim to slavery because those charged with the responsibility of promoting the general welfare are sending that much-needed-at-home tax dollar abroad to launch the offensive, to exploit, to subjugate, and when the need arises, exterminate.

It is no accident or coincidence that in the height of financial crisis, the prison-slave camps are being inundated with the poor, the black, the minorities of all levels and ideologies. It is no haphazard occurrence that all black and reform-advocating leaders are being exiled, imprisoned or murdered. Throughout history, the weakest groups were the first eliminated. We, the poor and black, are at present the weakest and least organized. This disorganization of the poor and black people is best evidenced by our numbers in prison slavery and also by the amount of time we must spend there, away from our families, friends, and loved ones.

Whatever artificial barriers you have erected in your mind about the good of prisons, we hope this article has enlightened you sufficiently as to leave no doubt that *prison is slavery.*

5

Black Prisoners, White Law

ROBERT CHRISMAN

The first black prisoners in America were the Africans brought to these shores in chains in 1619. Like our brothers in prison today—and like ourselves—those African ancestors were victims of the political, economic and military rapacity of white America. Slave camps, reservations and concentration camps; bars, chains and leg irons; Alcatraz, Cummings and Sing Sing: these are the real monuments of America, more so than Monticello or the Statue of Liberty. They are monuments of a legal inequity which has its roots in the basic laws of the United States and which still endures.

To justify and protect its oppression of blacks, white America developed an ideology of white supremacy which shaped the American state, its politics and all its interlocking cultural institutions—education, church, law. Apartheid, generally attributed to 20th-century South Africa, was developed as an instrument of oppression by this country in the 1600's and has its basis in the laws themselves, in the Constitution itself.

The function of law is to establish and regulate the political and economic franchise of the citizens within a given state. The Constitution, ironically hailed as a magnificent guarantee of human equality and freedom, deliberately refused franchise to black Americans and Indians and granted it only to white Americans of means. Indeed, black people were defined as a source of white franchise, in the infamous 3/5 clause. This clause gave the slaveholder a preponderance of political power by apportioning him 3/5 constituency for every slave he possessed, *in addition to his own free white constituency.*

Robert Chrisman is editor of *The Black Scholar* and vice-president of The Black World Foundation. A poet and fiction writer, he is a professor of creative writing at San Francisco State College. He holds a B.A. from the University of California, an M.A. from San Francisco State College and has had advanced study at Southern Illinois University. His essays and cultural analyses have been published in *The Saturday Review of Literature, Black World, Scanlan's* and *The Black Scholar.*

The right of slaves to escape bondage was also forbidden: In Article IV, Section 2, "No person held to service or labor in one State, under the laws thereof, escaping into another, shall in consequence of any law or regulation therein, be discharged from such service or labor, but shall be delivered up on claim of the party to whom such service or labor may be due." Escaped slaves were to be returned to the slaveowner—by national decree.

Designed by agrarian slaveholders and northern industrialists and merchants, the Constitution defined the relationship between their economic interests and their political franchise. Hence its preoccupation with finance and the divisions of power. The Bill of Rights, appended 4 years later, is an afterthought, as a concession to human rights.

Black people were governed by the infamous slave codes, which forbade manumission, voting, education, civil status and personal rights and privileges.

The Constitution was an apartheid document that guaranteed the continuance of slavery and racism as permanent institutions and perpetuated them as cultural realities. Despite the elimination by law of slavery and discrimination, we are still the victims of that racism sanctioned and encouraged by the Constitution.

Black people cannot be protected by American law, for we have no franchise in this country. If anything, we suffer double indemnity: We have no law of our own and no protection from the law of white America which, by its intention and by the very nature of the cultural values which determined it, is inimical to blackness.

In the literal sense of the word, we are out-laws. We are most subject to arrest—and the most frequent victims of crime. Over 40% of the prison inmates in the State of California are black. More blacks than whites are executed in the United States—and this does not include lynchings, "self-defense" or police killings. From 1930–1969, 2066 black people were executed to 1751 whites. Four hundred and five black men were executed for rape, as compared to 48 whites during the same period. In his article, "Black Ecology" (*The Black Scholar*, April 1970) Nathan Hare points out that "blacks are about four times as likely to fall victim to forcible rape and robbery and about twice as likely to face burglary and aggravated assault."

Being outside the law, black Americans are either victims or else prisoners of a law which is neither enforced nor designed for us—except with repressive intent. For example, gun control legislation was enacted by the United States only after black people began buying guns and endorsing the principle of self defense, which is a qualitatively different inspiration than the assassination of individuals such as John F. Kennedy and Malcolm X.

Furthermore, black leaders who address themselves to the fundamental question—that black Americans must have full political and economic franchise—are arrested or harassed. To list just a few black leaders who have been or are political prisoners: W. E. B. Du Bois, Marcus Garvey, Malcolm X, the Honorable Elijah Muhammad, Martin Luther King, as well as some of the currently embattled brothers and sisters: Rap Brown, Bobby Seale, Angela Davis, Ahmed Evans, Ericka Huggins, the Soledad brothers and Cleveland Sellers. The demand for black equality in America exposes its most basic contradiction: that as a democracy it cannot endure or allow the full liberation of its black citizens.

All black prisoners, therefore, are political prisoners, for their condition derives from the political inequity of black people in America. A black prisoner's crime may or may not have been a political action against the state, but the state's action against him is always political. This knowledge, intuitively known and sometimes transcribed into political terms, exists within every black prisoner.

For we must understand that the black offender is not tried and judged by the black community itself, but by the machinery of the white community, which is least affected by his actions and whose interests are served by the systematic subjugation of all black people. Thus the trial or conviction of a black prisoner, *regardless of his offense, his guilt or his innocence*, cannot be a democratic judgement of him by his peers, but a political action against him by his oppressors.

Grand juries, the state and federal judges of the Circuit Courts, Superior Courts and Supreme Courts, are appointed, not elected. This fact alone prejudices a fair trial and precludes black representation, for black people do not have a single official in this country who has the power to appoint a judge or grand jury to the bench. Furthermore, because of the appointive nature of most judgeships, judges have no direct responsibility to the persons they try, through recall or election. Nor do trial juries reflect the racial and economic compositions of the populations which they represent. If a city has a 40% black population it should have the same percentage on its juries, in its legal staff and in its judges.

It is of course obvious that mugging, theft, pimping and shooting dope are not themselves political actions, particularly when the victims are most often other black people. To maintain that all black offenders are by their actions politically correct is a dangerous romanticism. Black anti-social behavior must be seen in and of its own terms and be corrected for the enhancement of the black community. But it must be understood that the majority of black offenses have their roots in the political and economic deprivation of black Americans by the Anglo-American state and that these are the primary causes and conditions of black crime. The individual offender and his black community must achieve this primary understanding and unite for our mutual protection and self-determination.

Thus the matter of black prisoners and white law involves the basic question of self-determination for all black people. Black people must determine when a black man has violated the black community, and that black community must take the corrective action. As we drive for new economic and cultural institutions, we must also create new legal institutions that will accurately reflect the judgement, the social fabric, the conditions of the black community. As it stands now, only the white American community determines when a black person has offended the black community, and this is a colonial imposition and a political injustice.

Most important, the black community outside of bars must never divorce itself from the black community within bars. Freedom is a false illusion in this society; prison is a reality. Black prisoners must be supported by the black community during their incarceration and after they are released.

For the black prisoner is the most vulnerable member of our community—in a naked way he is directly at the mercy of the white power structure. It is also apparent that the black prisoner is one of the most valuable members of our community, as well—the organization, the discipline, the fraternity that black men have developed within prison to survive must be developed by us outside the prison if we are to survive.

We must employ all means necessary to protect and support black people within prison walls. We are all prisoners, and our unwavering task must be the achievement of organization, unity and total liberation.

6

W. E. B. DuBois:
Black Scholar and Prophet

LENNEAL J. HENDERSON, JR.

Now that black studies have etched their way into the swaying curricula of many American universities and colleges, it is difficult to imagine how dangerous, arduous, and, perhaps, impossible it was in the late nineteenth century to stimulate serious academic interest in black life in America. It is equally difficult to imagine how isolated and ridiculed an advocate of such interests would have been. "College-bred Negroes" advocating education for black improvement were quick to exhort young black people to take Latin and Greek, traditional liberal arts, or, more commonly, vocational education courses. Few dared to even dream of systematic studies of black social, economic, and cultural life or Swahili, Twi, or black literature.

Yet, in February 1893, a young black graduate student sat in a small room in Berlin, Germany, musing about his plans for the future. While he mused, Reconstruction in the United States was being savagely reduced to a mere transformation of conditions suffered by black slaves into more frightening and stringent conditions of racial segregation and socioeconomic deprivation. The son of a wandering mulatto man and an attractive ebony woman, he had been reared in the Puritan milieu of a small Massachusetts town, studied in the segregated edifices of Fisk University in Tennessee and in the ivy league glory of Harvard University. Having received a scholarship from the Slater Fund to continue his graduate studies in Germany, he attended political economy seminars un-

LENNEAL J. HENDERSON, JR. is Director of Ethnic Studies and Assistant Professor of sociology and government at the University of San Francisco. During the summer of 1971 he was à Visiting Professor of political science at Howard University and a Fellow at the Joint Center for Political Studies. Henderson received his Ph.D. in political science at the University of California, Berkeley. He is editor of *Black Political Life in the United States,* an anthology published by Chandler, San Francisco, 1972.

der the most prominent scholars in Europe. Handsome, brilliant, aloof, and proud, he had received a Bachelor of Arts and a Master of Arts degree and now advanced to doctoral study in history and sociology.

After sitting pensively for several moments, he made a bizarre "sacrifice to the Zeitgeist" of Mercy, God, and Work. After this little celebration with candles, Greek wine, song, and prayer, he made this entry in his diary:

These are my plans: to make a name in science, to make a name in literature and thus to raise my race; Or perhaps to raise a visible empire in Africa thro' England, France or Germany. I wonder what will be the outcome? Who knows? 1

Here, at age twenty-five, William Edward Burghardt DuBois (W. E. B.) pledges to distinguish himself in letters and science and thereby uplift black people throughout the earth. Beneath the inchoate, histrionic, grandiose pronouncement of this remarkable entry lies a prophecy which unfolded itself against many tumultuous decades of black struggle in the late nineteenth and twentieth centuries in a dramatic and memorable way. DuBois was many men to many people. A stirring orator, stinging wit, searing prophet, star poet, staunch propagandist, and stern leader, DuBois is perhaps the most outstanding and prolific black scholar in the black man's modern history.

He is also perhaps the most discredited and maligned black scholar in the twentieth century. Until very recently, his memory seemed to have been beaten into the darkness of oblivion, most of all by those he strove so diligently to improve. Perhaps because he identified with socialism and eventually joined the Communist Party; perhaps because he renounced his American citizenship to become a citizen of Ghana in 1961; perhaps because the trenchant words he penned and spoke assailed both black and white ears, DuBois has usually been relegated to the role of villain in American race relations. His legacy seems to be most obviously borne by the waning W. E. B. DuBois Clubs, more excited by his socialism than his black scholarship or race ideology.2 A growing aggregation of

1. Francis L. Broderick, *W. E. B. DuBois, Negro Leader in a Time of Crisis*. Stanford, California: Stanford University Press, 1959, p. 16. Broderick is thorough in this biography on DuBois but frequently harsh in his assessment of DuBois' aims and personality.

2. I must here record the exception taken to my interpretation of the W. E. B. DuBois Clubs noted in a letter to me by Herbert Aptheker, noted Marxist and historian and executor of DuBois' estate. Aptheker contends that the organization is just as emphatic about black liberation as it is about socialism.

black scholars and leaders, whose research and ideology was stirred and propelled by DuBois' writing, have also begun to seriously reconsider DuBois' writings and preachings. From that reconsideration comes a rejection of American scholarship's bypassing and discrediting of DuBois and a closer examination of the role he actually played in predicting and pushing the modern civil rights movement. Nevertheless, DuBois doggedly hammered out productive and insightful studies of black and African life as early as 1896 and certainly deserves the title of Father of Black Scholarship in America along with the titles of Father of Pan-Africanism, Dean of the Civil Rights Movement, Founder of the National Association for the Advancement of Colored People, Leader of Black Journalists, and Poet of Extraordinary Quality.

DuBois' life, as reflected by his scholarship, may be roughly divided into three major periods: (1) the intellectual-research period, 1881–1905; (2) the activist-polemic period, 1905–1935; and, (3) the internationalist-peace period, 1935–1963. Although this arbitrary division hides the fact that DuBois engaged in all these activities throughout his unusually long life, it demonstrates the emphasis DuBois placed on various strategies in the black struggle and elucidates more clearly the various intellectual influences on his scholarship.

DuBois returned from the radically idyllic milieu of the European universities to the United States in 1894 to complete the Ph.D. requirements at Harvard. Although he remained socially and intellectually aloof from all but a few of his fellow Harvard students, DuBois developed close relationships with some of the most distinguished scholars in the United States. He met most of these scholars prior to his departure for Germany and resumed his contact and association with them once he returned from Germany:

The Harvard of 1888 was an extraordinary aggregation of great men. Not often since that day have so many distinguished teachers been together at one place at one time in America . . . By good fortune, I was thrown into direct contact with many of these men. I was repeatedly a guest in the house of William James; he was my friend and guide to clear thinking; I was a member of the Philosophical Club and talked with Royce and Palmer. I sat in an upper room and read Kant's *Critique* with Santayana; Shaler invited a Southerner, who objected to sitting by me, out of his class; I became one of Hart's favorite pupils and was afterwards guided by him through my graduate course and started on my work in Germany. It was a great opportunity for a young man and a young American Negro, and I realized it.[3]

3. W. E. B. DuBois, *Dusk of Dawn*. New York: Harcourt and Brace, 1940, p. 37. DuBois' first autobiography which he writes as more a history of a con-

DuBois' vigorous studies at Berlin and Harvard stressed within him the necessity and importance of the 'scientific method' and nourished his born gift of precociousness in his thinking and research. Not only was he exposed to the latest methods in historiography, economics, and social science, but he paid close attention to the scientific analysis used in geology, mathematics, and metallurgy. He tasted James' pragmatism in psychology, Hart's interest in African history, and the emerging nationalism of the German nation. Most importantly, DuBois kept closely in touch with the social and political developments in the attitudes and activities of white people toward black people in the United States and Africa.[4]

DuBois' doctoral dissertation, *The Suppression of the African Slave Trade in the United States, 1638–1870,*[5] contained over three-hundred footnotes, 349 pages, and is still unsurpassed as an historical analysis of the political struggles which developed over the slave trade. DuBois consulted colonial statutes, public documents, ship diaries and accounts, as well as existing literature on the subject in developing his dissertation. That DuBois was not reluctant to scold the United States and England for playing with African lives in the slave trade is evident in the study. It was made the first volume of the newly established Harvard Historical Series and hailed as "the first scientific work of importance done by a Negro in America."[6] This work also led DuBois to Africa, the source of that people from whom he was partly descended and with whom he was so fascinated at Fisk University. He came upon the pernicious relations between imperialist activities in Europe and America and the rueful conditions of blacks in Africa and America. This led him to ponder seriously and study diligently the international implications of black bondage and to candidly question the very foundations of European and American imperialism and oppression.

His research also established within him an unflinching faith in science and knowledge as the best panacea for black America. If blacks and whites were rid of their ignorance about the race problem, they would correct their attitudes toward each other and collaborate to improve each other. DuBois began his research career

cept than an autobiography. A more recent autobiography is *The Autobiography of W. E. B. DuBois*, New York: International Book, Inc., 1968.

4. See W. E. B. DuBois, *The World and Africa.* New York: International Books, Inc., 1961.

5. Cambridge, Massachusetts: Harvard Historical Series, Volume I, 1896. Also reprinted by Schocken Press, 1969. Schocken has also reprinted *The Philadelphia Negro* and *Darkwater.*

6. Cursory mention of this is made in Ronald Segal, *The Race War.* New York: Bantam Books, Inc., 1967, pgs. 219-221 and Colin Legum, *Pan-Africanism: A Short Political Guide.* Praeger Books, 1963, pgs. 24-26.

in history, but his increasing concern with the larger dimensions of racism and oppression moved him beyond a mere consideration and admiration of the black biography and more toward social science in general. If science and knowledge were to erase the ailments of black and white people, all social institutions—the economy, the government, the psyche, cultural—had to be examined more carefully and more systematically.

The University of Pennsylvania offered to support his study of Philadelphia's squalid seventh ward to prove "that the Negro voters were primarily responsible for the scandalous Republican administration in Philadelphia." [7] Although he presented no verification for any of these assertions, he saw firsthand the startling poverty, cultural starvation and ravenous racism blacks suffered in this urban colony. He interviewed thousands of the residents, resided in the area with his young wife, and closely and meticulously examined every particular of the black man's life in the seventh ward. The result was his exhaustive study, *The Philadelphia Negro*,[8] published in 1899 and widely acclaimed as a seminal work and a major contribution to the development of the young discipline of sociology. It is evident that after completing this study, DuBois began to see the black man's bitter descent into lowest caste status in America as a sort of odyssey which confirmed not the black man's alleged inferiority to whites but the firm grasp whites had on the broken and starved institutions of black America. The vestiges of the so-called "gains" of Reconstruction faded before the mighty upsurge of private industry, economic gain, and white supremacy. Whites had neither the time nor the interest in black people to curb flagrant injustices against black people both in the North and in the South. Lynchings occurred an average of once a week. Merciless shootings and beatings were common. In Atlanta, DuBois read of and saw mobs of jeering, snarling whites storm through black neighborhoods, wantonly destroying black lives and possessions, while government at every level stood idly by and acquiesced. He prophetically proclaimed that "the problem of the twentieth century is the problem of the color line, the relation of lighter to darker peoples in Africa, Asia, America and the islands of the sea." [9]

7. Elliot Rudwick, W. E. B. DuBois, *Propagandist of the Negro Movement.* New York: Atheneum Press, 1968.

8. New York: Schocken Press, 1967. This work established the framework for later studies of black urban life, especially those of Myrdal, Frazier, Johnson and Clark.

9. W. E. B. DuBois, *The Souls of Black Folk.* New York: Fawcett Press, 1903, cited in the essay, "Dawn of Freedom." This passage is frequently quoted. One can see in this passage DuBois' growing global approach to racism and his perception of a potential Third World Movement.

DuBois saw and experienced the hopes of black people in the Reconstruction Era shattered by countless atrocities and an undeclared but prevailing national attitude and policy of apathy and indifference toward black people. Black folk again recorded their sorrow and aborted hopes in their spiritual strivings and songs. DuBois was not apart from this, though he did not profess faith in any one Christian denomination. The combination of his Puritan background and his unusual perception made him a gifted and extraordinary observer of the souls of black folk. DuBois recorded these spiritual strivings, including his own, in his most famous work, *The Souls of Black Folk*.[10] Even the title was striking at a time when most people preferred to believe that black folks had no souls. Nevertheless, this remarkable collection of spiritual and historical essays demonstrates DuBois' nimble pen, his stirring vision, and his thorough scholarship. The book talks about the Civil War, the crackup of Reconstruction, and the rise of Booker T. Washington.

It probes deeply into the nether region behind "the Veil," the line separating black people from white people. It shows black people in song, in spirit, in prayerful longing for release from a relentless predicament. DuBois vividly describes the passing of his first-born son in a moving essay. But most importantly, the book sums up the experiences and research of DuBois through 1903. He had seen atrocities and murders of black people. He had viewed their poverty and victimization in black colonies across Africa and America. His faith in science and knowledge as the sole cures for these ailments was abruptly and permanently shaken. He quickly concluded that knowledge alone could only at best be hoisted before whites in an impotent idealism; knowledge had to be complemented by direct action if anything was to be changed. But what kind of action, by whom, and what kind of program?

DuBois was slowly formulating an answer to this question as he watched one approach to this problem being pursued. Perhaps the most striking thing to happen to black people after the collapse of Reconstruction was the ascendancy of Booker T. Washington to national prominence.[11] Washington had gained the support of Northern philanthropists and Southern sympathizers for his program of industrial education at Tuskegee University, which he had founded. Washington, however, acquiesced in political and social crimes against black people and exhorted his followers to "cast down their buckets where they were." [12]

10. *Ibid.*
11. See DuBois', "On Booker T. Washington," *Ibid.*, pp. 41-59.
12. This was said in Washington's famous address at the Atlanta Exposition in 1895.

DuBois opposed Washington's submission to the myriad injustices against black people.[13] He was jolted by Washington's program and became the constant and persistent nemesis of Washington. He believed that the extension of the "palm branch" to Southerners enforced the disenfranchisement of blacks and created a separate status of inferiority through law for them. DuBois quickly assailed this "half-a-loaf program" in an eloquent essay in *The Souls of Black Folk*.[14] This essay outlined in detail DuBois' objections to Washington's program and thrust upon DuBois the leadership of a small band of black intellectuals who also took exception to the Tuskegeean's goals for black people. DuBois began to acquire the reputation of a polemicist and activist along with his reputation as scholar and man of letters. Moreover, DuBois was beginning to descend from his ebony tower of knowledge and science to the grim world of the black colony. Washington retorted with words, scorn and firm alliances with Southern whites who opposed DuBois' extremism and "arrogance," but DuBois persisted in his opposition.

The ingredients which led DuBois and Washington to their respective race ideologies lie largely in their different backgrounds.[15] Washington was a child of subservience. He was born a slave; his parents were slaves; he was raised in the Southern institutions of slavery. Throughout his adolescence he trained himself and was trained by whites to obey his master and to perform his lowly tasks with meticulous care. He gathered crumbs of knowledge and gradually developed an insatiable appetite for what was then considered learning. He struggled through trying times and steep climbs and finally obtained a college education at Hampton Institute in Virginia. Washington strongly believed that the solution to the race problem rested in knowledge. Knowledge not of himself and for himself, but knowledge of commerce, vocational education.

This belief was strengthened by his contact with representatives of a booming industrial and business establishment like Andrew Carnegie. He seems to have vicariously absorbed the vicious combination of Manchester liberalism, social Darwinism, *laissez-faire* capitalism and the prevailing economic interpretations of Christianity which America and Europe often used to justify their imperial activities in Third World countries. Washington felt that this knowledge could be best obtained through "temporary political submission" to white America. "Patting the lion" gained more than

13. DuBois did not wholly reject industrial education for blacks. He did, however, stress that it had to be complemented by a strong background in the liberal arts as well.

14. *op. cit.*, pp. 41-59.

15. It is here helpful to look at both DuBois' and Washington's autobiographies for major influencing factors on their lives.

the "extreme folly" of social equality. Industry, borne on black backs and thriving on black toil, seemed to him the ultimate benefactor of the black man and the best solution to race problems. Through industrial or vocational education blacks would supply a burgeoning American capitalism with skilled and freely available labor despite the growing competition from European immigrants streaming into the United States. The race problem, the problem of twenty-five decades of moral, physical, cultural, and lingual serfdom; the problem of countless and immeasurable injustices against black people; the problems of dehumanization, raped black beauty, broken ancestry and soul-shattered men would eventually through his program solve themselves.

DuBois, however, was a proud child from a long line of aristocrats and Africans. He proudly declared that, "he was black, of Dutch and French ancestry, but, thank God, no Anglo-Saxon." He was one of a handful of black people in the small town of Great Barrington, Massachusetts, and only occasionally bumped into discrimination. He far excelled whites in academic competition and in debate, proudly claiming that he "took pride in beating white students, whether in school, on foot, or beating their stringy heads." DuBois detested obsequity. He stressed that blacks would never taste freedom until they knew something of themselves, of their Africa, of both industrial and liberal arts and sciences, of the monstrous system suppressing their might, and, most importantly, of the urgency and necessity of incessant and tenacious struggle. Blending a profound understanding of the psychology of oppression with a natural spiritual vision, DuBois actually maintained that blackness is an essential and indispensable part of the black man's self-image concept.

Blackness was a positive and creative attitude about oneself, a remaker of the negative images thrust upon the black mind by futile attempts and faded dreams of becoming like that which enslaved him. The song, sense and perception hidden within the black man had its spiritual and cultural roots in Africa, from which he had been snatched. It had not been murdered with the countless murders of black men, women, and children but had swelled and sharpened with oppression. This preserved the black man. To deny and suppress it spelled the ultimate and complete ruin of Africa in America, thought DuBois. Even in 1899 DuBois wrote:

> I am the Smoke King.
> I am black.
> I am darkening with song.
> I am harkening to wrong;

I will be black as blackness can
The blacker the mantle the mightier the man! [16]

America had superimposed on black people a strong desire to emulate white culture and institutions and built into many black minds a hatred of all that was African in them. But no matter how diligent a black man was in hiding and destroying remnants and relics of his Africanness, as long as he lived he lived with it. This created a burning contradiction within the black man. His strivings were at once for all that was American and, unknowingly and unwittingly, for all that was African. DuBois understood this dual quality in the black mind and soul better than most "Negro leaders" of his age.

Unlike most black leaders, DuBois did not bend with the prevailing view that Africa was a vast pasture of untamed and cannibalistic savages, a race of people one small step above apes and one large step below *homo sapiens*. His unusual concern with conditions of blacks in his childhood Great Barrington, in his *alma mater* Fisk, and in the United States, north and south, naturally rolled backward chronologically to their origins on the African motherland. His doctoral work demonstrated his unhappiness with the slave trade. At Fisk he was captivated and transfixed by the "whole gorgeous color gamut of the American Negro world," as well as by the black man's "three gifts of song and story . . . the gift of sweat and brawn to beat back the wilderness." [17] He identified the gnawing and everpresent paradox of the American-African clash within the black man:

It is a peculiar sensation, this double consciousness, this sense of always looking at oneself through the eyes of others, of measuring one's soul by the tape of a world that looks on in amused contempt and pity. One ever feels his two-ness—an American, a Negro; two souls, two thoughts, two unreconciled strivings; two warring ideals in one dark body, whose dogged strength alone keeps it from being torn asunder.[18]

Thus DuBois' profound awareness of black conditions and his staunch opposition to Booker T. Washington moved him into action. With other brilliant black intellectuals—among them William Monroe Trotter, a Harvard schoolmate of his; J. Max Barber of Memphis; and F.H.M. Murray and L. M. Hershaw, both of Washington, D.C.—DuBois organized, in 1905, the Niagara Movement,

16. Herbert Aptheker, "The Unpublished Essays of W. E. B. DuBois." *Freedomways*, 1968. A marvelous memorial edition to DuBois which should be consulted to see how others viewed DuBois and his contributions.

17. J. A. Rogers, *The World's Greatest Men of Color*. J. A. Rogers, 1946.

18. *op. cit., Souls of Black Folk*, p. 46.

designed to carry on the black struggle for full manhood and citizenship rights. This was a pioneer, organized black opposition to Washington's Tuskegee school of thought. The new movement rejected segregation as a way of life which Washington had condoned, if not fully approved. From this sprang the National Association for the Advancement of Colored People, which DuBois helped found in 1910. Unfortunately, liberal whites controlled most of the executive positions of the infant NAACP with DuBois, who had resigned his position at Atlanta University (after conducting and directing the writing of 2172 pages of scholarly fact and opinion on black people in America) as the only black official. DuBois was made Director of Publications and Research and Editor of the *Crisis* magazine, which he edited for twenty-three years.

DuBois attracted national and international attention as editor of the *Crisis*. He wrote and spoke against lynching, eco-political oppression, Booker T. Washington, imperialism, and even against white liberals in the NAACP. His extensive and pioneering sociology studies of black America at Atlanta University well equipped him with the facts and insights to support his controversial positions.

DuBois saw the drift of international affairs toward world turmoil and alluded that nineteenth-century-colonialist policy lay at the heart of most of the conflict. At the beginning of World War I, he urged blacks to "close ranks" and fight side by side with white soldiers. Many thought DuBois a turncoat and traitor for taking this position, but it is possible that he saw the necessity of keeping European hegemony out of the United States so that the vicious oppression of black people would not be accented by the internecine battles between European and American whites.

DuBois was also worried over the status of Africa in the oncoming war. Actually, he had been introduced to Africa long before the First World War and had worked with Sylvester Williams of Trinidad to sponsor a seminal Pan-African conference as early as 1900. Many African and Afro-American writers had written poems and novels about Africa which showed a growing love for the motherland and a growing dislike of colonial attempts to beat down African culture and traditions among the black diaspora. By no means the first but perhaps the most important link between the "literary" and political streams of Pan-Africanism was DuBois. For almost half a century he dominated the Pan-African movement. As early as 1897, DuBois had said that "if the Negro were to be a factor in the world's history it would be through a Pan-Negro movement."

DuBois kept in constant contact with African political leaders and shrewdly used the *Crisis* to expound his ideas of a unified black people throughout the earth. After the First World War, DuBois urged the allies to emancipate the African colonies, and out of that grew the Mandates Commission and an inquiry into the colonial status of Africa. In 1919 DuBois wrote, "The American movement means to us what the Zionist movement must mean to the Jews: the centralization of race effort and the recognition of a racial fount."

DuBois was not the only black leader interested in Africa after the First World War. The startling ascendancy of Marcus Garvey in Harlem compelled DuBois to reconsider seriously the relation of the black movement in the United States and the restlessness of native Africans on the motherland. DuBois and Garvey became formidable enemies. Garvey, snarled DuBois, "was a little fat black man; ugly but with intelligent eyes and a big head." Garvey dismissed DuBois' light-skinned complexion as "hybrid." More important, however, was the stance adopted by DuBois toward Africa. While Garvey advocated the return of blacks to Africa, DuBois, strongly influenced by socialist thought, envisioned a unified and powerful Africa dressed in "the beautiful robes of African Socialism." He continued his extensive research into the African past and black American institutions and culture. It is interesting to note that no matter how engrossed DuBois was in the political struggles he engaged in with whites or Negroes, he always continued his research and writing. DuBois the scholar always supplied DuBois the leader with a generous store of fact and analysis, and DuBois the leader always supplied DuBois the scholar with an equally generous store of empirical and theoretical problems to work at. Writes DuBois:

In 1909, I published my biography of John Brown which I regarded as one of the best things I had done; but it met a curious fate. Unconsciously I had entrenched on the chosen field of a writer who controlled two powerful literary vehicles. He severely criticized the work, most unfairly as it seemed to me, and would give me no chance for rejoinder. In 1911, I tried my hand at fiction and published "The Quest of the Silver Fleece" which was really an economic study of some merit. Beginning in 1910, I published "The Negro," a sketch of racial history, in 1915; and a series of essays called "Darkwater" in 1920. In 1924, with the subvention of the publishing fund of the Knights of Columbus, I brought out "The Gift of Black Folk," basically sound as I believe, but too hurriedly done, with several unpardonable errors. In 1928 came another novel, "Dark Princess," my favorite book. In addition to this I published a considerable number of magazine articles in many of the leading periodicals.

DuBois had started and continued an unprecedented movement of black leaders in America, the islands of the Caribbean and the womb of Africa. His scholarship and journalism and Garvey's leadership triggered the famous "Negro Renaissance" in Harlem.

The *Crisis* awarded prizes to young black poets and writers, and many famous black poets and authors published their work in the *Crisis*. This stimulated a new and widespread interest in black writing in the late nineteen twenties, especially in Harlem, but in other cities and towns as well. Claude McKay, Langston Hughes, Jean Toomer, Countee Cullen, Arna Bontemps, Anne Spencer, Abram Harris, Jesse Fauset, and Roscoe Johnson were among many prominent young authors who were a part of this amazing literary movement. DuBois himself had turned from scholarship to creative writing and during this period produced some of his finest fiction and poetry. Unfortunately, the Depression helped smash this thriving literary movement. Black writers had to turn from black themes to themes they thought white people would enjoy and buy.

DuBois once again turned to history after the Renaissance subsided. With the assistance of a grant from the Rosenwald Foundation, he undertook an exhaustive study of the Reconstruction Era. In 1935 his *Black Reconstruction* was published. Unlike hordes of previous and subsequent studies on Reconstruction, DuBois was far more concerned with the economic aspects of the era than with retelling the supposed attempt of the federal government to involve blacks in southern politics. He analyzed the roles of the black and white workers and planters, attempts to revive southern agriculture and the role of labor in a rapidly growing industrial country. This emphasis on economics also shows DuBois' increasing use of Marxist theory in viewing the racism and capitalism of the white world. He began to lose faith in America's desire and ability to change itself.

In 1936 an aging but still energetic W. E. B. DuBois journeyed to the Soviet Union at the invitation of the Soviet government. He closely observed Soviet social and political institutions and learned more about international relations from a different perspective than he had before. He continued his journey, eventually lecturing in many nations in Asia and Africa. Many whites and blacks began to question his increasingly candid admiration of socialist regimes. His views on international peace and Pan-Africanism were inseparably permeated with socialist theory. He resumed his teaching at Atlanta University, edited a magazine entitled *Phylon* (Race) and continued to dig into the black man's past and social predicaments. For a brief time DuBois returned to the NAACP but soon resigned because of his frequent clashes with Walter White, then Executive Director of the NAACP.

Perhaps the temerity with which DuBois advocated his beliefs led to his confrontation with the United States government in the early 1950s. DuBois had helped organize a Peace Information

Bureau, which attempted to accumulate and file information on peace efforts throughout the world but which included a large number of socialist and Communist delegates. The witchhunt for Communist sympathizers had begun in Congress, and DuBois received an order to register as an agent of a foreign power. He replied that he only represented peace and was not involved in any clandestine machinations against the American government. He was finally indicted and faced trial for "subversive activities." With the aid of his friend and attorney Vito Marcantonio the move was finally thrown out of court, but DuBois' pride and reputation were seriously damaged.

DuBois spent the remainder of the decade assailing the injustices of imperialist governments and the arrogance of plutocratic America. He continued his prolific writing and speaking engagements, although he now assumed a background role in the black liberation movement. In 1958 he received the Lenin Peace Prize for his peace activities. Finally, disillusioned with American racism, DuBois applied for membership in the Communist party and became a citizen of Ghana. President Nkrumah, his old friend, prepared a comfortable study for him and made him head of a gigantic project, multinational and all-inclusive, called the Encyclopedia Africanus, scheduled for completion in 1969. DuBois died in 1963, one day before the great march on Washington.

The life of DuBois is itself a monumental chapter in world history. His published work includes 18 books, more than 20 long pamphlets, and a plethora of articles, columns and commentaries. He had been among the chief forces behind the great black movements throughout the world in his lifetime and finally became a major figure in the peace movements following World War II.

More importantly, DuBois fathered what we now know as black studies. His studies on the African slave trade, urban colony life, business and economics in the black community and his profound analyses of black social institutions were the most comprehensive that had ever been undertaken. He pioneered the vast range of the black universe, and his pen and tongue dispelled many myths and falsehoods about the history and culture of the African in Africa, America, Asia, and the islands of the sea. He brought to his work an extraordinary intellect, a transcendental insight, an unusual candor and frankness, and a thoroughness which is unmatched even today. DuBois embodied the ideal black scholar in that he carefully analyzed the black nation, and, not content to sit around and intellectualize with white scholars, he took his learning into the black world and strove to assist in the vital institution-building which is now occurring. He was far ahead of his time, and those phenomena which he predicted are certainly occurring with alarming precision.

Truman Nelson amply describes DuBois' insight in this moving paragraph:

In the beginning the prophet sees pre-conditions, the explosive present and the transcendental future like a man sitting by the window of a darkened room, reading by strokes of lightning. A flash of insight, of foreboding, flares across his consciousness, and then he is plunged back into the confusions and the doubts of the ordinary mortal, groping his way through what may always be a total darkness and incomprehension of his private world and his fate in it. In time the flashes come closer and closer until the world he is destined to illumine lights up under his hand with an incandescent glare and he is able to hold its crimes and secrets, its dungeons and despairs, to a steady cleansing glow which crackles and consumes like a forest fire.

7

Black Liberation and World Revolution

ROBERT L. ALLEN

Any attempt to discuss the political economy of black liberation must first confront the problem of selecting an adequate framework of analysis. We can hardly expect to arrive at valid conclusions if our interpretive basis is faulty. For example, if we choose a framework that is temporally restricted to a few decades of previous history and that limits itself to considering only developments internal to the U.S., then we invariably find that our analysis ends in frustration. If we examine almost any randomly selected ten, twenty or even thirty-year time span of modern U.S. history, we find racism solidly entrenched. There may be minor fluctuations in the degree and extensiveness of racial oppression; new forms may replace outmoded institutions, but the basic power relationships undergo little change. Black people are a racially oppressed, powerless group, and that painful reality cannot be avoided. Such a conclusion, of course, leaves us very few options. We can retreat into apathy and hopelessness, giving up the struggle for liberation altogether as an impossible fantasy. We may engage in nihilistic outbursts of retaliatory violence which are more self-destructive than liberating. We may prostrate ourselves before the white ruling class and appeal to its moral conscience. Or finally, we may dream of escaping by emigrating *en masse* to Africa or South America or even some other part of the United States. We aspire toward full independence—

ROBERT L. ALLEN is widely known for his book *Black Awakening in Capitalist America*. Allen has extensive experience in the Movement and in Movement journalism. For two and one-half years he was a byline correspondent for the *Guardian*. Originally from Atlanta, Allen worked with the black student groups of the 60s during the civil rights movement. Allen taught in the Black Studies Department for three years at San Jose State College. He is Associate Editor of *The Black Scholar* and Vice-President of The Black World Foundation.

self-determination—yet history seems a conspiracy to frustrate us at every turn in the road.

Yet we are well aware that others among the wretched of the earth have somehow broken free of the strait-jacket of oppression and misery. People who were labeled as "primitive" and "savage," "backward" and "stupid" have somehow taken charge of their own history in a way that their oppressors never imagined possible. Intuitively, we feel that our fate is bound up with these, our brothers and sisters. We reach out for contact, sometimes daring to think that we will lead them, other times pleading for their aid and support—but always the connection seems to be an illusion, and we fall back upon ourselves still empty-handed. After all, we are not a majority, nor do we possess the land. What can distant struggles in the Third World offer us? Is it not more sensible to confine our attention to our immediate situation and let the rest of the world take care of itself?

I contend that the answer to this latter question must be no. The fluctuations and contradictions within our immediate struggle cannot be understood purely on their own terms. The conflicts between accommodation and resistance, integration and separation, violence and non-violence, struggle and apathy can be understood only by transcending the immediate context and viewing these matters from a much broader perspective. I submit that we can find no way out of these dilemmas until we recognize that the oppression of black people in the U.S. is an integral part of an epoch of world history. Our problems are the result of the flow of global history over the past several hundred years, and hundreds of millions of other people have been affected by the political and economic relationships stemming from this historical development. We thus make a mistake in viewing our situation in isolation from the larger context. Indeed, it is essential that we grasp this broader perspective because, as I will attempt to show, there is an intimate interdependency between the struggles of Third World people inside the U.S. and the struggles of Third World peoples around the world. Both components are necessary if complete liberation from racial and economic oppression is to be achieved.

To begin with, it is necessary to examine the dialectic between imperialism and national liberation.

The outlines of this dialectic have been traced by such contemporary scholars as Paul Baran (*Political Economy of Growth*) and Oliver Cox (*Capitalism as a System*). Briefly, it was the rise of capitalism in Western Europe and the spread of capitalist colonialism to virtually all parts of the world that shaped the present historical epoch.

It is important to recognize that the early development of capitalism in Europe was not simply an accident, nor was it due to the supposed racial or cultural "superiority" of Europeans. Baran argues that three basic pre-conditions were requisite for capitalist development: (1) a steady increase in agricultural output accompanied by massive displacements of the traditional peasant population, thereby creating a potential industrial labor force; (2) society-wide propagation of a division of labor resulting in the emergence of a class of merchants and traders (incipient bourgeoisie); and (3) massive accumulation of capital in the hands of the developing merchant class. It was the convergence of these historically conditioned processes that precipitated capitalist development. The first two processes were maturing in many parts of the world during the pre-capitalist era, but it was the spectacular development of the third process in Europe that shaped all subsequent history. We may say that the first two conditions were *necessary*, but by themselves they were not *sufficient* to lead to capitalist development, since without massive capital accumulations large-scale capitalist manufacture could not have been organized. Mercantile capitalist accumulations were rapidly acquired in western Europe, because (1) the geographical location of many European countries gave them the opportunity to develop maritime and river navigation and trade at an early date, and (2) such trade paradoxically was stimulated by Europe's relative lack of economic development and paucity of highly valued natural resources. Thus European traders journeyed to the tropics in search of spices, tea, ivory, indigo, etc.; to Asia seeking high quality cloth, ornaments, pottery, etc.; and finally engaged in vicious plundering of gold, silver and precious stones from many parts of the world. In short, Europe's location at a crossroads of trade routes between more economically developed civilizations and/or countries more richly endowed with natural resources stimulated an explosive advance of trade and capitalist accumulation by European merchants. At the same time, the requirements of long-range navigation and trade fostered rapid development of scientific knowledge and weapons technology that enabled Europe to begin the colonial plunder and subjugation of other areas.[1]

Wherever it has penetrated, capitalism has brought about basic changes in social life. At the most basic level it completely altered the process of production. Capitalism "socialized" the production process by (1) replacing the individual producer of pre-capitalist societies with an organized social work force, and (2) it replaced

1. Paul A. Baran, *The Political Economy of Growth*. New York and London: Modern Reader, 1968, pp. 137-139.

individual tools with social tools (e.g., plantations, factories, etc.). Thus the individual craftsman working with his own tools, for example, was replaced by modern assembly line production involving hundreds of workers engaged in synchronized labor activity. This revolutionary reorganization of production brought about a tremendous increase in the productive powers of human societies. It liberated untapped potentials of human organization. At the same time, however, the developing capitalist classes assured their control over this social process by imposing the concept of capitalist private property, which made possible individual ownership (control) of a process that was inherently social in nature. This is the fundamental contradiction of capitalism. Almost all social conflicts are either traceable to this contradiction or are basically remolded by it, including racial conflict.

The alienation of the worker from the land and the means of production via capitalist property relations combined with the money-wage system made the capitalist class—always a small majority—the dominant class in the political economy of capitalism. The worker, compelled to sell his labor power in order to live, was thereby reduced to a mere cog in the capitalist social order. Hence, the fundamental contradiction of capitalism expressed itself in terms of a class conflict between workers and capitalists.

However, it is imperative to realize that the class conflict within capitalism took place in the context of colonialism and imperialism. Internationally the emergence of capitalism resulted in the concentration of capital in a small part of the world—western Europe and, later, North America. The early colonial plunder of the non-European world provided a global base for the accumulation of capital in Europe. These accumulations made industrial and cultural development possible. The development of the steam engine, heavy industry, ship-building, manufacturing, and many modern financial institutions were all financed directly or indirectly by the slave trade and other forms of colonial exploitation.[2] Indeed, it is no exaggeration to suggest that the Industrial Revolution, which enabled Europe and North America to leap far ahead of the rest of the world in material welfare, would have been delayed by several centuries if not for the capital yielded by colonialism.

For the peoples of the colonial world capitalist penetration was disastrous. They were bequeathed all the evils of capitalism and none of its benefits. Their wealth was mercilessly plundered by European pirates disguised as traders. Moreover, colonialism disrupted their traditional agricultural economy, forced them to grow

2. Eric Williams, *Capitalism and Slavery*. New York: Capricorn Books, 1966.

exportable commercial crops, and thereby undermined the self-sufficiency of the colonized societies. Among the basic techniques employed in colonial exploitation were included commercial pressure on local rulers to extract land grants and trading commissions, and imposition of taxes to compel the local population to produce commercial crops or to go to work on plantations and in the mines. Outright slavery was resorted to in many instances. Thus, the colonial societies were brought into the worldwide system of commodity circulation, contributing their economic "surplus" to the growing capital of Europe. Their economies were distorted by the demands of colonialism, and their traditional industries and handicrafts were destroyed by competitions from European industrial exports. Consequently they were forced onto the path leading to economic underdevelopment.

In essence capitalist colonialism produced a worldwide division of labor in which the colonized world "specialized" in providing cheap raw materials (mainly agricultural but lately mineral), in becoming markets for goods manufactured in Europe and North America, and in constant hunger, disease and squalor; while the industrial capitalist nations "specialized" in the white man's burden of collecting profits.

Very few areas of the world escaped the devastation wrought by colonialism. One such was Japan, which managed to avoid being colonized, and after 200 years became itself a major capitalist industrial power. Within the colonial world there were variations which led to different courses of development. In North America, for example, white settlers encountered a relatively small native population which they proceeded to exterminate in order to gain control of the land. They then imported slave labor from Africa to provide a work force for their vast plantations. Taken together, the slave trade controlled by the North and the plantations controlled by the South created the conditions for independent capitalist development in North America. The American Revolution marked the decision of the white capitalist classes of North America to break their colonial bondage to Great Britain and strike out on their own as an independent capitalist nation. In parts of Africa, Asia, and Latin America (especially Mexico and Peru), on the other hand, European merchants encountered large and economically well-developed populations. Hence, large-scale European settlement was precluded. Instead, the European "visitors" proceeded to extract the largest amount of wealth possible, while taking no interest in encouraging independent capitalist development in the host countries. Thus a growing economic imbalance developed between Europe and the colonial world.

The rise of economic imperialism in the nineteenth century institutionalized this imbalance and condemned the colonial nations to "permanent" underdevelopment. Where colonialism plundered nations, imperialism sought to block their economic development by actively preventing capital accumulation and the creation of an industrial base. As Oliver Cox has observed: "No backward people under imperialist control has ever been transformed from an essentially agricultural and mining nation to an essentially manufacturing one. Technological progress has never become a positive movement in countries subject to imperialism. Backwardness for most of the people of the world seems to be a relatively permanent condition of the mature capitalist system." [3] Thus development and underdevelopment are opposite sides of the same imperialist coin.

Backwardness and underdevelopment, however, are not the irreversible fate of most of humankind. In dialectical fashion, the globalization of monopoly capital (imperialism) has produced the social forces capable of bringing about its destruction. Indeed, the main dynamic of modern history has become the contradiction between the imperialist nations and the colonial and semi-colonial parts of the world. Beginning with the 1917 revolution in Russia, a backward and semi-colonial nation, socialist national liberation movements have sprung up throughout the world to challenge and overturn imperialism. China, Korea, Cuba, Vietnam, as well as other parts of Asia, Africa, and Latin America have followed this course and are providing a dramatic and viable alternative to the misery of permanent underdevelopment. In effect they have counterposed national self-determination to imperialist subjugation, and socialist central planning to the social anarchy of capitalist economics. The ramifications of this worldwide struggle transcend our conceptual abilities.

We seem to be standing on the threshold of a new epoch of human history. The capitalist imperialist system finds itself embattled and in retreat. It is no accident, for example, that the present international monetary crisis can count among its major causes the economic strains provoked by an imperialist war—the American aggression in Vietnam. Thus, the Vietnamese, in their struggle to oust imperialism, have not only defeated the U.S. military aggression, but they also helped to generate a major crisis for international capitalism. Most recently, pressure from anti-imperialist Third World and socialist nations forced the U.N. to open its doors to the People's Republic of China, thus improving the chances of prying that organization loose from the domination of the Western im-

3. Oliver C. Cox, *Capitalism as a System*. New York: Monthly Review Press, 1964, pp. 149-150.

perialists. Despite some disastrous setbacks, it appears that anti-imperialist forces are gaining new strength in parts of Africa and Latin America. In short, imperialism has created its own destroyer, and the process of dismantling imperialism is gaining momentum today. Many nations in the colonial world are breaking free of the fetters imposed by imperialism and are restructuring their economies to facilitate industrial growth.

However, we must always remember that the dismantling of capitalist imperialism is a highly complex process involving many factors. International capitalism may be in crisis, but it is not moribund. It is still a strong and resilient system, possessing great military might and also quite capable of prolonging its life by offering limited reforms and concessions to its opponents as the price for keeping the basic system intact. In the past few decades rebellious colonies have faced both military repression and cynical manipulation. Some former colonies were granted formal political independence on the one hand, while at the same time they have been kept under tight economic domination by the imperialist nations. The new domination was accomplished in part through the imperialist tactic of encouraging the growth of comprador or buffer classes within the former colonies which have an economic stake in maintaining capitalist relations with the former mother country. Hence a native ruling class is created which can act as liaison between the imperialists and the exploited native masses. True self-determination is thereby subverted, and imperialism remains in the saddle, although it now wears a new hat. This is what Kwame Nkrumah and others mean when they use the term neo-colonialism.

Of equal importance in deciding the final outcome of the struggle between imperialism and national liberation is the question of the internal strength of the imperialist powers. Obviously an imperialist nation whose population is unified in support of imperialism will make a much more durable adversary than an imperialist nation whose population becomes divided. We need only look at the French withdrawal from Algeria or the present U.S. de-escalation in Vietnam to appreciate the truth of this assertion. National unity, however, is a matter of ideology. A nation unites around an ideological concept of itself and its role in history. Thus the imperialist nations initially justified their colonial activities as a matter of Christian religious duty. Unfortunately from their standpoint, the possibility of religious conversion posed dilemmas that made this rationale somewhat less than satisfactory. For example, should a slave who converted to Christianity be set free? In the view of those who benefited from slavery and the slave trade the answer was obvious. Hence, beginning in the seventeenth century, we note a

steady shift in ideological perspective from religion to race and culture as the prime justification for imperialist exploitation. It became
the "sacred trust" of the European nations to "civilize" the racially
inferior peoples of Africa, Asia, and the Americas. Since the peoples
of these continents could not change their racial status (as defined
by Europeans), racism proved to be an ideal ideological tool for
unifying the white Europeans in support of imperialism.

It is imperative to realize that racism was more than merely an
ideological distraction foisted upon European workers to gain their
support for imperialist adventures. On the contrary, the myth of
white racial and cultural superiority corresponded to the underlying immediate interests of many workers in the imperialist nations.
The more exploited segments of the working class and lumpenpro-
letariat embraced racism because this was the only basis on which
they could justify their hopes of escaping to the colonies or the
New World and of establishing themselves as exploiters of the available natural and human resources. Colonialism made it possible for
even poor white settlers to acquire land and laborers cheaply;
hence their wholehearted support of colonialism's ideology: racism.
Among the more economically privileged segments of the working
class an additional dynamic was at work.

These workers were the indirect beneficiaries of European ex-
pansion. It was the capital accumulated through colonialism and
imperialism that made possible the industrial advancement of
Europe. Although the lion's share of this new wealth went to the
capitalist classes, European workers still benefited, because the new
trade and industries pushed their standard of living to higher levels
than ever before. Indeed, a "labor aristocracy" developed within
the white working class. This privileged stratum grasped that its
favored status was based upon the success of monopoly capital and
imperialism. Hence, it proceeded to reproduce the ideologies of
monopoly and racism within its own ranks.[4] It was no accident that
trade unions among skilled workers attempted to monopolize job
opportunities by excluding other workers, especially members of
subjugated racial groups, who might threaten the privileges enjoyed
by the organized minority. Thus, all classes in the imperialist nations opened their hearts to racism, because colonialism and imperialism offered them unprecedented opportunities for individual
material advancement.

Significantly, the only occasions on which imperialism and its
racist ideology have been modified are (1) when a particular form
of imperialist exploitation outlives its usefulness, and (2) when the

4. Martin Nicolaus, "The Theory of the Labor Aristocracy." *Monthly Review*, Vol. 21, No. 11, April, 1970.

victims of imperialism have risen up to challenge it. The abolitionist ideology, for instance, gained strength only when slavery and the slave trade were no longer consonant with the new level of capitalist development. More recently the necessity of granting political independence to many former colonies precipitated a shift in emphasis in the imperialist ideology from racial to cultural factors: it was those native intellectuals and politicians who assimilated "western culture" who were granted the privilege of becoming the local ruling class in the former colonies. Today, imperialism has been forced to retreat from many parts of the world, and the objective basis is thereby being laid for the breakdown of racist and cultural chauvinist ideologies within the imperialist nations themselves. How successful the imperialist nations are in maintaining the ideological unity of their domestic populations thus becomes a crucial problem to which we will return shortly.

For the "domestic colonies" of imperialism—e.g., black and other colonized peoples in the U.S.—these developments are of momentous importance. In the first place, the rise of domestic colonialism and imperialism has paralleled the rise of colonialism and imperialism on the world stage. In fact, American domestic imperialism is in large degree a continuation and further development of European imperialism. The United States began as a collection of settler colonies. The Europeans who came here displaced the native American population by trickery and brute force. Their campaign of physical and cultural extermination eventually whittled the Indian population down to less than 25% of its original size.

At the same time that the settlers were seizing Indian land, they were kidnapping a colonial work force from Africa. As was the case with Great Britain, the slave trade and slavery had a multiplier effect on the economy of the American colonies. The traffic in slaves was a strong stimulus to northern shipping and ship-building. Slavery was of course essential to the development of the southern plantation economy. In turn, the products of southern agriculture fed the fledgling industries of northern capitalists.

Not only did capitalists and plantation owners gain from slavery but so also did many of the white workers who emigrated to the New World. As James Boggs has observed: "To white workers at the very bottom of white society, African slavery also brought substantial benefits. First, the expanding industry made possible by the profits of slave trafficking created jobs at an expanding rate. Second, . . . white indentured servants were able to escape from the dehumanization of plantation servitude only because of the seemingly inexhaustible supply of constantly imported slaves to take their place . . . For the individual white indentured servant or laborer, African slavery meant the opportunity to rise above the status of slave and become farmer or free laborer." [5] In *Black Reconstruction* W. E. B. DuBois noted the other side of this process; namely, the wholesale social and cultural corruption of the "poor whites."

It is generally established that the origin of racism as a systematic ideology accompanied the institutionalization of capitalist slavery in North America, just as on the world scene racism grew as colonialism became more entrenched.[6] As happened in Europe, virtually all segments of the white population in North America embraced racism since slavery in its heyday yielded direct and indirect economic bonuses to all classes. However, as is always the case in settler colonies, the racist ideology became much more virulent and intense than anything seen in Europe. The white settlers, living in intimate contact with a domestic colonial population, found it constantly necessary to affirm their racial superiority in order to justify the daily crimes they were committing against other human beings. Whites in Europe could afford to be a bit more detached about the matter.

Once industrial capitalism in the U.S. had matured to a certain point, it no longer needed the crutch of slavery. In fact the slave system became a hindrance to further industrial development. A similar dynamic had occurred earlier in the relationship between Great Britain and the West Indies, as Eric Williams has described in his book *Capitalism and Slavery*. The Civil War signaled the triumph of industrial capitalism in North America.

Black workers were emancipated from slavery, but their oppressed colonial status changed very little, if any. Indeed, by making black workers wage slaves, it was now possible to exploit them even more mercilessly. With blacks thrown on their own as individuals

5. James Boggs, *Racism and the Class Struggle*. New York and London: Monthly Review Press, 1970, pp. 150-152.

6. Oliver C. Cox, *Caste, Class and Race*. Garden City, N.Y.: Doubleday, 1948, Chapter 16. Some contemporary scholars have denied that there was a causal link between capitalist slavery and racism. These writers place greater stress on psychological variables or pre-existing attitudes to account for the development of racism; yet their own evidence reveals the crucial role played by the institutionalization of slavery in the English colonies (and English contact with other slave-trading nations such as Spain and Portugal) in fostering and shaping the ideology of racism. See Oscar Handlin, *Race and Nationality in American Life*. Garden City, N.Y.: Doubleday-Anchor, 1957; Carl Degler, "Slavery and the Genesis of American Race Prejudice," in Melvin Drimmer (ed.), *Black History: A Reappraisal*. Garden City, N.Y.: Doubleday, 1968. For a detailed examination of this question see Winthrop D. Jordan, *White Over Black: American Attitudes Toward the Negro, 1550–1812*. Baltimore, Md.: Penguin Books, 1969.

instead of being the collective responsibility of the white master class they could be used to increase the marginal profitability of industrial capitalism. Under slavery the worker represented both labor and a capital investment, but the sharp separation of labor and capital under mature industrial capitalism offered more opportunities for exploitation of a colonial work force. Already, on the West Coast, Chinese contract labor was proving the value of a colonized but ostensibly "free" labor force.

Thus, black workers were reduced to a subproletariat, a reserve army of labor for industrial capitalism. This process took place in the fifty years between 1870 and 1920. Several steps were involved: (1) the agricultural depression of the 1870s, the counter-revolution against Reconstruction, and the failure of the Populist movement, all of which combined to force blacks out of the rural areas and into the cities in search of jobs; (2) The rise of monopoly capital, which actively pitted black workers against white workers in the allocation of jobs and wages; (3) the growth of opportunism in the labor movement as labor leaders established job monopolies and used racism to gain privileges for their followers at the expense of unorganized non-white workers; (4) the spectacular upsurge of American imperialism in the 1890s which greatly intensified racism among both capital and labor within white America. The rise of monopoly capital, imperialism and opportunism in organized labor are inseparable processes which combined to entrench racism both as an ideology and as a set of discriminatory social, economic, and political institutions. Segregation, disenfranchisement, lynching, and trade union and employer discrimination all reached a fever pitch at the turn of the century as the U.S. launched its career as a major imperialist power.

Ironically, the new European immigrants, who poured into this country by the millions during this period, fell right in line with American racism. Although they themselves were discriminated against and divided into competing nationality groups by employers, they were unified in their determination to reap the direct benefits of racism that had not been possible in all-white European countries.

With the outbreak of World War I blacks were cast in the role of internal immigrants of the U.S. urban economy due to the virtual shutting off of European immigration and the mechanization of agriculture in the South. Unlike other immigrants, however, black workers were kept permanently at the bottom of the urban economy as the result of segregation, discrimination, and monopoly capital's declining demand for unskilled and semi-skilled labor.

The use of blacks as an industrial reserve army had major consequences for the structure of American society. To quote Boggs

again: "Instead of the vertical color line dreamed up by white radicals, there has actually existed a horizontal platform resting on the
backs of blacks and holding them down, while on top white workers
have been free to move up the social and economic ladder of advancing capitalism. This horizontal platform, a ceiling for blacks and
a floor for whites, has created and maintained a black labor force
serving the economic needs of advancing capitalism, as it has developed, stage by stage, from manufacturing capitalism to indus-
trialism to monopoly capitalism to its present stage of military-
industrial capitalism, or what is more popularly known as the
'military-industrial complex.'" [7]

Boggs extends these remarks to apply to all colonized workers
in the U.S., for over the past century the capitalist-imperialist system of North America has recruited a nonwhite colonial work force
from China, Japan, the Philippines, Mexico, Puerto Rico and other
areas. All of these workers, to a greater or lesser extent, were forced
into the same racist mold first imposed on black workers. All of these
workers were assigned to be the scavengers of American capitalism,
and institutionalized racism has kept the majority of them from
escaping this role. Although today all Third World peoples in the
U.S. are not necessarily in the same boat, they are certainly all
caught in the same turbulent sea of racial oppression.

Given this analysis, the interrelationship between the growth of
capitalism and imperialism and the entrenchment of domestic racial
oppression should now be more apparent. The former directly stimu-
lates and shapes the development of the latter. However, there is
another side to the imperialism-racism coin. The worldwide anti-
imperialist revolt is shattering the foundation of racism. This has
had important consequences for the domestic colonial population of
the U.S. In fact, an intricate and interconnected process has been
set in motion that links the domestic struggle against racism with
the world struggle against imperialism.

Perhaps the most fully developed example of this process can be
seen at work in the history of Pan-Africanism and African nationalism. In the last part of the 19th and first half of the 20th
centuries, blacks from the West Indies and North America traveled
to Africa or met with Africans in Europe. Among these Pan-African
travellers were such well-known figures as Edward Blyden, Henry
Sylvester Williams, W. E. B. Du Bois, Marcus Garvey, George Pad-
more and C.L.R. James, to name a few. Although these men differed
in their political and economic views, all were staunch advocates of
black self-determination. Taken together, their activities in the Pan-
African movement contributed directly to the ideological birth of

7. Boggs, *Racism and the Class Struggle*, p. 152.

African nationalism and the consequent rise of national liberation struggles in Africa.

Conversely, the growth of national liberation movements and independent states in Africa spurred the black revolt against racism in the U.S. It was no mere coincidence, for example, that the black student sit-in movement got underway as African nations were winning political independence. Secondly, the anti-colonial revolt helped undermine racism as an ideology and correspondingly increased the chances for success in attacking institutional manifestations of racism in the U.S. For example, it is only in recent years that significant segments of white society have at least admitted for the first time that there is a problem of racism, instead of a "Negro problem." There can be little doubt that the development of independent African states was a major factor in discrediting the racist myth of black inferiority, thereby shifting world attention to the underlying problem of white racism.

In sum, the African revolution, which was partly inspired by blacks from the Western hemisphere, has in turn directly affected the consciousness of racism among both blacks and whites in the U.S., and it has thus contributed to the domestic struggle against racism. This is one example of a broad interconnected process in which we are deeply involved and whose ramifications are of greatest importance.

If we admit that racism and cultural chauvinism are ideological and institutional components of imperialism, as I have tried to show, then it follows that their ultimate destruction will require the overthrow of imperialism. Furthermore, the international defeat of imperialism will compel a thorough-going racial and economic reorganization inside the U.S. When the U.S. can no longer monopolize the resources and labor of the exterior Third World, then it will no longer be possible to grant privileges to a minority of capitalists and white workers, and instead the entire labor force, led by domestic Third World workers, will have to be brought into the mainstream of economic life and political power. Of course, there is a real danger of a fascist reaction to imperialist decay, but if the fascists can be isolated and kept from power then for the first time in American history true economic democracy will replace the capitalist system of economic monopoly and privilege.

Today the major political and military forces capable of setting the stage for the final destruction of imperialism are gathering in the Third World. This is the chief dynamic of modern history. What does this maturing historical constellation imply concerning tasks thrust upon blacks and other colonized peoples in the U.S.? Does it place us in the role of mere spectators?

On the contrary, the domestic colonial population has a unique and crucial role to play in the dialectic of world revolution. Just as imperialism created the external forces capable of rolling it back, so did it also create the internal forces necessary to promote and consolidate domestic opposition to imperialism. The institutional arrangements of domestic colonialism have meant that millions of people in the U.S., the chief bulwark of imperialism, have been systematically excluded from the spoils of imperialist exploitation. The objective situation of black and brown people has left them little option but to oppose racism and imperialism with as much power as they can muster. This struggle has had many setbacks and defeats, but it is significant that the greatest advances in the struggle against domestic racial oppression have come in an era when imperialism is in forced retreat. Imperialism has thus created within itself an *independent ideological force,* a social force that gains strength as the tentacles of imperialism are pried loose from the Third World.

Not only does this independent ideological force exist, but it has also proven capable of precipitating large-scale social dislocations in American society. Over the past fifteen years the black struggle has acted as a catalyst, setting off revolts among other Third World groups, white youth, and women. In each case there were underlying economic questions, but the black liberation movement, directly or indirectly, provided the ideological trigger. This is most apparent in the ethnic revolts. Each of these groups has a long history of struggle, but it is quite apparent that the most recent phase of their activities bears a direct relationship to the black struggle.

The white youth revolt is directly traceable to three factors: (1) the black revolt against racism, (2) the Vietnamese struggle against imperialism, and (3) social dislocations caused by economic stagnation. While the third factor may be considered the most fundamental, it was the first two that shaped the ideological thinking of the student rebels.

Similarly, it was mainly among black and white women activists in the student and New Left movements that women's liberation got its start. The rapid growth of the women's movement was stimulated by the realization that in modern America, women, who comprise 51% of the population, are economically and socially exploited citizens. Presently this new movement is composed chiefly of middle-class white women who are angered by the limited job opportunities open to them and the stereotyped roles into which they are cast at home and at work. Yet the double oppression of working class white women—as the result of class and sex—and the triple oppression of Third World women—as the result of race, class, and sex—mean that the issue of women's equality has very far-reaching implications for American society as a whole.

We may say therefore that the black liberation movement has had a multiplier effect of its own, sending shock waves of social unrest throughout many strata of U.S. society. This is clearly one of the most outstanding, although largely unintended, results of the black movement. Moreover, it demonstrates forcefully that the black movement is fated to play a vanguard role in breaking down the ideological unity that imperialism has generated in American society. Earlier I noted that the ideological unity of the domestic population in support of imperialism was crucial to the continued survival of the imperialist system. Now we see that imperialism itself has generated social movements that are ripping apart its internal cohesion and laying the basis for a possible anti-imperialist coalition.

I say "possible" because it is all too obvious that many problems have cropped up. When we examine the contemporary situation we find that these various social movements often have serious conflicts with one another. The white movements, although they sprang from an anti-racist struggle, have been unwilling or unable to purge their own ranks of racism due to the long conditioning to social corruption fostered by imperialism, and this has cast doubt on their reliability. At the same time, some Third World groups (including some black organizations) have adopted an extreme form of nationalism that makes them hostile toward and unwilling to cooperate with other colonized groups, thereby closing off avenues for the multiplier effect. All of these movements, and their most recent offshoots, waste incredible amounts of time and energy arguing about who is more oppressed than whom—a debate which no doubt gives the white ruling class much to laugh about. This constant chaos and conflict poses serious problems for black leaders who recognize the historic necessity of a Third World-led anti-imperialist coalition in the United States.

Perhaps it is best to sort out these problems and then analyze each separately. First, there is a host of problems arising from black attempts to relate to white social reform movements. These problems have deep historical roots that are often overlooked in the search for instant answers. Secondly, there are problems that arise in our attempts to relate to other Third World groups, both inside and outside the borders of the U.S. Finally, interwoven with the other two are problems encountered in dealing with the white ruling class, e.g., the dangers arising from repression and co-optation.

The continuous development of the capitalist-imperialist system produces strains and conflicts which tend to split and divide the white population. Consequently reform movements spring up and address themselves to what they perceive as the injustices or unfair social dislocations caused by economic development. Very frequently blacks are hardest hit by these stresses in the social system. However, the pervasiveness of racism as an ideology usually prevents these reformers from adopting a sharply anti-racist position, unless they are confronted by independently organized militant blacks or other external forces. A few examples will clarify this point.

In the decades prior to the Civil War the growing tension between the slave-plantation system of the South and the industrial system of the North laid the basis for the development of a strong abolitionist movement. Composed chiefly of middle-class professionals and intellectuals, the white abolitionist movement opposed slavery but often accepted other elements of racism, such as the various colonization schemes aimed at deporting the black population. They accepted the racist contention that blacks were undesirable and should be removed. It was the black abolitionists, organized independently into the Negro Convention Movement, who confronted the white abolitionists and compelled them to oppose all attempts at colonization.

The fifty years between 1870 and 1920 witnessed the triumph of the industrial system, the consolidation of monopoly capital, and the rise of American imperialism. The effect of these developments was to undermine the old independent middle class of small farmers, professionals, and small businessmen which, until then, had been a major component of white America. At the same time Reconstruction was overthrown, and racial oppression settled even more heavily upon the black population of the South and the Asian population on the West Coast. Populism and the Progressive movement represented the revolt of the rural and urban middle classes against the encroachments of monopoly capital. In the South the Populists tried to gain control of state governments in order to impose restrictions and controls on the railroads, banks and other giant corporations whose monopoly practices were destroying the class of small farmers. In this campaign they turned to black voters for support.

The terrorism that accompanied the downfall of Reconstruction had effectively wiped out independent black political organizations in the South. Consequently, black farmers and sharecroppers, who were also victims of monopoly, found themselves virtually helpless pawns in a violent political struggle between Democrats and Populists. Both sides sought to control the black vote, and eventually they agreed to disenfranchise blacks altogether. Since blacks had no independent organizations (the black farmers' alliances, which had a total membership of one and a quarter million, were organized and controlled by the white rebels), they therefore lacked a base from which they could challenge the racism of the whites.

In the North militant blacks possessed an organizational base in the National Afro-American League and its successor, the Niagara Movement. However, these organizations were elitist; they represented the Talented Tenth and were largely divorced from the masses of black people. As a result these organizations tended to be weak and constantly on the brink of financial collapse. Consequently, they could be co-opted by the well-heeled white progressives who organized the NAACP. Despite their weaknesses, the independent militant black organizations played a crucial role, because they developed an anti-racist program, and they succeeded in getting the interracial NAACP, which was to wield much greater social and legislative influence, to adopt a watered-down version of this program.

Industrialization and urbanization also stimulated a large reform movement among middle-class white women who demanded the same rights and privileges as the men of their class. Middle-class black women also organized independently to demand their rights. However, middle-class black women by themselves were not strong enough to prevent the white women reformers from capitulating to racism as an expedient in gaining the vote for themselves.

All in all the upsurge of middle-class reformism at the turn of the century did not halt the advance of monopoly capital. Instead, it culminated in the creation of the modern corporate liberal state in which government and big business are partners. This new system works smoothly because of the regulatory laws and agencies introduced by the middle-class reformers. At the same time the white middle class itself was assured a secure niche as a professional, managerial and bureaucratic elite within the new system. As for blacks, these developments hardly represented a blessing. In the South, where black people had no independent organizations outside of the church, they were victimized by the white reformers. In the North, middle-class blacks organized independently, but they had no real power base. Nevertheless they did succeed in getting some of the white reformers in the NAACP and the National Urban League to oppose the more blatant manifestations of racism.

The Great Depression of the 1930s provoked another outburst of reform activities, this time among the white workers. The massive CIO organizing drives and the demand for social welfare legislation were aimed at protecting the working classes from economic disaster. During this period much attention was focused on black workers. There were two reasons for this. In the first place, black workers had made tremendous inroads into the mass production industries of the North and consequently they could not easily be ignored or excluded, as had been the policy of trade unions in the AFL. Secondly, many of the labor radicals of the CIO were influenced by the racial equality ideals of the Communist Party, which was very strong at that time. It should be remembered, however, that the racial policies of the CP were not homegrown. They were the product of Lenin's analysis of imperialism and national oppression, as interpreted by the Communist International. Thus we see another impact on the domestic scene of the international dialectical process.[8]

The period of racial enlightenment in the CIO lasted only a decade. The anti-Communist hysteria which followed World War II coincided with the launching of the CIO's southern organizing drive. The combination of virulent anti-Communists and aggressive white supremacists caused a turnabout in the CIO's policies. The leadership became more cautious and conservative, and all suspected radicals were purged. By the beginning of the 1950s the CIO was well along the path toward the political conservatism and bureaucracy that had always characterized the AFL.

Within the AFL the great proponent of racial equality was, of course, A. Philip Randolph. Randolph had organized the Brotherhood of Sleeping Car Porters Union in 1925. The Brotherhood not only sought to protect black porters, but it also provided Randolph with an independent base for attacking the racism of the AFL. The March on Washington Movement of 1941 represented another creative use of independent organizing which Randolph used to gain concessions from the federal government. Randolph's activities graphically demonstrated the value of independent organization at the mass level in confronting both white reformers and the white power structure.

This was also one of the main lessons of the civil rights movement. The civil rights movement began as an independent black struggle, but it started declining partly because it merged with white liberals and allowed them to call the shots. Black Power was a direct response to this situation. Black Power did not reject tactical alliances with white reformers, but it insisted that black groups

8. Of course this coin also had another side. Although the Communist Party advocated black self-determination, it consistently sought to manipulate the black movement to suit the foreign policy needs of the Soviet Union. Since there was no independent party of black socialists, this manipulation was not effectively challenged. Instead black Communists became disillusioned and tended to drop out of the movement altogether.

must maintain their organizational integrity and establish strong ties with a black community base.

These examples could be multiplied, but I think they are sufficient to establish that blacks must maintain independent mass-based organizations in dealing with white reform movements. Otherwise the needs of the black community will be totally ignored. Historically most white reformers refused to confront racism unless prodded into doing so by outside forces. Today we see the same story repeating itself in the peace movement, New Left, women's liberation, etc. Unless militant blacks possess an independent base they will be unable to impose the ideological leadership necessary to prevent these movements from becoming totally racist.

There are some who say we should ignore so-called progressive or radical forces in the white community because they are in fact racist. While the pervasiveness of racism cannot be denied, I think it is politically very short-sighted to take this position. There are several reasons why we must struggle to inject our ideological and survival concerns into white reform movements. In the first place, we have an obvious stake in any changes which are brought about in the social, economic and political conditions in the U.S. White reform movements have played a key role in precipitating such changes in the past and probably will continue to do so in the immediate future. Hence we cannot afford to ignore them. Secondly, the activities of white reformers often create rifts within the white community and the white power structure. Such splits in the white community can open new options for the black freedom movement by expanding our area of maneuverability. Therefore, it is again imperative that we actively seek to influence and guide the social change forces in white society.

Finally, we must constantly bear in mind that we have a long-term reason for dealing with white social reformers. Not only do we want to gain some tangible benefits for the black community, which is no different from our objective in dealing with the white power structure, but there is an additional consideration posed by the fact that reform movements are a manifestation of strains and contradictions within the capitalist-imperialist system. Insofar as we are concerned with basically transforming the system then we must seek to maximize those of its internal tensions that are progressive in character. Social reformers are to a greater or lesser extent alienated from and critical of the dominant social system. Each time we effectively challenge the racism of progressive reformers we thus heighten a basic ideological contradiction in the system. Moreover, we must unceasingly push white social reformers to perceive the connection between racism and imperialism. The ideological struggle against racism can thereby become an effective weapon in undermining the legitimacy of imperialism and the internal unity of the imperialist state. As I argued earlier, breaking the internal cohesion of imperialist nations is a key factor in the ultimate dismantling of imperialism.

I am not suggesting here that individual black people should dash out and join white reform movements. On the contrary, as individuals we have no power and will only be absorbed and ignored. We do, however, have a political responsibility to ourselves and to our brothers and sisters in the Third World to make every effort to shape the ideological development and practice of white reformers. Since we live in imperialism's strongest fortress, this task is of urgent importance. Past experience shows that this task demands independent mass-based organizations which can effectively confront and challenge white reformers, and white society generally, at every step of the way. Hence it is imperative that we continue building militant black organizations and institutions that can provide this kind of independent base for black leadership. But only by institutionalizing channels of communication between these independent black organizations and social reform groups can we maximize the multiplier effect, disseminating anti-racist and anti-imperialist thinking throughout the more progressive segments of American society.

In assessing our relationship with other Third World groups in the U.S. today, the chief problem we encounter is extreme nationalism, which fosters jealousy, rivalry, and dissension. We have already seen the debilitating effects of extreme arrogance and nationalism in the black movement. Bickering and name-calling have escalated into fratricidal violence. The combatants seem to forget that while they may have legitimate ideological differences, the main enemy is still the white ruling class and its allies. Among Third World groups extreme nationalism promotes cultural arrogance between different but equally oppressed ethnic groups. It therefore hinders the development of a unified struggle of all colonized peoples against capitalist and imperialist oppression. The only people who can benefit from such divisions are the white oppressors.

It is therefore incumbent upon militant blacks to establish working relationships with their counterparts in various Third World communities in order to build viable alliances. Certainly there are legitimate differences in political consciousness and economic development between different Third World communities. But all these communities share parallel histories of domestic colonialism, and this creates an objective basis for unity among Third World militants. Black and other Third World leaders must seek to realize this potential unity by actively opposing chauvinist tendencies within their own communities, and by establishing working links between militant Third World organizations.

Our relationship to the Third World outside of the U.S. is somewhat different. The main struggle in the world today is between imperialism and the nations seeking to break out of imperialist bondage. As I have argued, the fate of black people is linked to the outcome of the world struggle. In this international conflict black and other ethnic groups in the U.S. are not the leaders. On the contrary, we must look to anti-imperialist Third World nations and national liberation movements to gain a perspective if we are not to fall into serious political errors. Again it is the Pan-African movement which can serve to illustrate my point.

The early Pan-African movement, led by black Americans and West Indians, attempted to build a racial unity of all black people without regard to class or political ideology. This movement helped give birth to African nationalism and the African independence movements. Imperialism responded to these developments by creating class divisions within African nations that could be exploited by the imperialists. Thus, an African bourgeoisie arose which in effect became an internal enemy of genuine African liberation. Kwame Nkrumah has summed up this neo-colonial situation: "Political independence did not bring to an end economic oppression and exploitation. Nor did it end foreign political interference. The neo-colonialist period begins when international monopoly finance capital, working through the indigenous bourgeoisie, attempts to secure an even tighter stranglehold over the economic life of the contingent than was exercised during the colonial period." [9]

According to Nkrumah, who is the foremost contemporary leader of Pan-Africanism, this new stage of imperialism has necessitated a class and ideological struggle within Africa. Racial unity alone is no answer to neo-colonialism.

Pan-Africanists and other militant blacks in the U.S. may study and attempt to understand the implications of these developments. To the extent that domestic imperialism is a reflection of international imperialism, the tactics of neo-colonialism will have repercussions in our own communities. This is a point which I have argued in detail in my book, *Black Awakening in Capitalist America*.[10] I will not repeat that argument here. Suffice it to say that monopoly capital is in fact fostering class divisions within the black community in an effort to recruit black people who will cooperate in exploiting the black community by acting as a buffer group. Al-

9. Kwame Nkrumah, *Class Struggle in Africa*. New York: International Publishers, 1970, p. 87.

10. Garden City, N.Y.: Doubleday-Anchor, 1970.

though this neo-colonial tactic is not as far advanced in the U.S. as it is in Africa; it still poses a real threat, and we must develop a clear understanding of its meaning. Moreover, we must develop organizational forms, such as an independent black political party, which can combat these insidious tactics. Again, we would do well to look to anti-imperialist Third World movements to gain a better perspective on our own situation.

Of course, it may be objected that we cannot look to Third World movements for leadership because these movements have many ideological differences with one another. How are we to pick and choose among them? Certainly differences exist on a number of specific questions in the Third World. Our job, however, is not to decide which Third World movement has a corner on absolute truth. Rather our task is to study and learn from the *general* experience of Third World struggles and to apply this *general* knowledge to our particular situation.

For example, the whole history of Third World national liberation struggles points up the necessity of steadfastly opposing imperialism in all of its guises. It is impossible to compromise with imperialism, because it does not accept genuine compromises. It may change its method but not its purpose. This chameleon-like quality also exists in domestic forms of imperialism and presents special problems for black leadership. As U.S. imperialism suffers setbacks around the world, the white ruling class can be expected to do everything in its power to maintain the internal unity of American society. There are two extreme forms that this process can take.

On the one hand the white ruler may openly embrace fascism and attempt to brutally repress all dissident elements. This danger calls for a careful historical analysis of those forces in American society that might tend to support or oppose the development of fascism. Such an analysis should not be made in isolation. Rather it should draw upon the experiences of African and other Third World movements that have had to struggle against fascism; and it should attempt to assess fascism as part of an international dialectic. Once such an analysis is made then black militant leaders must act to deepen the ideological understanding and commitment of all anti-fascist social forces in the U.S. On the other hand the white rulers may choose co-optation instead of repression. As a last-ditch effort, the black communities may be offered a slice of the imperialist pie in return for supporting imperialism. This is like a wagon train of white settlers surrounded by an overwhelming force of Indians who then offer their black slaves "freedom" and "equality" in return for helping the whites fight the Indians. Because imperialism is in crisis, offers such as this are little better than death warrants. Racial integration will not save the U.S. imperialism, but it could conceivably commit black people to the defense of a dying imperialist system. Black leaders must therefore be vigilant against and undermine the attempt to attach ideological strings to any concessions the white power structure may offer the black community.

Repression and co-optation are well established in the tradition of imperialist oppression. I contend that by studying the history and ideological development of Third World struggles we can learn much that will aid our own struggle for independence. In this sense we will be responding to and effectively allying with Third World struggles—not mechanically marching in lockstep, but creatively applying a general body of accumulated experience to our specific situation.

What I have offered here is obviously no program, but a perspective. It is a perspective that attempts to sort out in at least rough terms the main dynamics of modern world history and to locate the black struggle within this broader context. As such it is a perspective which I think should be borne in mind as we formulate concrete strategies and programs, because it gives us a valid way of assessing our actions aside from the question of their immediate "success" or "failure." This is not to imply that success and failure are irrelevant, only that they are relative. The fact that Marcus Garvey was confused on some questions and that his movement eventually collapsed does not mean that we should discount Garveyism as a failure. On the contrary, Garveyism inspired more politically mature forms of black nationalism both in U.S. and Africa. Despite its weaknesses, Garveyism was on balance an important contributor to the world struggle against imperialist domination.

This paper has tried to show that the black freedom movement is intimately tied up with the political-economic dialectic operating between imperialism and national liberation movements on a world scale. In this dialectic the leaders of black and other colonized peoples in the U.S. have a special role to play, because these groups represent the main contemporary domestic forces that are objectively opposed to imperialism and racism. Although by ourselves it is doubtful that we have the power to topple the system and end our oppression, as part of the world dialectic our independent struggles within the U.S. still can play a key role in undermining the hegemony of the imperialist ideology and thus weaken imperialism itself. This task demands organizational integrity and working relationships between black and other Third World groups, both within and outside the U.S.

Although this is an ideological struggle, it does not operate solely in the realm of ideas. On the contrary, to attack all institutional manifestations of racism in employment, housing, education, etc., is in fact to challenge the ideology of racism. In this manner our domestic struggle for survival will itself become a vital contribution toward not only our own liberation but also toward the liberation of our brothers and sisters in Africa, Asia, and Latin America.

8

Black Politics:
Third Force, Third Party
or Third-Class Influence?

CHUCK STONE

In this era of the Black Revolution—a period that demands revolutionary action and a break with the conventional modes of action of a white racist system—black people have yet to formulate a precise *modus operandi* for the acquisition of power and the politics of survival.

We have gotten hung up on militant rhetoric that is a marvelously emotional bowel movement, but a non-fulfilling nourishment for life. Because American honkiedom has been so totally oppressive in its programming of black people into a separate but equal subculture, the understandable conclusion has developed in the black community that the present system is so bad: (1) it must be completely overhauled, and (2) change should be effected by working outside the system and not utilizing any of the apparatus of the system. Its values should be rejected and its political methods eschewed. As Mao Tse-tung wrote: "What my enemy affirms, I reject. What my enemy rejects, I affirm."

That defines a philosophical parameter for action, but in the

CHUCK STONE, writer and political analyst, is the author of *Black Political Power in America* and of the novel *King Strut*. From 1965 to 1967 he was Special Assistant to Adam Clayton Powell, then Chairman of the House Education and Labor Committee. He has edited a number of newspapers, among them *The Chicago Daily Defender*, of which he was Editor in Chief 1963-64. Chuck Stone recently resigned from his position as Director of Minority Affairs of the Educational Testing Service, Princeton, New Jersey. Brother Stone is presently a columnist for the *Philadelphia Daily News*, in addition to doing radio and television commentaries, teaching and writing.

unique experience of the black American, a rejection of the apparatus of the majority leaves no alternative. If black people refuse to operate within the system in the belief they will be co-opted, what kind of alternatives are open to acquire black power and insure black survival?

The road to success in fulfilling the black revolutionary imperative is neither ideologically singular nor operationally monolithic. It is divergent, many-splendored and filled with options. Here again, Mao is instructive. "A revolution does not march a straight line. It wanders where it can, retreats before superior forces, advances wherever it has room, attacks whenever the enemy retreats or bluffs, and above all, is possessed of enormous patience."

If that political sentiment makes sense—and the possession of enormous patience is always a requisite in the ultimate achievement of any people's liberation—then we should examine how black people can rise to a position of massive political empowerment that does three things: controls the black community, proportionately controls the decision-making apparatus of a white racist government and guarantees black survival. This can only be done by acquiring political power. There is no other course.

Political power is government control or the ability to decide who shall control.

Black political power, a direct function of numerical weakness, is limited solely to the ability to infrequently influence that control and then, only on the most peripheral levels. Black political power has rarely been in the forefront of controlling or influencing the control of government. White political power has maintained a monopoly on the apparatus of control by winning elections and in so doing, demeaning black political power.

Ever since 1860, national elections have been won by one of the two major parties, the Democrats or the Republicans. They have done so by putting together the broadest base of the electorate. The history of American politics, however, demonstrates that both third parties and "third forces" have occasionally been able to disrupt the dreary normalcy of the two-party system by doing one of two things:

(1) Becoming a dominant force in itself. When the Republican Party was formed in 1854, it was a "third party," but within six years it became one of the two major parties. In 1912, however, this same Republican Party was an object lesson that no major party can survive a strong third party challenge. Theodore Roosevelt's liberal "Progressive Party" split the Republican national vote almost in half by polling 4,216,000 votes to GOP nominee William H. Taft's 3,483,932 votes. The Democrats' Woodrow Wilson

thus won the Presidency with 6,286,214 votes—a million and a half votes less than the combined total of the two Republican candidates.

(2) Becoming a cohesive force which shifts its political loyalty as a "balance of power," either as a "third force" or as a Third Party. The "third force" has been successfully practiced by the Catholic vote, the Jewish vote and the labor vote. A Third Party has dominated New York state and city politics in the form of the Liberal Party and was the one political instrument Mayor Lindsay was able to use as a respectable base for his re-election after he had been rejected by his own Republican Party.

The black vote—or more properly called today "the Negro vote" because black people are still voting as "Negroes"—has rarely affected the outcome of an election. In some of the major cities, there is increasing evidence that this myopia is being cured, and black people are demonstrating a ferocious commitment to black political unity. But, nationally, black people are owned lock, stock and barrel by the Democratic Party, which has as much contempt for them as it has Governor Wallace and Richard Nixon.

The reason the "Negro vote" has rarely decided the outcome of an election is because of its political ignorance and blind single-party loyalty. For example, in 1932 and 1936, when Americans voted overwhelmingly for a Democratic President, black people in opposite numbers voted for the Republican candidate because a Republican President had freed their ancestors 70 years before. They were still paying political booty. Then, in 1952 and 1956, America shifted its political sentiment and voted in equally overpowering numbers for a Republican President, but black people voted Democratic 74% and 77% respectively in those two elections. This time, they were paying political booty to a Democratic President who had put food in their stomachs.

Only in the 1960 Presidential election, did black people play a decisive role for the first time in history in a national election. Kennedy won by 116,550 votes out of a total 63,335,642, in effect a split vote. But Kennedy was able to capture 77% of the national black vote, winning three key states, Illinois, South Carolina and Texas, by the exact margins of the cohesive black vote for a total of 69 electoral votes and the Presidency.

Today, political powerlessness dominates black communities. Bearing in mind that black people represent 12% of the population, look at the unhappy statistics of black politics:

United States Congress: Of 435 Representatives, only 9 or 2% are black, of 100 Senators only one or 1% is black, and it is an absurdity to characterize him as a black man, since he spends most of his political energy trying to justify his non-involvement as a black man. He is, in reality, a colored honkie.

Federal Government: Of 77 independent federal agencies, not one is headed by a black man. Nor is there a black cabinet official.

State governments: In only one state, Connecticut, does a black man hold one of the major elective offices of the state.

Municipal governments: Of the 130 cities with 100,000 or more population, only two (1.5%) have black mayors, Cleveland and Gary. *Yet, 39% of all black people are concentrated in the 10 largest cities in America.* What a fantastic power base! In 10 years, all 10 of these cities— New York, Chicago, Los Angeles, Philadelphia, Detroit, Baltimore, Houston, Cleveland, Washington, D.C. and St. Louis could have black mayors. At the present time, Cleveland has a black mayor and Washington, D.C. has a Presidentially appointed "Negro" whose shuffle is among the most fastidious in American politics.

In light of the history of white political contempt for black political power, the issue of amassing black political power reduces itself to one question. How can black people achieve lasting and total political power under the present white racist system that is becoming increasingly oppressive and aggressively hostile—as a Third Force, a Third Party or by remaining within the two-party system as a third-class influence?

By continuing to do the latter, black political power can only be a third-class influence, because predictable loyalty is always expendable and is rarely rewarded or cultivated.

As Adam Clayton Powell pointed out in Point 4 of his 17-point "Black Position Paper" issued in 1965: "The black masses must demand and refuse to accept nothing less than that proportionate share of political jobs and appointments which are equal to their proportion in the electorate. Where we are 20% of the voters, we should command 20% of the top jobs, 20% of the judgeships, 20% of the commissionerships and 20% of all political appointments."

In no major political situation in America—since Reconstruction— has Point 4 ever been fulfilled.

But this proportionate control of the political process has been manipulated by the Irish, the Italians, the Jews and the Polish in virtually every major city in America. Ethnic bloc voting and ethnic political loyalty has been a feverish adjunct of every ethnic group in America except black people. We've been too busy trying to get "integrated" and listening to the black surrogates of white racism such as Roy Wilkins, Whitney Young and Bayard Rustin instead of trying to build political power bases.

Take Chicago. That city's 298,000 Polish-Americans comprise *one-ninth* of the population. Chicago's 980,000 black people comprise *one-third.*

Yet, political power in Chicago's Congressional representation is precisely diametric. Of Chicago's 9 Congressmen, only one, or one-ninth, is black and three, or one-third, are Polish-Americans.

That's black powerlessness. Chicago should have three black Congressmen and only one Polish Congressman.

But blind single-party loyalty has permitted this political charade.

Blind single-party loyalty has given black voters only nine black Congressmen out of 435.

Blind single-party loyalty enabled the Democrats, with impunity, to get rid of the highest elected black official in America in 1960, Manhattan Borough President Hulan E. Jack.

Blind single-party loyalty encouraged the Democrats to strip the most powerful black politician, Adam Clayton Powell, of his committee chairmanship, kick him unconstitutionally out of the Congress and in effect, tell all the black voters in America, if you don't like it, kiss both our Democratic and Republican asses!

Aware that black people are compulsively loyal to one party, the Republicans neither want nor are wooing their political favor. Instead, they are hard at work getting the concentration camps ready for the black populace. The Nixon administration had served notice on black people that as far as it is concerned, black people are not only subhuman, they just don't exist in the political spectrum.

Taken together, these historical and contemporary instances represent a depressing confluence of the black man's third-class influence within the two-party system.

To exchange that status for first-class influence, first-class power and first-class control, black people have no choice but to become either an independent "Third Force" or a Third Party where the peculiar circumstances of the loyal community warrant it.

A Third Force is, by definition, independent, unpredictable and totally black-oriented. It asks only one question: what do you intend to do for black people? A "Third Force" is a cohesive vote which oscillates at will between the candidacies of a Democrat, a Republican or a Third Party black man, depending upon which one the black Third Party can more effectively control. (A black Third Party is not going to be able to control an Uncle Tom, nor is he going to want their support.)

Another principal advantage of the black Third Force is its flexibility in forming alliances. As a continuing balance of power force in politics, the Third Force must be prepared to accept the logic of an alliance with radical or liberal white groups that will establish a coalition of unassailable political strength. It is irresponsibly visionary for blacks to believe that they alone can sway the political process without some coalition with whites committed to the same goals of radicalizing the existing society. This does not suggest that without white allies a black Third Force could not be a determinant of election outcomes. But it does postulate the thesis that for optimum political strength over a long haul, an occasional alliance with white groups will maximize the Third Force's ability to achieve its end for black people. The important factor here is flexibility to do either.

America is entering an era started under the Johnson administration and one which the Nixon administration is neurotically pursuing with a vengeance.

It is the era of White Consensus politics.

"Come, let us reason together," exhorted Lyndon Johnson in a terrible bastardization of the sentiments of one of the greatest Biblical prophets. What Mr. Johnson really meant was come and reason *my* way or I'll knock the hell out of your side.

Mr. Nixon has now called on the American white class to unite under his banner of White Consensus. Although he denies this is his purpose, he is attempting to create a climate in which dissent is unpopular, opposition is unhealthy and blackness is unpretty. There is no room for black people in Mr. Nixon's society except in the subculture of their underclass. Responding to white middle-class America's demands to resist any further "encroachments" by blacks on the bastions of white power, the Nixon administration will religiously foster and preserve a society which prepares Americans to accept the morality if not the practicality of black preventative detention areas, similar to the reservations now occupied by the Indians and concentration camps inhabited by the Japanese-Americans during World War II.

Anticipating the gruesome possibility of the era of White Consensus, black people must begin to form a Third Force or Third Party that maximizes their political strength. They will be unable to turn to the Democratic Party, since the Democratic Party must move in the identical direction in order to recapture those white voters who have become disenchanted with the so-called "liberal" tendencies of Democrats. In a political atmosphere of repression, the smart politician adopts some of the same coloration of the repressor in order to win votes.

As such, black people owe no loyalty to either of the major political parties, because there is absolutely no difference between the two. This was dramatically illustrated in the 1968 Presidential campaign. Nixon and Humphrey differed only in style, not in convictions. One of Humphrey's closest political advisers was a practicing white supremacist. Vice President Agnew is a Republican carbon copy of Democratic Mayor Richard Daley. They're both political neanderthals whose mental processes are stimulated by the cloacal juices of their spleen. The movement toward the establishment of concentration camps for black people which both Attorney General Mitchell and his deputy, Kleindienst, have implicitly reserved on their agenda, began in the Johnson administration.

While a black Third Force must become operative in most major cities, a Black Political Party—what I have tentatively called the Liberation Party—must be formed on a national level. This gives an additional *option* to black people in the political process.

In those cities where there has been a history of periodic oscillations in power between the Democrats and the Republicans, the Liberation Party can become an instrument of power at the local level.

Where black politicians elect to work *within* the system by remaining a Democrat or a Republican, black people should only support them if—and this is important—if they are responsive first to black people, are responsible first to black people and place the black community first in their commitment to the political process. It is exceedingly critical to black unity that we accept the right of black politicians to exercise *their* options for black people. We must not disavow those black politicians who are determined to remain relevant to the black community and who, in the words of Maulana Ron Karenga, accept their blackness as their ultimate reality.

Thus, in addition to Harlem's Congressman Adam Clayton Powell, Brooklyn's Congresswoman Shirley Chisholm, Detroit's Congressman Charles Diggs, Jr. and St. Louis' Congressman William Clay are just a few examples of black politicians who have placed the welfare and political empowerment of the black community first in the use of black politics.

At the same time, they cannot but help be educated in their thinking and political activities if a black Third Force or Liberation Party manages to either win an election or be the fulcrum in that election's outcome. Just the existence of the Third Force and the Liberation Party is going to enable some party-loyal black politicians to extract more from their political base than would ordinarily be expected. They still will not be able to revolutionize the political process, but they will be compelled to move toward black unity. And as long as black people are the principal beneficiaries, we should have no quarrel with their slowness of foot. They will eventually come on board the ship of black nationhood.

The main task before us, however, is the establishment of a black Third Force and a Liberation Party controlled by black people.

They represent the development of new political options. We

must unleash a *proliferation of political options* that allows black people the same political flexibility that has characterized the rise of white ethnic political power in America.

- We must acquire a political sophistication that not only disciplines and empowers but punishes and extracts its pound of political flesh when we have betrayed.
- We must plunge into the political process, learning how to manipulate and control.
- We must become a strong political striking force that prepares the foundation for the ultimate achievement of a Third World dedicated to the love of humanity, the dignity of each individual and the unity of all peace-loving peoples.
- We must plant our own flag and affirm our nationhood to insure black survival and preserve our black heritage.

Those are the goals of black politics in America.

The most magnificent drama in the last thousand years of human history is the transportation of ten million human beings out of the dark beauty of their mother continent into the new-found Eldorado of the West. They descended into Hell; and in the third century they arose from the dead, in the finest effort to achieve democracy for the working millions which this world had ever seen. It was a tragedy that beggared the Greek; it was an upheaval of humanity like the Reformation and the French Revolution. Yet we are blind and led by the blind. We discern in it no part of our labor movement; no part of our industrial triumph; no part of our religious experience. Before the dumb eyes of ten generations of ten million children, it is made mockery of and spit upon; a degradation of the eternal mother; a sneer at human effort; with aspiration and art deliberately and elaborately distorted. And why? Because in a day when the human mind aspired to a science of human action, a history and psychology of the mighty effort of the mightiest century, we fell under the leadership of those who would compromise with truth in the past in order to make peace in the present and guide policy in the future.

W. E. B. DUBOIS, *Black Reconstruction*

IV

ECONOMICS

1

Black Labor and the
Black Liberation Movement

JOHN OLIVER KILLENS

Between us club members in the Brotherhood of Blackness, it is no
secret that the Black Liberation Movement is running out of steam.
The civil rights integrationist organizations are deathly stricken
with senility and obsolescence. The Black Power detachments are
at the moment powerless. "Race riots" as a form of struggle have
become a terrible bore to the sophisticated white establishment.
Indeed, in many cases, the metropolitan police forces looked forward eagerly to those famous long hot summers as a means of killing off a few of the "natives" and as proving grounds for testing
new anti-riot weapons. Witness also the current plight of the Pan-
thers in all their heroic innocence. Beautiful, desperate black
youth are now referring to the "lumpen element" of the black
community as the most dependable source from which a vanguard
will spring forth to spur the revolution onward, a revolution that
has not really gotten underway, rumors to the contrary. It is
suicidally naive to depend on lumpen elements to spark the "revolution." It is precisely this group that helps to bring dope into the
community, snatches pocketbooks, mugs helpless old black women,
hustles young black women for white men, makes the streets unsafe
for black mothers. The winos and dope addicts may very well be
pathetic and worthy of our deep compassion, but they, like all the

JOHN O. KILLENS teaches creative writing at Columbia University. He is also
a professor of creative writing at Howard University. He is renowned as a
novelist and essayist. His works include *Odds Against Tomorrow, Black Man's
Burden, Youngblood, 'Sippi,* and *And Then We Heard the Thunder.* Killens
studied at Columbia University and Howard University Law School before
turning to writing as a career. For two years he was Writer-in-Residence at
Fisk University. His recent novel, *Cotillion,* has been wide aclaimed. His latest
publication is *Great Gittin' Up in the Morning,* a book for children on the life
of Denmark Vesey.

other lumpens, are the ranks from which the police get most of their informers. We romanticize the lumpen at our gravest peril.

"Revolutionary suicide" has become a slogan for some young and righteous "militants," a slogan born of pure and tragic desperation, and no less desperate or futile or unrealistic for all its purity of purpose and nobility of posture and righteousness of cause. "Revolutionary suicide" is about as realistic in terms of furthering the liberation of black people as Buddhist immolation by fire has been in ending the war in Vietnam. It should be clear by now that wars of liberation are not won by death wishes or "Because God is on our side," or "Ours is a just cause."

As the Bible reports, and a Negro spiritual sings beautifully of, the prophet Ezekiel might very well have seen wheels way up in the middle of the air, but the wheels of liberation and revolution do not run by faith, nor do they run by the grace of God. The wheels of liberation run by power, manpower, a power generated and kept in motion by the exploited, disinherited masses. Muscles, brains, blood, sweat. A vanguard is worthless without troops committed to the struggle.

Brown-versus-the-Board-of-Education, Montgomery, Little Rock, Freedom Rides, Sit-Ins, Lowndes County, Oakland, Harlem, Watts, Washington, Detroit; all were great historic moments in the black man's freedom struggle. Moreover, they were necessary and inevitable moments in the evolution of our struggle from one level of revolutionary sophistication to another. Men like Stokely Carmichael, Cleveland Sellers, Rap Brown and Stanley Wise put their lives on the line in the name of non-violence and integration before they moved to the higher level of struggle under the banner of Black Power. Each level had its own integrity. Historically, this kind of evolving development is legitimate and inevitable. Martin Luther King was an authentic leader of the black movement, which is probably why the white establishment is not satisfied with destroying him physically, but has also decided now to assassinate the memory of the dead Messiah. It is a very peculiar bit of irony and white sophistication the way the white establishment is apparently quite willing to make a saint out of Malcolm and a devil out of Martin. The white boy is a gaming dude. Witness the job *Time* magazine is doing on a black hero who a few years ago was their "Man of the Year."

All this is by way of saying that in order for a people to move forward they must understand their past, even their immediate past. A people ignorant of their history are condemned to repeat their history. And we black folk cannot afford that kind of deadly repetition. As legitimate and heroic as the movement has been since the

1954 Supreme Court decision, there have been major weaknesses from then till now.

But one of the major weaknesses has been the lack of a black dynamic organized-labor force in the ranks of the Movement as well as in its leadership. Millions of black men and women now stand in the ranks of labor. These are troops needed desperately in the freedom struggle. It is past time now for them to step forward and give their strength and leadership to the Liberation Movement. The vanguard is beautiful, dramatic, inspirational and necessary, but the army is where it's at. The key question is—How many troops can you put in the field? Afro-American labor can become the Great Black Hope. But first, or simultaneously, they must liberate themselves from the Great White Father bosses of the American labor movement. This in itself is a formidable task. I know, because I was once a union organizer.

The whole history of the American labor movement has been a history of white racism and apartheid. From the American Knights of Labor and the American Federation of Labor to the Congress of Industrial Organizations, black men have been second, third and fourth-class citizens in the labor movement. For a couple of very brief moments in the history of labor in the U.S.A., it seemed that the working class might live up to its "historic" commitment, i.e., to liberate the nation. The AFL was always openly racist and anti-skilled labor. But in the thirties, when the young dynamic CIO (Congress of Industrial Organizations) was born, everywhere they shouted the slogans: Organize the unorganized!" "Black and white, unite and fight!" In its constitution, the CIO declared piously that black and white labor would be organized on the basis of equality. There would be no jim crow locals in the CIO. I recall as a young man of about twenty years attending a congress of black people in Washington, D.C., and John L. Lewis (then International President of the CIO) wrapping himself in the star spangled banner and screaming to thousands of gathered blacks: "Organize! Organize! Organize!" Lewis was probably the last of the authentic American labor leaders of any national stature.

Black men stood side by side with their white counterparts and fought and bled to build the CIO and industrial unionism. They were a decisive force in organizing auto plants at Detroit and the Chicago slaughter and packinghouses. They were the main organizing force at Bessemer in Alabama, where they paid some terrible dues. It was already three strikes against you if you were black in Alabama, but to be a black "commonist" CIO union agitator was to call down the wrath of the southern gods, to invite the KKK and lynching and the tar-and-feather. Blacks bled and died at

Bessemer to bring the union to the steel mills. The industrial unions promised black people everything and gave them disillusionment.

In the forties, of course, came the "patriotic war" and the complete sell-out of the trade union movement and the rest of the so-called left wing and progressive moments. It was a time of no-strike pledges. It was a time when the struggle for Black Liberation should have gone full speed ahead, but instead, it slowed down to a crawl. It was all-out for the war effort to defeat Fascism. Everything was going to be peaches and cream after the war ended. Blacks would be given their freedom automatically. No longer would labor be exploited. Supposedly, we were going lickety-split into the era of "Progressive Capitalism." Can you dig it?

The bubble burst after the war. Labor had lost considerable ground, American capital had become all-powerful throughout the world. The CIO made another brief commitment to the under-classes. In the latter half of the forties, the CIO put together "Operation Dixie." They would go into the basically unorganized South-land and organize the unorganized. They would put together an organizing drive that would be based on the proposition that all men are created equal, and that labor with white skin could never be free as long as labor in black skin was in chains. Karl Marx had made a similar statement about a century before. Booker T. Washington said essentially the same thing when he said that in order for the white man to keep the black man in the ditch he, the white man, would have to stay in the ditch on top of the black man.

Historically, the American bosses of industry had set white workers against black workers and vice versa, the easier to exploit them both. The employers would tell the white workers, "Don't let the niggers into your union, they'll think they're as good as you are. Pretty soon they'll be marrying your daughters." The whites agreed, kept the blacks out of their unions. When the unions struck for higher wages and better working conditions, the bosses would entice the blacks to be strike breakers with: "Why should you support the white workers' strike? They wouldn't let you join their union. You don't owe them crackers no loyalty." The blacks agreed and came to work until the strike was broken, at which time the white workers came back at the same low wages, and blacks went back to join the ranks of the unemployed, black and white workers hating each other more than ever. The name of the game was *divide and conquer.*

Karl Marx, great European philosopher that he undoubtedly was, made a fundamental mistake in his evaluation of the role of labor vis-a-vis national liberation. He appeared to think that the revolutions would first occur in those countries having a high degree of industrialization. The revolutions have in fact occurred in countries where the economies were basically agrarian, i.e., Russia, China, Cuba, etc. He reckoned without taking into consideration the absolute corruption of the white working classes in the highly industrialized countries, England, Germany, U.S.A., etc. The working classes in these countries, especially England, France and America, ate high on the hog precisely because of the super-exploitation of the so-called "native" populations, the so-called "niggers" of the earth. Marx reckoned, without fully appreciating, the influence of racism and colonialism on the white working classes of the world.

When the CIO's *Operation Dixie* came into the Southland, blacks mistook it for the Freedom Train and leaped aboard by the thousands. *Operation Dixie* came to my home town, Macon, Georgia. Black folks got aboard the "Freedom Train." Workers, teachers, preachers got on board. An elderly black businessman, Larkin Marshall, threw his support behind the organizing drive, despite the fact that it did not affect him directly (he was not a worker), and in spite of warnings from the white establishment of Macon to him and others to "stay away from that union mess. It's nothing but a whole lot of commonism!" His newspaper backed the organizing drive, and the white establishment put it out of business. Black churches opened their doors to the *Operation*. One of the largest black churches in town, the one I grew up in, was a regular meeting place for the union. And what happened? The CIO kept its word. It did not bar blacks from the union. In fact, it organized the blacks. It emphasized the blacks. Of an evening white and black organizers could be seen visiting and proselytizing in the black neighborhoods, but practically no one went into the white neighborhoods. The white organizers had no stomach for struggling with the white racism which was rampant in the white community. Therefore, the drive resulted in an all-black union. The boss could still divide and conquer.

Years later, the young people of SNCC and CORE met the same problem. White and black young folk worked in the black communities of Mississippi and the rural South, where it was relatively safe. But where were the white troops ready to do missionary work to civilize the ignorant white masses and struggle with their racist attitude? Larkin Marshall told me once, "Hell, son, them union people seemed to think it was a Negro problem. But it's a white problem. It always has been. We always been ready for the country to be free ever since the first black slave set foot on this devilish land." The fact of the matter was—black folk didn't need anybody to come into their neighborhoods and tell them they were exploited. They knew they were. It was the backward whites who thought their whiteness was some kind of charm or juju which warded off all kinds of evil spirits, including poverty and exploitation. *Operation Dixie* failed because the CIO did not see itself as a force of liberation. *Operation Dixie* failed because the CIO played footsie with the racism of the white working class.

At how many international AFL conventions did A. Philip Randolph speak to deaf ears about the unions' jim crow policies? It was a ritual that they tolerated year after year. "Let Randolph have the floor, and then go on as we have always done," was the attitude. At the so-called left wing and progressive international trade unions, civil rights were usually the last thing on the agenda of the last day of the convention, when all the important issues had been settled, when half the delegates were leaving for home and the other half were restless to be on their way. If a group of black trade unionists called together a black caucus before or during the convention, everybody else got uptight. The brothers getting the caucus together were accused of racism, black nationalism, discrimination-in-reverse, anti-leadership tendencies and so on. We were the terrible black racists of 1948. We hear the same song being sung today. "Segregation-in-reverse," "crow jim" and so on. We even hear some black civil rights brothers mouthing such sentences as, "Black racism is just as bad as white racism." We went down that road twenty years ago. But a people ignorant of their history are condemned to repeat it.

Let us look at one of the more "progressive and liberal" trade unions in the country. Take the United Auto Workers for example. Sure, during the bus boycott in Montgomery, Reuther's union contributed monies, moral support and a couple or more station wagons to the cause. Reuther spoke at the historic March on Washington in 1963. The auto international can be depended on to pay lip service to the cause of civil rights. But about a decade ago, some black brothers in the union took notice of the glaring lack of color on the auto union's international Executive Board, and the brothers raised the issue with the union leadership. Whereupon Mr. Reuther came forth with his famous color-blind statement. To paraphrase: "In this union we do not practice color prejudice. On this board there are no black men, there are no white men. There are only human beings."

Apparently, the pallor of the Executive Board was merely a coincidence. Or, more likely, the black brothers were considered not within the pale of humankind. Two years ago, a Detroit friend of mine, black ex-labor leader, told me, "They used to say that Detroit was run by the Big Three—Ford, Chrysler and General Motors. But now they say the Big Four—Ford, Chrysler, General Motors and

General Reuther." He said further, "Ironically enough, Reuther's political power in the Democratic Party is based on the black workers of Detroit. Most of the white workers have moved to the suburbs and are voting Republican." It could be added that many of them are voting George Wallace. Obviously it is time for black workers to flex their black muscles and begin to exert the power that is potentially theirs.

In New York City, unions like District 65 and Local 1199 wear an aura of militancy and liberal respectability about them, because they pay lip-service identification to the Black Liberation Movement. It is a respectability they do not deserve. Historically, 65, a union of retail and warehouse workers, was made up mostly of Jewish workers, so naturally the leadership was a white Jewish leadership. That is how it should have been in those days. Today its membership is fundamentally black and Puerto Rican, but the membership is still saddled with a bunch of Jewish Great White Fathers. If the slogan of Black Power meant that Charles Evers be elected mayor of a town in Mississippi, it certainly means that black and Puerto Rican workers should hold the reins of leadership in District 65. Are the New York union leaders more racist than the crackers in Mississippi?

The same situation exists in 1199, a union of drug and hospital workers. Black membership—white leadership. This is not to comment one way or another on the integrity or effectiveness of the present white leadership. Suffice it to say that white leadership cannot serve the profounder aspirations of black memberships. Period. The leadership in 65 and 1199 should be black and Puerto Rican leadership. The leadership of the International Ladies Garment Workers Union and the Amalgamated Clothing Workers should be black and Puerto Rican. The subways and buses of New York City are manned in the main by blacks. Most of the bus drivers, the subway motormen, the conductors and the token sellers are black, but the leadership is white and mostly Irish. Historically, the New York subways were a domain on which the Irish staked their claim successfully.

It means also that if the transportation workers, the retail and warehouse workers, the garment workers and the hospital workers were led by blacks and Puerto Ricans, the number-one priority of these powerful unions would be black and Puerto Rican liberation. It means that a black-led Industrial Union Council in a city like New York could wield a lot of political power in the interest of black people. It could also turn its attention to cracking the lily-white policies of openly-racist unions like Construction, Sanitation, Printers, Plumbers, Electricians, etc., etc.

The most substantial, most stable, most reliable, most politically sophisticated element in the black community is black labor. It should also be the most influential. A black community is made up primarily of workers, not doctors, or lawyers, or even teachers, and this fact should be reflected in its leadership on a local and national level. Remember the 1963 March on Washington? The top leadership was made up of almost every other element of the black community except black labor. This statement is not meant to derogate A. Philip Randolph. He was there, but he is an old warrior, an elder statesman who exerts no real influence on the Movement. His union is almost a myth. The National Negro Labor Council is more illusionary than real. Its fundamental loyalty is to the white labor establishment, not to black liberation. The most powerful labor leader on that platform at the Lincoln Monument was not black, but white, and his name was Walter Reuther. General Reuther of the Detroit Big Four.

The whole struggle for jobs and union membership in the movie industry, in the various tight and white "family" unions such as camera and carpenters and designing and so forth should be led by black labor, not by the labor secretary of the NAACP. This is not to put down the job attempted by NAACP. Somebody had to fill the void.

A National Black Labor Congress is needed, an organization whose first loyalty and primary concern is with the problems of black people. Jobs, housing, education, culture, political and economic power, black control of black rank-and-file unions. In a word, Black Liberation. During the past two decades, leadership and spokesmanship in the Movement have come mostly from preachers, lawyers, intellectuals, businessmen, artists, teachers, students. This leadership has not on the whole been negative. But it has been middle-class leadership, and as such has oftentimes been out of touch with the aspirations of the vast majority of black people who are working class. The middle class did not, could not, speak the language of the masses.

For example, the black student has contributed greatly to the more militant attitude of the Movement, but the middle-class student movement is at best a transitory one. The students are here today and gone tomorrow. College is usually at most a four-year experience. Sometimes it is much less than that in these days when copping out by dropping out has become so fashionable. Oftentimes even the most militant of black students see the Liberation Movement as a part of that four-year experience, a happening. But black labor is a lifetime commitment to the black community. It cannot help but be so.

Can you dig how different and more effective the fight in New York City for school decentralization could have been had there been a Black Labor Congress in New York in the leadership of the struggle? A leadership that could have organized the black masses of the community and the black labor movement (they're both made up of the same people), a leadership that could have been able to defeat the power-drunk strategies and racist tactics of Albert Shanker and his clique of the Federation of Teachers. A black labor-community force that could have stopped the trains and buses from running in support of decentralization.

It is significant that, of all the Black Liberation conventions held over the Labor Day weekend in Atlanta, Mobile, Philadelphia, not one of them saw the importance of involving black labor in a meaningful way. Yet each convention sincerely claims to speak for the black community. But black labor is the heartbeat of the black community, the core of its existence. Not students, writers, lawyers, doctors, artists, all of whom have important roles to play. But the role of black labor is decisive; it is time for black organizations serious about liberation to make one of their primary tasks the liberating of our black brothers and sisters from the bonds of the white labor establishment, either by helping them in a struggle for power inside the existing unions or by helping to establish new black unions of our own. In cities like New York they would be black and Puerto Rican unions. Brother Chavez is waging a similar fight in California to liberate the Mexican-American workers from the gringo-dominated unions.

Can you dig what a liberated black labor force could do for the Liberation Movement? A truly liberated black labor could have its own black studies program, its own black theater, its own publishing, its own Black-Book-of-the-Month, its own black communiversity. Can you dig what a happening it would be if black artists and black labor got together regularly; if they were, in fact, a part of one another, giving mutual sustenance and nourishment? A Black Labor-Community Art Festival every day and twice on Sunday.

It will not be an easy task to get rid of the great white fathers of the labor movement. It will not be an easy task for black workers to achieve the right of self-determination. Taxation without representation is, in truth, tyranny. And that is what black and Puerto Rican workers are faced with, especially in unions in the transport and garment industries. Tyranny is hard to displace without a revolution. The white union bosses are so deeply entrenched it will take considerable excavation to dig them out. Maybe nothing short of dynamite will do the job.

Meanwhile, for starters, the existing civil rights and black power organizations could be of great assistance if they oriented themselves toward black labor and its struggle for liberation from the white union bosses. Unions like 1199 in New York hold "Negro History Celebrations" once a year and invite black leaders, artists, and various assortments of black celebrity to participate, thereby conferring upon the white entrenched leadership a kind of black respectability. It is time for our celebrities to cease and desist from helping to perpetuate the rule of whites over black and Puerto Rican workers.

Some of the black second-line leadership will of course feel threatened by the slogan of black power in the labor movement. The little power they do exert comes from above and not from the black rank-and-file. But what the master giveth he can damn sure take away. The unions are like vast plantations. The second-line colored leadership is like the house slave that Malcolm spoke of. The rank-and-file are the field slaves. What the house slave must be made to understand in this instance is that his true strength can only come from the rank-and-file, and only when he is elected by them and if they become his sole allegiance and concern.

Certainly it will not be easy, but nothing worthwhile is easily achieved. But the victory, when and if achieved, can have a tremendous significance for black liberation and will be well worth the effort. While millions of white workers will see a conflict of interests between black liberation and the white-oriented labor movement, there can be no fundamental contradiction between black labor and the black community. Objectively, every aspect of black life can go forward through black liberation. There is no contradiction in the slogans—"*Up Pan-African Unity!*" "*Up the Black Nation!*" and "*All Power to Black Labor!*"

I have always believed that the basis of colonialism is economic, but the solution of the colonial problem lies in political action, in a fierce and constant struggle for emancipation as an indispensable first step towards securing economic independence and integrity.

KWAME NKRUMAH

2

The White Foundation's Role in Black Oppression

CHUCK STONE

In a white racist society built upon the economic exploitation of black people, the tax-exempt foundation has been the supportive cruelty that permits American industry to justify its continued subjugation of black people.

First, American industry refuses to hire black people (and when it does it hires black people in the most demeaning and unskilled jobs). Next, it sets up tax-exempt foundations which employ only white people and which address themselves to innocuous and irrelevant issues in American life. And finally, these foundations, by an enormous dispensation of funds, become a controlling influence on the intellectual development, employment of scholars and formulation of research programs within the American educational community.

Throughout this sequence of developments, white supremacy has remained the dominating ethic. The foundations, as do their industrial sires, exclude black people with the same abundance of ethnic contempt. As far as they are concerned, there is no room for black people in their organizations as employees, executives, consultants or subject studies. It is no accident of history that the Ford Foundation, by far the largest of the 6,803 foundations in America, hired its first black program specialist only four years ago, and it is well known that this black man has little or no power to make final decisions on grants.

While foundations can be expected to adopt the same racist pat-

CHUCK STONE, writer and political analyst, is the author of *Black Political Power in America* and of the novel *King Strut*. From 1965 to 1967 he was Special Assistant to Adam Clayton Powell, then Chairman of the House Education and Labor Committee. He has edited a number of newspapers, among them *The Chicago Daily Defender*, of which he was Editor in Chief 1963–64. Chuck Stone recently resigned from his position as Director of Minority Affairs of the Educational Testing Service, Princeton, New Jersey. Brother Stone is presently a columnist for the *Philadelphia Daily News*, in addition to doing radio and television commentaries, teaching and writing.

terns as their corporate sponsors, the right of *tax-exempt* institutions to perpetuate white supremacy is especially iniquitous. It is comparable to an organization being given a donation just to maintain racial segregation. And this is precisely what 6,803 American tax-exempt foundations have done.

Who are these foundations? What do they do? How much money do they control? What kind of programs do they support?

The following statistics were true as of 1966:

- There are 6,803 foundations.
- They have combined assets of $19,927,000,000.
- They made a total of $1,212,494,000 in grants that year.
- They operate programs in seven major fields:
  Education
  International activities
  Humanities
  Welfare
  Sciences
  Health
  Religion

Because the foundations must maintain their tax-exempt status, they fund no political programs, and any study dealing with politics must be theoretical in nature, non-partisan and as close to non-active as possible. Foundations also avoid controversial programs, particularly racial, to avoid the scrutiny of Congress, which has never been enthusiastic about their existence.

Just as monopoly has become the prevailing practice in American business, the same game has been played by the foundations. Of the 6,803 foundations, 13 or 0.1% hold $7,750,000,000 or 38% of all the listed assets of these foundations.

These 13 foundation giants are:

Foundations	Assets (in millions)
Ford	3,050
Rockefeller	854
Duke	692
Kellogg (W. K.)	492
Charles Stewart Mott	424
John A. Hartford	342
Lilly Endowment	320
Alfred P. Sloan	309
Carnegie Corporation of New York	289
Pew Memorial Trust	273
Longwood Foundation	251
Moody Foundation	244
Rockefeller Brothers Fund	210

It would be hoped, but not expected, that the combined assets of these foundations dedicated to everything from world peace to more effective methods of birth control *would be* a major force for the betterment of racial relations and resolution of racial tensions in America, the country which provides their tax-exempt status. *But they are not.*

The fact is that the overwhelming majority of foundations vigorously eschew any programs which affect, influence or improve race relations. The indictment by the Kerner Commission that *America is a racist society* discovers its justification in the programs of these foundations.

Of the 6,803 foundations, only 40 or 0.5% made grants (94 in 1966) in the field of race relations. These grants totaled $5,767,000 or 7% of the total $80,512,000 allocated to welfare programs. (In itself, the categorization of "race relations" as a component of the welfare division is a sorry commentary on the foundations' mentality and lack of urgency in resolving the racial crisis in America.)

Of the 6,803 foundations, less than five employ a black man in any major planning or policy-making position. In fact, these tax-exempt foundations practice employment apartheid as assiduously as their corporate founders. Black experts are not utilized, and consistently the white "urbanologist," the white sociologist, the white political scientist, the white educator, the white economist, the white urban planner, the white housing expert, the white journalist, the white anthropologist, the white historian and the white writer are hired as consultants and specialists, are awarded fellowships and given the opportunity to write foundation books. But the black professional, to the average foundation, is the "invisible man."

With malice aforethought, the foundations deliberately exclude black persons from the execution of programs.

What, if anything, can be done to change this racist pattern? Are these foundations capable of changing? Do they want to change? Can they be made more relevant to the black community and if so, how? What specifically can the black community do to achieve greater black participation in the decision-making process of these foundations and to insure the employment of more black staffers, more black consultants and more grants to black-oriented programs?

The answers are not simple. In fact, they are difficult. But they are answers which must be accepted. Foundations, in this era of burgeoning racial confrontation, have no alternative if they are to accept their responsibility to help effect a peaceful change.

The 3rd International Conference on Black Power, therefore, calls on the 6,803 foundations of America to undertake the following measures:

1—Elect immediately at least one black man to their boards of directors or boards of trustees. Where there is already a token black man on the board, a second, preferably a black militant, should be elected.

2—Appoint at least one black man in one of the foundation's top policy-making positions and as one of the foundation's executive officers. (For example, if a foundation has a president, vice-president, secretary, treasurer, etc., one of these officers should be a black man.)

3—Appoint a black man to serve on the policy-making committee that reviews all grants. This requirement demands that a black man have the power to help approve or disapprove grants and, more importantly, submit programs for funding.

4—Each foundation must fund programs involving at least 10% of their grants which concern themselves with race relations. Thus, a foundation whose grants are limited to medical research would award grants to black medical schools, black colleges and universities, the National Medical Association (predominantly black professional society) and other black professional groups capable of conducting research. The important aspect of this measure is that it forces the foundations to refocus their attention toward the black community in areas they heretofore have never considered pertinent to their program areas. This applies whether it's the arts, international activities, the humanities, religion, health or the sciences.

5—Black consultants must be hired by the foundations. There are black experts in every discipline and area of life. As a matter of policy, foundations should attempt to hire a black consultant in preference to a white consultant. It is a grinding insult to black people for foundations to hire white consultants to "study" us.

6—Black writers and applicants for grants must be given preference over whites. Unless this is done, black people will never be able to overcome the disadvantages under which they suffer—disadvantages built up by the foundations in the first place.

7—A black man must be hired as an executive in the personnel departments of the foundations to help integrate the staffs of these foundations. Where such a department is too small to hire a black man to concentrate on fair employment, then the foundations should be encouraged to utilize such minority-group specialists as Richard Clarke and Associates in Rockefeller Center, New York City.

The days of "we-just-can't-find-a-qualified-black-person" are over. They are gone. They don't exist anymore. That excuse is no longer acceptable to the black community, and its continued exploitation by the foundations as a white racist alibi will only escalate the cold war between whites and blacks into a hot civil war.

American industry, the most inventive and imaginative complex in the history of mankind, which has been able to orbit men in space, send rockets to the moon, cure incurable diseases, build gravity-defying skyscrapers and weave an intricate web of intercontinental highways must surely be able to encourage its tax-exempt write-offs known as foundations to solve the problems—not of mankind—but between white Americans and black Americans.

If there is no change in the employment and granting pattern of American foundations, then the black community *next year* must mobilize its political strength to spotlight these foundations by publishing a detailed investigation of their activities and by energizing a full-scale Congressional investigation at both the House and Senate level and by demanding an investigation by the state legislatures where these foundations now operate.

It is to be sincerely hoped that the foundations, with their heightened sensitivities to the manifold problems of society and man's relationship to his fellows, will move forthrightly to become relevant instruments in the cause of racial peace. Law and order start with this requirement.

3

The 1972 Homestead Act

DEMPSEY J. TRAVIS

Historically, because of our position of servitude, we were never permitted to be counted among the landed gentry. When land in America, during the late 18th century, was selling for 8 and 9 cents an acre, most black people in this country were in shackles and chains or prohibited by law from becoming landowners. In those few instances where we were permitted to buy, the absence of security was always present because of the fear of being dispossessed by an angry white individual or mob. Many instances are recorded in history where blacks had to leave land, home, and personal effects in the middle of the night, simply to escape with their lives.

The 1785 Ordinance of the Continental Congress set the price of land at a dollar per acre, plus expenses. It was usually sold in sections of 640 acres each, and larger quantities were sold, by negotiations with the Congress, at a few cents per acre. Such cities as Cleveland, Cincinnati and Marietta were developed by the Ohio Company, which purchased 1½ million acres at a price of 8 to 9 cents per acre in 1787. If we compare the price the Ohio Company paid for its land with the current prices of from $500 to $800 per acre for raw farmland and $2,500 to $3,000 an acre for land adjacent to metropolitan areas, I think we can readily see that some economic innovations will have to be applied, if the black man is ever to participate in the mainstream of our capital development.

Regrettably, our founding fathers and their successors never saw the need of a land reform act that would include the black brother.

DEMPSEY TRAVIS is President and Chairman of the Board of Directors of Sivart Mortgage Corporation, the largest black-owned mortgage banking company in the United States, founded in 1953. Active in urban affairs, Mr. Travis is President of the Travis Realty Company in Chicago. He is founder and President of the United Mortgage Bankers of America, Inc., a national association of black mortgage bankers founded in 1961. He received a B.A. from Roosevelt University in 1949 and completed an M.B.A. in mortgage banking from Northwestern University in 1969.

Even though blacks fought in every battle, including the American Revolution, when land grants were given to soldiers in lieu of pay, the historians have yet to find any recorded documentation showing that black soldiers participated in the 1776 G. I. Bill.

If black America is to get off of the welfare treadmill, the Congress must enact a 1972 Homestead Act that would be solely applicable to the disenfranchised black Americans, in light of the fact that blacks did not participate when the federal government handed out to homesteaders 250 million acres of land, granted the railroads some 90 million acres of land and sold, at subsidy prices, some 430 million acres of land; these figures do not include the 225 million acres that were granted to the states for public purposes. It appears that America has now come to a crossroads where it must keep its commitment of 40 acres and a mule, or rather, "40 acres and a Ford!"

As of January 1, 1968, the federal government owned 760 million acres of land—354,182 acres of which were located in Alaska. With this available land in Alaska, the cry at this time might possibly be: "Black man, go north, to Alaska!" But, who wants to go to Alaska, since they have told us, and we believe it, that we are better acclimated to warm climates such as Mississippi?

Land reclamation should take place in the inner-core areas of every major city in America. The vehicle for reclaiming the land would be an urban fund to be used by blacks throughout America for the purpose of acquiring land in the inner city. The basis for funding this account by the U.S. Government would be based on 40 acres per individual of those 3,600,000 black people who were in bondage in 1862, at the time the Homestead Act was passed. At 40 acres per person, this would amount to 144 million acres of land, and at $150 per acre, this would amount to $21,600,000,000 (21 billion, 600 million dollars). While this figure might appear staggering, it is only one-fourth of the annual national defense budget!

The presence of this fund would serve to eradicate, once and for all, the "hat-in-hand" posture that the black man has had to assume over the past hundred years in his effort to procure loans for private and commercial uses. As an example of how much this type of funding is needed, the largest black publishing company and the largest black manufacturing company—both headed by "Johnsons" (not related)—were started with small loans from loan shares. As a matter of fact, in talking to George Johnson, the head of Johnson Products Company, Inc., which manufactures Ultrasheen hair products, I learned that he needed $250 to capitalize with a partner so that they would have a $500 capital base. He went to the small loan company he had used in the past to get money and told the man he wanted to open a business. Of course, the man told him that the money was not available and sent Johnson away, although there had been four previous occasions when he had been granted such loans. Then Johnson decided a week later that he would try another office of the same company. When he applied for a $500 loan for the purpose of taking a vacation trip to California, the loan was made at once. Historically, it has been true, not in the distant past, but in the recent past and even today, that white folks don't think in terms of making loans available to black folks for any purpose other than buying Cadillacs, mink coats, and taking vacations—things that will not lead to capital formation. The type of sensitivity that is needed, in my opinion, can only be found in the black community, with people who have had this kind of experience themselves; that is, the black bank or the white bank within the black community.

The new urban fund, therefore, should be administered by the 20 black banks who have shown their sensitivity to the needs of the black and rural urban communities. These black banks currently have assets in the amount of 200 million dollars, as compared to white banks with assets in excess of 200 billion dollars. If we are to judge from the black banks' rate of growth in the past, we would still be playing a "mickey-mouse" role in the capital structure of America—in the year 2170.

This money could be used for equity capital, land acquisition, the establishment of industrial parks, commercial shopping centers, housing developments, and to get the black man into business areas which heretofore have been closed because he never had the capital to compete. The result of this would be a self-contained community, black-controlled.

Although the financial umbrella would be black, we must look at all the ingredients needed to achieve our end.

We must recognize one grim fact.

We are appallingly short on the necessary industrial and managerial black technicians necessary for realization of a 1972 Homestead Act. The deliberate exclusion of blacks from positions of capital and professional power has left us without the necessary black personnel. We would draw that personnel from three probable sources, with black control and veto operating at all times:

  · non-black Americans—which would include whites and various personnel of Third World background;
  · our African and Third World brothers from abroad who have similar problems of development. Their expertise and insight could perhaps aid us in developing a community which is not a carbon copy of the white community. New concepts of space, land use, design, with

correspondingly different demographic and topological and cultural considerations could be introduced;

- young black students and college graduates, newly trained specifically for our tasks. Such a program is implicit in many of the black studies programs throughout the country. We could make it explicit and train a cadre of young black nation builders. Land grant or normal colleges are a possibility here and could be funded through the 1972 Homestead Act, as well as existing colleges modified to this purpose. Most likely the necessary personnel would derive from a combination of these three.

We would need architects and land planners for our building programs and land development. In view of there being only 690 black architects out of a total of 29,720 in the United States, this means that black architects represent only 2.3 per cent of the total number, or less than 50 per cent of the number employed by the two top architectural firms in America, and this is by no means adequate. Engineers will be needed, and there are only 9472 black engineers compared to more than half a million whites—to be exact, 552,398 whites. This means that we represent about 1.7 per cent of the engineers in the country.

In the very fields we are discussing here today, we represent less than 1.4 per cent of the total industry. In other words, there are only 4,041 blacks involved in finance, insurance, and real estate, out of a total of 295,267 whites. In these latter areas, all of our talents could be meaningfully absorbed in two major cities, and still there would be need for more blacks. In addition, white participation is required in the area of managerial guidance—the same guidance this country offers to Africa, India and other undeveloped countries under the government's technical assistance programs. These managerial areas are still off limits to black men. Since there are only 5400 black accountants out of a total of some 400,000 in the entire country, we will require assistance in this area, too. There is a great need for an amalgamation of talents and direction; however, there is a greater need for the black man to assume his dignity as a man and lose forever his historical image as a boy—and a white man's boy at that.

The funding of the black community in this magnitude is absolutely necessary, if we are to get a capital structure off the launching pad. The wheels that move the American capital structure are credit. Unfortunately, the black community has no wheels. The funding of the 1972 Homestead Act would enable black and white America to close the books on past wrongs and stamp them: "Account closed . . . paid in full!"

> *I have always believed that the basis of colonialism is economic, but the solution of the colonial problem lies in political action, in a fierce and constant struggle for emancipation as an indispensable first step towards securing economic independence and integrity.*
>
> KWAME NKRUMAH